A CLOUD OF WITNESSES

*Personal Stories of God's Presence
In Today's World*

A CLOUD OF WITNESSES

Personal Stories of God's Presence
In Today's World

For you, Susan ~
Thank you for all you
do for Shalem! I hope
you enjoy this book ~
Blessings always,
Joan Hickey

Joan S. Hickey, *Author/Editor*

SERAPHINA
PRESS

Seraphina Press
212 3rd Avenue North, Suite 290
Minneapolis, MN 55401
612.455.2293
www.SeraphinaPress.com

ISBN-13: 978-0-9848028-5-2
LCCN: 2013931194

Distributed by Itasca Books

Cover art by Jacqueline Saunders

Printed in the United States of America

This book is

lovingly and gratefully

dedicated to

that Divine Reality

whose nature

is

Boundless Love.

Contents

Foreword
The Rev. Tilden Edwards, Ph.D.

THE deepest desire in us is for the deepest kind of intimate love. Love is freely given, life-giving communion, mutual indwelling. On the mature person-to-person level we can touch the wondrous hem of such deep love, even to the graced point of its becoming sacramental. But there remains an exclusive and erratic quality to our human loves: they are subject to our mutual ego possessiveness and to conflicting needs and limited understanding. In religious spiritual history we find evidence of a deeper love in human experience, the one from which all true loves emanate. In Christian tradition we see this especially held up in the mystical experiences reported in Scripture and in the lives of the saints.

In mystical experiences something breaks into our awareness that reveals an inclusive, interdependent deep reality, pervaded by mysterious but palpable radiant light and love. We are shown a radiant love beyond the telling, beyond what the mind can adequately translate into its categories. Sometimes the experience goes beyond such a general awareness to a sense of personal encounter with the gracious One who affirms us in love and calls us to particular ways of loving in our lives; it is a transformative encounter. In its most graced form we know the gift of union: full mutual indwelling in God, firsthand realization of the image of God in us that we most deeply are.

Joan Hickey masterfully clarifies this often confusing range of mystical experiences in Christian tradition and provides very helpful, classical ways to discern the authenticity of such experiences. In her personal spiritual maturity and broad understanding of mystical tradition drawn from scientific and psychological as well as religious interpreters, she wisely affirms that our goal in the spiritual life historically is not for any particular religious experience, but for our deep desire for God and for our trust in the divine hidden presence lovingly at work in our lives, however that may show itself.

This view, along with her sense of the need to ground our intellect and feelings in our direct open-hearted presence in God, reflects Joan Hickey's deep grounding in Christian contemplative tradition. That tradition of the first-hand spiritual experience of great mystics walking in the footsteps of Christ shows great respect for the evolving and mysterious lifelong nature of the spiritual journey, as we move from the image of God in which we were born, to the full likeness of God for which we are made (as the early Church Fathers would put it).

In recent decades we have seen the re-awakening of the mature wisdom and practices of contemplative tradition, reflecting the hunger of many people around the world for a deeper personal and communal life in God. The Shalem Institute for Spiritual Formation was born as a response to that hunger.

The many inspiring personal stories of mystical experience Joan Hickey has collected for this book are, as she well says, reminders to us all of God's real presence among us. Since these people are ordinary people like you and me, rather than great saints of the tradition, we can identify with them more easily, realizing that mystical experience is an ordinary human phenomenon, claimed by close to half the population in some polls. In reading these accounts I found my own trust in the elusive elusive-yet-so-close divine presence was quickened. I also found my awareness of the rich array of ways the great Radiant Love can show itself greatly broadened.

Anyone reading these stories I'm sure will share with me a sense of having touched moments of profound firsthand awareness of the Radiant Love at the heart of what is, however veiled it may be to us in our own busy daily consciousness. I believe we are made for that Love, indeed made of that Love. Our yearning is for our full home in that Love, and to help the world to realize its belonging to it. We plant seeds of its glory whenever we participate in the divine shaping of a world of just peace and mutual belonging—the kingdom of God relentlessly growing in our midst.

The great Jesuit scientist Teilhard de Chardin once said that we are not human beings on a spiritual journey, but spiritual beings on a human journey. The stories in this book help us to see that truth. We are in the world, as Jesus said, but not of it, except as we perceive it shining with Presence, and as we participate in that gracious Presence's loving intimacy and callings. Each of us is a unique and evolving personal story of God's Presence in the world. In this book we find ourselves among a great cloud of witnesses to that spiritual truth.

෴

Tilden Edwards, an Episcopal priest, is the founder and, for many years, the director of the ecumenical Shalem Institute for Spiritual Formation. Besides creating and leading many of Shalem's programs, he has led retreats and lectured throughout the United States and abroad. He is the author of eight books related to contemplatively grounded living, leadership, and compassionate action. Although now retired from administrative duties he continues to be involved in most of Shalem's programs and in the larger movement for contemplative awakening in the world today.

A Preliminary Note

This book is being produced in collaboration with the Shalem Institute for Spiritual Formation, a primarily Christian contemplative prayer, resource, and educational center located in Washington, D.C. Almost all of the original stories shared for this book come from persons with a Christian background who have been participants in various Shalem programs over the years and who remain a part of Shalem's network, and Christianity is also the faith tradition of the author/editor. This book, therefore, is written from the perspective of Christian faith and theology.

Mystical experiences, however, are universal among human beings, and all of the world's great faith traditions have well-developed histories and traditions of contemplative prayer and mystical phenomena, Judaism and Islam together with Christianity in the West and, in the East, Buddhism and Hinduism in particular. Shalem has, over the years, been in dialogue with a number of these traditions, especially Tibetan Buddhism, and Shalem participants, both Christians and those of other faiths, have found their spiritual journeys much enriched from these contacts. Though this book is written from within the Christian tradition, it is our hope that others may find value in the book as it connects with their own experiences, since mystical experiences themselves transcend religious boundaries.

Introduction

THIS IS a book of true stories, stories of ordinary people in today's world who have had extraordinary experiences of God. Or perhaps they were not extraordinary after all! The Reverend Andrew Greeley, a research sociologist and Roman Catholic priest, says that his research indicates that roughly 43 percent of contemporary Americans have had a mystical experience at least once in their lives. Five other studies conducted in the United States in the same time frame, the 1970s, found the incidence of such experiences to be between 40 and 50 percent. A contemporaneous study in England reported the percentage of these experiences to be as high as 56 percent among church-going Christians. But ordinary or extraordinary is not the point here—the people and the experiences themselves and what they may mean for all of us, are the focus of this book.

But what do we mean by "mystical experience"? The words mysticism and mystical experience are used so loosely today to speak of so many different things, sometimes even to refer to occult events, that some definition is surely in order. Entire books could be, and have been, written just to arrive at a suitably complete yet nuanced definition, but for the moment let us just settle for a short version and say that a mystical experience is an unmediated, direct experience of the immediate presence of God.

But what, exactly, does that really mean? Do such things actually happen? Do they happen to anyone other than the greatest of saints? Are they truly "normal" or is there something pathological about them? How do we know that they are real and not just some kind of hallucination? Can they be faked? In other words, how do we know if they are authentic or not? What are their causes and effects? Why is it that some people don't believe that such experiences have anything to do with God at all? And, if these events really do happen to the extent that the studies indicate, why haven't we all heard a lot more about them before now?

Those and many, many more questions besides, can come into our minds about this fascinating subject. That is exactly why this book is planned as it is, in two main parts. Part One provides an overview of the subject, offers background and context for the stories included here and answers many of those questions, while Part Two is where you will find, in their own words, accounts of the mystical experiences they have had from fifty-eight different writers. The information in Part One of the book is of extreme importance and can greatly enrich your understanding of the stories that follow in Part Two. If your eagerness to get to the stories right away is truly pressing, however, of course you do not need my permission to skip over Part One (for the moment only, of course!) and go directly to Part Two. Though, should you decide to do so, I do urge you to be sure to return to and read Part One later. The background and context for the stories included here is not only important to understand the stories themselves, but also will provide a much richer and more complete understanding of these fascinating experiences in general.

I first became seriously interested in Christian mysticism and mystical experiences in the fall of 1949 when I was a senior majoring in English literature, with a minor in philosophy, at Dunbarton College of Holy Cross, a small Catholic women's college then in Washington, D.C. In a class on medieval literature, we were assigned readings from the works of some of the fourteenth-century English mystics. I was enchanted, so much so that I read well beyond the assignment and wrote my major senior paper on the subject. Their words were so simple, yet also so profound and so beautiful, and they introduced me to a spiritual path that I had never encountered before. At the same time, there was something that I can only call a down-to-earthness about them—I'm not sure whether or not that had anything to do with the fact that so many of them were lay people, as opposed to monks, nuns, or clergy, though it can be interesting to speculate about that. But even beyond those qualities of their work, some of these writers had the most delightful names; names that flowed out of one's mouth like music—Dame Wiggins of Wye and Richard Rolle of Hampole, for example. I simply fell in love and have continued to read and research in this field of Christian mysticism for all of the years from 1949 until today—that adds up to just over sixty years of pursuing more and deeper understandings of this spiritual "way." Of course, I learned in short order that there had been a vast flowering of mysticism all over Europe in the fourteenth century, so I spent some years pursuing what had happened there. Later still, I returned to the very beginnings and early growth of Christianity, both in the Western and Eastern Christian Church, and followed the path of mystical spirituality as it appeared and flowed through the life of the Church in the following centuries. It was in midlife that I was to discover, research, and come to understand the mystical traditions in the other major religions of the world and to appreciate the commonalities that we share in this spirituality despite the differences that exist between us in terms of doctrine.

After those studies from the 1970s were published indicating the unexpectedly large number of today's Americans who reported having had at least one mystical experience in their lives, of course I wanted to jump right in and see if I could follow up on those studies by contacting and interviewing some of these people. However, there was just no way for me to do so then. Having completed a master's degree in pastoral counseling at Loyola College, Baltimore, and four years of graduate study in theology and pastoral studies at the

Washington Theological Union along the way, my time was taken up by full-time duties as a pastoral counselor for the Church and as a leader and teacher of contemplative prayer groups and facilitator of silent retreats throughout the United States. Quite simply, wish though I might, there just wasn't enough time for me to also follow through with this at that time. When I retired from my professional work five years ago, however, I noticed rather quickly that my old desire to delve more deeply into this issue of mystical experiences in our own contemporary world and how they affect our lives, was still alive and well—and beckoning. My path ahead was clear. A Cloud of Witnesses: Personal Stories of God's Presence in Today's World is the result of following that path.

My deepest hope is that this book may be as interesting and enlightening, and as much of a pleasure for you to read, as putting it together for you has been for me.

Now let us begin . . .

PART ONE
Background and Context

MOST OF US who grew up with any brush with the idea of mystical experiences at all will no doubt have come across the subject in connection with the lives of some great saints, many of whom, over the centuries, are reported to have been blessed with such gifts. The amazing thing about these studies referred to on the preceding pages is not so much that they report mystical experiences to be events that happen in the lives of "ordinary" people as well as great saints, but the extent to which they occur at all. Rather than being quite rare, as we have been likely to suppose, it turns out that mystical experiences are, in fact, a relatively widespread phenomenon. If it is true, as these studies have indicated, that 40 to 50 percent of contemporary people in America have personally had such experiences, that can hardly be considered insignificant and, I believe, warrants a much deeper and more serious consideration of the issue of such experiences in our lives.

So let's begin to look at some of the questions that are asked—and that we, ourselves, ask—about these phenomena. One of the first questions that comes up for me is, if these experiences do occur so frequently and are as widespread as is being suggested, why is it that we haven't heard more about them before now? I believe there are a number of reasons. For one thing, many people who have such experiences, perhaps even most who do, are left with such an overpowering sense of awe at the unutterable holiness of the experience that they simply feel no desire at all to speak of it publicly as the experience is just too personal and intimate to be shared. To the contrary, their natural tendency is to be silent and hold it close within their hearts. One potential contributor to this book, who had had an experience of the risen Jesus, changed her mind about writing an account of it and, when asked her reason, said, "I know this is ridiculous, but it feels like I would be dragging Jesus out into the public square to be spat upon again. I just can't do it." Of course, her feelings were honored.

People often hold their counsel, too, because of numerous different forms of fear. Because these experiences involve an altered state of consciousness, one so radically different from the normal, everyday state of consciousness that we are used to, some people have an instantaneous fear that they may be becoming unhinged or even possibly losing their minds and so hesitate to speak of it at all to anyone. Others fear that, if they talk about the experience, other people will think that they are crazy, something that actually happens with some frequency. Others fear that if they say anything about it, people may suspect that they think they are some kind of saint or are trying to promote themselves as a special holy person in some way.

And there is yet another reason why we rarely hear of these powerful encounters with God. Many, many years ago, the late Gerald May, a board-certified psychiatrist who was for many years the director of spiritual guidance for the Shalem Institute for Spiritual Formation held a Psychology/Spirituality Day, the first of what would soon become an annual event. He spoke of subjects that are taboo in our society. There was a time, he said, when money was a taboo subject; persons of good breeding simply did not discuss money with anyone but their banker or investment counselor, whereas today, people tend to talk about money quite freely with anyone who might be interested. Then there was a time when sex was very much a taboo subject, even to the point where parents often refrained from giving their children the information they needed about the subject. In today's world, he remarked, there is barely anything that cannot be said about sex. He went on to say that he believed the only remaining, truly taboo subject in our world today is the subject of religious experience.

Then he asked each of us present to turn to someone sitting beside us and share with each other an account of a religious experience that we had had. I turned to the woman seated at my right, who was probably forty-five years old or so. She was very anxious and the first words out of her mouth were, "Oh, I can't possibly do this! I am a psychiatrist and when I have told my colleagues about some of my experiences, they tell me I am having psychotic episodes." To reassure her I said, "That's all right, I'll go first then," and spoke of one experience of my own. When I was done, the floodgates opened and she shared a number of beautiful, clearly mystical experiences she had had over a number of years, in her case primarily after having been to confession. As a psychiatrist herself, she knew full well that she was not having "psychotic episodes" but her experience with her colleagues had made clear to her that the idea of such experiences should be considered a taboo subject when speaking with them and so she gave up trying to do so.

And so here is another reason why people often don't share these most intimate moments of their lives with God. We have no idea how many people just never share their experiences of these moments of profound apprehension of God's presence because of their sense that these are things that just ought not be spoken of in polite society. It should be noted that this reticence to speak of religious experiences is more evident in some of our Christian denominations than in others. Within the Catholic, Orthodox, Anglican, and other mainline Protestant churches, churches where liturgy or worship tends to be more formal, members are much less likely to speak about their personal religious experiences, except, possibly, in a one-to-one talk with one's pastor, spiritual director, or guide, while Evangelical and Pentecostal churches as well as Charismatic groups value and encourage emotional experiences of God, to a greater degree along with the full, open, and public expressions of such experiences.

Another possible barrier to talking about religious experiences may be the simple fact that words that seem appropriate to discuss the subject are hard, if not often actually impossible, to come by, and those we do find are rarely satisfying to those of us who might, otherwise, at least try to speak of them.

THE PROBLEM OF WORDS

One of the marks of profound religious experiences is that they are "ineffable," that is, that we are essentially incapable of finding words to adequately describe them. But long before we arrive at the point where we are trying to describe such an experience, we have already run into difficulties with language. In Evangelical and Pentecostal churches as well as in many Charismatic communities, it is common to hear people using phrases such as, "The Lord told me . . ." or "God says that . . ." and this can leave the rest of us wondering exactly what this means. Does it mean that the person has literally heard these words from God, either audibly or in some inner way? Does it mean that the speaker has a profound intuition that this is true and is giving God credit for the insight? It generally seems to be more the latter. During the 2008 campaign for the presidency, the subject of "God's will" came up through the vice-presidential nominee of the Republican party, Gov. Sarah Palin of Alaska, who is a member of a Pentecostal church. She spoke often and confidently of this or that action as being "God's will," referring on one occasion to the potential building of an Alaska natural gas pipeline, as "God's will." I believe it is fair to assume that most, if not all, serious Christians wish to know God's will, but most will readily admit that they find difficulty, sometimes even grave difficulty, in arriving at such a sure sense of knowing what actually is, in fact, God's will. As a result of this reticence, many listeners expressed some surprise at the facility with which Palin used those words. Questioned about this, Pentecostal scholar Cecil M. Robeck Jr., director of the David du Plessis Center for Christian Spirituality at Fuller Theological Seminary, explained, "Oftentimes, within our circles, people will say that they think something is God's will if they have a strong inner sense that something is right."[1] Within the Pentecostal community this would be readily understood, but it could lead to some serious misunderstandings in the context of an ecumenical dialogue. This is most especially true when we are trying to understand profound religious experiences in the course of which people often do, indeed, claim with some frequency that they actually have heard words from God, not usually audible to their physical ears but in a manner markedly distinct from words they are familiar with as expressions of their own thoughts. In the interests of clarity and to avoid any misunderstanding, let it be said here that this voice within and yet not of one's self is exactly the claim of many of those who have shared their stories for this book. So it is of supreme importance, as we begin to explore the world of mystical experiences, that we are diligent about using language carefully and clearly so as to be as specific as possible when describing the particular religious experiences called "mystical," the experiences reported in this book.

But the difficulties involved in speaking of these experiences goes well and far beyond the challenge of understanding the use of words like "God's will" by fellow Christians. There is a lot more that needs to be said about the problem of words.

DEFINITIONS

The fact is that there is probably no field of interest in which it is harder to find words that adequately, clearly, and coherently describe what we are talking about than the field of religious, spiritual, or mystical experiences. And even when we, ourselves, have found words that satisfy us, and someone else speaks to us using the same words, we have no sure way of knowing immediately whether we are talking about the same thing or not.

Mountains of parchment and paper and oceans of ink have been used up over millennia discussing this subject. Still there are vastly different ways of understanding and presenting these ideas. There must be literally hundreds of definitions proposed today. This book in no way purports to present a comprehensive history or analysis of these experiences. You will find numerous resources in the bibliography if you wish to delve more deeply into this subject matter. My aim here is just to provide the simplest possible framework within which to look at and begin to understand these kinds of experiences in a way that gives us some common ground of understanding as we go forward.

For the purpose of this book, I will be using the words religious experience as an umbrella term to cover a variety of different events all focused on an encounter with or an experience of a Divine Reality in some way. This may be as simple and ordinary as being lifted up in spirit and experiencing God's closeness during a worship service, after receiving Holy Communion, or in solitary prayer. It may come through reading and meditating on Scripture or through the serious study of Scripture, which sometimes sparks a sudden new insight that brings with it a powerful sense of God-with-us in that moment. It may, in fact, come through the study of many subjects; let's say, for example, the study of physics or astronomy. Perhaps even just seeing photographs beamed back from the Hubble telescope could instantly transport us into an immediate sense of holy awe at the magnitude and beauty of creation in which we find ourselves looking, un-self-consciously and without defense, into the face of that Divine Reality that we suddenly perceive to be in and behind it all. Religious experience also includes those moments of deep and peaceful stillness during meditation when we are aware of God's immediate presence and experience a sense of peace and of being at one with God as well as those sudden and startling moments when we are surprised by a sudden "in-breaking" of God that is immediately recognized as "given," neither self-created nor "accomplished" in any way by ourselves. In other words, a "religious experience" has something to do with or is oriented toward that Transcendent Reality we usually simply name as God.

Among the many definitions of religious experience that exist, one that is particularly appealing to me because it is so simple, succinct, and comprehensive comes from the late German-American theologian and sociologist of religion, Joachim Wach, formerly of the University of Chicago Divinity School. In his words, Dr. Wach defines religious experience as ". . . a response of the whole person to what is perceived as ultimate, characterized by a peculiar intensity, and issuing in appropriate action."[2] He intends the word peculiar to mean unusual, not odd. We might paraphrase this as follows: A response of our whole being, thoughts, and emotions, and in the depths of our hearts, to God that is characterized by an unusual intensity that leads, in some fashion, to a transformation of our life.

It is more difficult to define spiritual experience because, much of the time, we all use the term interchangeably with religious experience. These, however, are not synonyms. In light of Wach's definition of religious experience, it is really important to be more precise about the differences between the two. There are two reasons for this. First, the distinction is important because today we often hear someone say something

like, "I'm not religious but I am a very spiritual person."
Generally, this seems to mean that the speaker is not
affiliated with any particular church or other religious
body and does not hold to any specific religious dogma; rather, the speaker knows himself or herself as a
person who often has experiences of life that clearly
transcend our "everyday Tuesday" mind-set and lift us
to another level of experience that seems to us to be
clearly more of spirit than of body. Such a person may
or may not have a clear concept of or explicit belief in
God, as we ordinarily think of and speak about God,
but may speak more easily of respect for the mystery
that they acknowledge to be at the heart of all life.
These individuals often speak easily of hearing great
music, magnificently performed, which provided them
with a spiritual experience, or of having had a spiritual
experience in special moments of deep personal closeness with someone they love very much. Other triggers
for spiritual experiences might be the birth of a child
or being in the presence of great natural beauty or
sometimes in the presence of the created beauty of
fine art. From the outside, it may be impossible to know
whether, for them, this means being in touch with God
or not and, if so, how that God might be understood.
This is why we must let them speak for themselves and
honor the beauty of their experiences, which may or
may not also aptly be called "religious."

But there is a second reason for honoring this distinction between "religious" and "spiritual" experiences. All

of us, including those of us who would readily acknowledge ourselves as religious persons, do, at various times, have the same kinds of wonderful experiences of music, love, and beauty described above. We may well be lifted up by them to the point where we might feel that we could easily fly if we jumped off of a building, and yet not experience in those moments any explicit sense of the presence of God. Perhaps it would be better for us to think of such moments as examples of what psychologist Abraham Maslow called "peak experiences," moments when we are truly experiencing life "to the full." In this sense, we, too, need an apt way of saying how glorious such experiences are and what they mean to us. Without an explicit awareness of or connection to God, to call these "life to the full" moments "spiritual experiences" may work well for us all.

Or may not! Is that really all there is to a "spiritual experience"—just that glorious "high" that we feel on a particularly happy day? Or might there be something more not yet factored in? I do believe there is another highly important element that needs to be identified and so I would like to finally define a "spiritual experience" as an experience springing from any source that touches us in the depths of our being in such a way that it brings us to an immediate awareness of our unity, our oneness with "all there is," all of life or Ultimate Reality. Such moments are generally referred to as "unitive" experiences.

I think a story about the lyrics of a song that was popular in the late twentieth century may help us see the subtle difference between these two kinds of experiences.

In 1965, Alan J. Lerner and Burton Lane composed the song "On a Clear Day" for a Broadway musical, On a Clear Day You Can See Forever. I have been told that the original lyrics were these:

On a clear day, rise and look around you
and you'll see who you are.
On a clear day, how it will astound you
That the glow of your feelings outshines
every star. You will follow every mountain, sea and
shore,
You will see from far and near a world
you've never seen before.
On a clear day, on a clear day, you can
see forever, and ever, and ever more.

However, by the time the show had opened on Broadway in the fall of that year, and thus well before May of the following year, 1966, when the singer Frank Sinatra made his famous recording of the song, a few adaptations in the words had been made. They were so small as to be almost unnoticeable, and yet those few words radically altered the overall meaning of the song. Here is the final version:

On a clear day, rise and look around you,
and you'll see who, just who you are.
On a clear day, how it will astound you
That the glow of your being outshines
every star.

*You feel part of every mountain, sea and
shore,
And you can hear, from far and near, a
world you've never heard before.
And on that clear day, on that clear, clear
day,
you can see forever, and ever, and ever
more.*

This second version speaks clearly of a spiritual experience, as opposed to the simple delight of enjoying a lovely day.

Does this mean that we always need to be analyzing our experiences or those of other people and placing them into one category or another? By no means! Especially with regard to the experiences of others, this is inappropriate; since we have no way to access or understand the subjective experience of another person, we must always respect each other's self-understanding and description of his or her own experiences. What it does mean, however, is that when we want to talk about these things with other people and it seems necessary or important to distinguish authentic religious experiences from other types of meaningful or even, in some sense, transcendent experiences, we have at least the beginnings of development of some common understandings that can clear a way in which we can do that.

Mystical experiences, which I consider a category under the umbrella of religious experiences, are experiences of a markedly different character since, throughout the centuries as well as today, it is the constant witness of those who have had such experiences that they are totally and completely "given" and usually surprisingly so. Mystical experiences seem to break into an individual's awareness with unmistakable authority and clarity, usually lasting only for a few moments (though there are exceptions) and leaving the recipient with a stunned sense that, for those few moments, a veil was lifted and a greater and more real reality than the one with which we are familiar has been shown to them. We might think of something as dramatic as the blinding light that burst upon St. Paul on the road to Damascus, followed by the words, "*Saul, Saul, why are you persecuting me?*"—an experience that transformed his life completely and forever—or the three simple words that Francis of Assisi heard as he prayed before the painted crucifix in the little half-ruined chapel of San Damiano, "*Rebuild my church.*" Francis's first thought was that Jesus wanted him to rebuild the little chapel, which he immediately set out to do with help from some friends. Only later did he come to understand that the request was for something infinitely larger—that he was being asked to undertake the task of rebuilding the institutional Church. (Perhaps it is just as well that the full meaning of those words came to Francis slowly and over time. Had he understood the full commission instantly, might he not have been tempted, like Jonah, to head immediately in the opposite direction?)

Some people who have similar mystical experiences do, indeed, understand immediately and with great clarity what they are to do in the wake of their experience. In contemporary times we might think of Mother Teresa's mystical experience on the train as she was leaving Calcutta to go to Darjeeling for her annual retreat; in its wake she seems to have known almost instantly that she was meant to leave her religious order and return to India with a new mission— to care for the sick and dying poor. Others, like Francis and many of us, need time to grow into a deeper and more complete understanding of the call on our lives. As one of the contributors to this book said, "As I look back over my life, I see that every path taken, as well as every side trip, was an attempt to follow and live out the implications of that moment." In all cases of mystical experience, however, the final authentication of the experience itself is that it is transformative in the life of the person who experienced it.

Notwithstanding the experiences of St. Paul and St. Francis, and so many others, as the literature about mysticism and mystical experience has built up over the centuries, many, though not all, scholars, historians, theologians, and especially philosophers of religion have chosen to restrict the use of the term mystical experience to only the highest state of religious awareness that we humans can attain in this life, a state of complete union with God, a state that seems usually to have been invited and facilitated by years of ascetic practice and contemplative prayer. I believe this is unnecessarily and unhelpfully restrictive. For one thing, most religious experiences occur when we are in our normal state of consciousness and are aware that that is so, while, in the case of mystical experiences, we sense ourselves as being in a radically and strangely different mode of consciousness, one that we cannot explain and have difficulty describing. (In an attempt, once, to do so, the great Carmelite mystic and saint, Teresa of Avila, finally gave up and said, "I wish I could explain it to you, but I can't.")

This shift in one's state of consciousness is universally described by those who experience it as associated with something like a powerful "in-breaking" of God into their awareness, which captivates their attention completely and overrides virtually everything else for the few moments that it lasts. As mentioned before, people often describe this experience in terms of a veil being lifted for those moments, as they experience a dimension of reality that they never had experienced before, and that they knew immediately, with apparently infused knowledge, that God was fully and immediately present to them right there in that moment. There may or may not be a spoken or unspoken but understood word or message in that moment. They describe being in touch with their surroundings, that is, not "taking leave of the world" in any way but rather seeing through their present physical reality to the more fully Real—the transcendent and eternal Reality beyond.

These experiences, like those of Paul and Francis and so many other thousands, perhaps even thousands of thousands, of both saints and ordinary people are not experiences of union with God, but of encounters with God as Other, or, in the words of the Jewish philosopher Martin Buber, profound "I–Thou" experiences of God. We need a word or phrase that can help us distinguish these unusual experiences from both the graced encounters with God that we often experience in our day-to-day consciousness and also from the high states of complete union with God. Buber's description seems to meet that need perfectly, so I will gratefully adopt it to designate this different type of mystical experience.

Some writers, as a way of acknowledging these I–Thou experiences of God without putting them into the category of "mystical" have settled for calling them "mystic (or mystical) apprehensions," as a way of distinguishing them from the great states of union with God that often grow out of long years of dedicated spiritual practice. While there may be important reasons to maintain the distinction between these two different types of experiences, I fear that this solution may cause more of a problem than it solves because it seems to suggest that such "mystic apprehensions" come about because of the action of the subject who, on a particular occasion, somehow by her or his own power, apprehends the presence of God, not by grace but by self-capacity. Yet those persons who have had such experiences universally identify God as the one who acts, who acts alone and in the Divine Being's own time and manner, breaking into their lives without any action on their part, as well as in the complete absence of any expectation on their part of such a thing ever happening at all.

Nelson Pike, professor emeritus of philosophy at the University of California, Irvine, has written at length about mystical states and, though he uses the designation "mystic apprehensions" for these powerful I–Thou experiences of God (again, to distinguish them from the states of mystic union with God), he does consider them to be another kind of mystical phenomenon. He speaks of them as, "gratuitous graces . . 'extraordinary' gifts tailored to meet the needs of particular individuals at particular times."[3] That is an exact description of the experience of those who have such experiences.

In view of all this, and the fact that far and away the greatest number of experiences of God's immediate presence and action in the lives of people throughout history as well as today do not seem to be experiences of union with God as much as they are, like the experiences of Paul and Francis and many of the writers of this book, I–– Thou experiences, I am going to choose to differ with some other writers and ally myself with Pike in seeing these experiences as unambiguously "mystical."

As additional justification for that position I cite the thoughts of Luke Timothy Johnson, Woodruff Professor of New Testament and Christian Origins at Emory University's Candler School of Theology. Dr. Johnson uses a wonderful analogy from music in thinking about mystical experience. He says, "We can appreciate the greatness of music through the genius of a Mozart but we can see, too, that piano students struggling with simple tunes also participate in music. In the same way, the great mystics and visionaries show us the range of what is possible in the life of devotion to God while including those at a much lower level of [experience]."[4] Incidentally, Dr. Johnson's definition of a mystic is anyone who "seeks a personal and passionate devotion to the divine."

With that in mind, since we all have the option of seeking such a devotion if we choose, we can say that none of us need be cut off from the mystic's journey. Our potential for enlightenment regarding God, like our ability to dream dreams for our own lives and for the world, depends to a large extent on our openness to the mysteries and possibilities in this life and beyond.

HOW TO IDENTIFY AUTHENTIC MYSTICAL EXPERIENCES

Earlier, I defined mystical experiences as the unmediated and direct experience of the immediate presence of God and also described such experiences from the point of view of subjective experience. It is time now to look at such experiences from an objective point of view—how can we go about discerning whether any such experience is authentic or might, instead, be the result of self-delusion, illness, or fabrication? Most of us are wise in many ways, but not one of us is wise in all ways, so it would be a mistake for us to overlook any shred of hubris that might lurk within us and conclude that we have it within our own power to decide infallibly whether any given experience is authentic or not. We can, however, follow some ancient and traditional guidelines that can help us conclude whether it is most likely, likely, or questionable that a particular experience is, indeed, authentic.

I believe that we can begin to get some sense of the authenticity or falseness of accounts of such experiences by answering five questions. I will identify these question areas first and then go back and look at each in more detail. First we must ask, what is the personality and character of the person reporting the experience? Second, does the experience being reported give evidence of the classic qualities of such experiences as described over the centuries through others who have had them? Third, does all content involved in the experience meet the test of orthodoxy? Fourth, is the experience life-enhancing and does it foster integration in one's life? Fifth, and the ultimate test of authenticity, is the experience transformative for the subject? This, of course, is the ancient standard of, "By their fruits, you shall know them."

I. What Is the Personality and Character of the Person Reporting the Mystical Experience?

It is important to begin our evaluation by asking, is this person well grounded in reality, not given to creating dramatic fantasies for the entertainment of either self or others, nor to lying? In other words, is he or she what we might call a "down-to-earth" person, honest and straightforward, a person of good character? Is the person free of any need for an inordinate amount of personal affirmation or any desire to be seen as a spiritual "star" or to routinely be the center of attention in a group? Is this person free of any physical or mental illness that might mimic mystical experience or interfere with the person's ability to accurately assess the difference between what is real and what is unreal in day-to-day life?

Some people are of the opinion that near-perfect physical and mental health in the subject are necessary to authenticate any mystical experience the person may claim; the nineteenth- and twentieth-century French Jesuit Augustin Poulain, author of The Graces of Interior Prayer, is of this mind. However, the contemporary professor and scholar of mysticism Luke Johnson, of Emory University, sees this differently and points out a number of saints and mystics who had human illnesses and problems of one sort or another. He mentions the great abbot and saint Bernard of Clairvaux, who suffered for years with a chronic illness, and St. Catherine of Siena, who is thought today to have been anorexic and whose death at the early age of thirty-three was likely caused by self-starvation. We know that the beloved fourteenth-century anchoress Dame Julian of Norwich, newly popular in our time, once had three straight days of mystical experiences during which she was given numerous "showings," as she called them, and this happened while she was severely ill, an illness she had prayed for in order to understand and share the Lord's sufferings more fully. Lest we suspect that her experiences were the result of delirium rather than a genuine encounter with God, consider that she wrote a brief account of them soon afterward, meditated on the experiences for the next twenty years, and finally wrote a longer account, available today under the title Revelations of Divine Love, spelling out her theological conclusions. This account caused the twentieth century's great contemplative monk and writer Thomas Merton to name Julian as one of the Church's most eminent theologians. (I think most of us could agree that good theology is highly unlikely to grow out of delirium.) In our own time we might think of the much revered Italian monk, Padre Pio, now formally St. Pio of Pietralcina, who died in 1968 and was canonized in 2002. Padre Pio, whose life was marked by both mystical and awesome paranormal gifts as well, was so sick for much of his early years in the monastery that he often had to leave and return home for months at a time to recover before he could return to the rigorous life of the monastery. In fact, if we merely scan briefly the history of those holy people in the Church who have had mystical experiences, we can hardly avoid agreeing with Johnson that neither physical illnesses nor less than perfect psychological health seem to pose a barrier to God's gifting anyone with experiences of the Divine Presence since, in so many cases, we see these human handicaps often noted more for their presence than for their absence.

In view of all of this, it seems reasonable to let the idea of such physical and psychological perfection go as a criterion for validating or invalidating any reported mystical experience. After all, in his earthly life Jesus does not seem to have made such perfection a prerequisite for approaching and interacting with others; rather, to the contrary, he seems to have sought out the sick and distressed, and on one occasion is reported in all three synoptic Gospels (Mt 9:12, Mk 2:17, Lk 5:31) as saying, *"Those who are healthy do not need a physician, but the sick do."* Why ought we expect that he would act any differently in his risen life?

Still, as we let go of such extreme requirements in our attempts to discern the authenticity of any reported mystical experience as much as we can, we do, at least, want to see no evidence of any disorder that would render the subject's "in-touchness" with reality questionable or any confusion about the difference between internal and external reality.

Part I: Background and Context

II. Does the Experience Reflect the Classic Qualities of Genuine Mystical Experience as Reported Through Time?

In attempting to understand the qualities of genuine mystical experience, we can do no better than to refer to the work of the late-nineteenth and early twentieth-century psychologist/philosopher/physician William James in his book The Varieties of Religious Experience, published in 1902 after first having been presented as a series of lectures at the University of Edinburgh in Scotland in that and the previous year. Virtually every scholar, researcher, writer, or teacher since James who deals with this subject depends on and quotes James's analysis of the qualities of authentic mystical experience, as will I.

James identified the following four characteristics of genuine mystical experience that seem to be universal:

1. They are "ineffable," that is to say that they are beyond adequate description in words. Remember Teresa of Avila's words, "I wish I could explain it to you, but I can't." This is primarily because they occur in an altered state of consciousness for which we have no agreed-on vocabulary and, thus, we must fall back on analogy or metaphor. It is interesting that persons who themselves have had such experiences will generally recognize the reality and truthfulness of another's descriptions of such experiences even if they are expressed in halting and approximate words and even if their personal attempts to speak of their

own experiences would be phrased in a totally different way. At the same time, the words or attempted
descriptions of both may be puzzling and unrecogniz-
able as a reflection of any known reality to someone
who has not had such an experience.

2. They are "noetic." In James's own words, "Although
so similar to states of feeling, mystical states seem
to those who experience them to be also states of
knowledge. They are states of insight into depths
of truth unplumbed by the discursive intellect. They
are illuminations, revelations, full of significance and
importance, all inarticulate though they remain; and
as a rule they carry with them a curious sense of
authority for aftertime."

James says further of ineffability and noetic quality
that "These two characters will entitle any state to be
called mystical, in the sense in which I use the word. Two
other qualities are less sharply marked, but are usually
found." These are as follows:

3. They are transient. Far and away most mystical experiences last only for moments in linear time, though
James acknowledges rare circumstances when they
may last half an hour or at most an hour or two. An
example of the latter would be the well-known event
experienced by the French mathematician and philosopher Blaise Pascal on the twenty-third of November, 1654, which he described in his journal with these
words:

FIRE
GOD of Abraham, GOD of Isaac, GOD of Jacob,
not of the philosophers
and of the learned.
Certitude. Certitude. Certitude. Feeling. Joy.
Peace.
GOD of Jesus Christ.
My God and your God.
Your God will be my God.
Forgetfulness of the world and everything.
except God . . . .
Joy, joy, joy, tears of joy . . .
Let me not be separated from him forever.

For the rest of his life, Pascal carried a handwritten account of this experience sewn into the lining of his coat.

It should be noted that even the briefest of these experiences, however, are almost universally seen by the recipients as a watershed event in their lives, never to be forgotten and marking a radical change from those moments on in how they understand reality.

4. They are experienced as completely "given." James calls this "passivity" and says that "Although the oncoming of mystical states may be facilitated by preliminary voluntary operations" such as meditating, praying, and so forth, yet when the characteristic sort of consciousness once has set in, the person "feels as if his own will is in abeyance, and, indeed, sometimes

as if he were grasped and held by a superior power." This sense of being "grasped and held" seems not always to be the case; most persons who have such experiences and with whom I have spoken describe themselves as being more "transfixed and powerfully drawn" to the One whose Presence is apprehended. They speak, not of having their will "in abeyance" but rather of accepting and rushing toward the Transcendent One they perceive with their whole hearts, minds, and fully operative wills.

III. Does All Content Involved in the Experience Meet the test of Orthodoxy?

Over the centuries, this has been a consistent and primary standard for use in evaluating mystical experiences on the basis of the belief that God's Spirit, having guided the Church, the People of God, to come to know certain truths about God's Self, it is inconceivable that God would then contradict those very truths in an encounter with any single individual. I understand this to refer to core doctrine; perhaps we might think of those things contained in the Nicene Creed. What we generally see is that mystical experiences seem to deepen and make more real for the one who has them, truths that have been learned through orthodox teaching but which had little life or liveliness or actual sense of reality before the mystical experience. One person with whom I spoke said, "It is as if my experience of God that day put flesh on the bones of what I had been taught my whole life." A beautiful example of this comes from the Quaker Thomas Kelly and is reported in his wonderful little book, Reality of the Spiritual World, in these words:

> *One may have said all of one's life, "God is love." But there is an experience of the love of God which, when it comes upon us, and enfolds us, and bathes us, and warms us, is so utterly new that we can hardly identify it with the old phrase, God is love. Can this be the love of God, this burning, tender, wounding pain of love that pierces the marrow of my bones and burns out old loves and ambitions? God experienced is a vast surprise. God's providence experienced is a vast surprise, God's guidance experienced is a vast soul-shaking surprise. God's peace, God's power—the old words flame with meaning or are discarded as trite, and one gropes for new, more glorious ways of communicating the reality.[5]*

So, far from challenging orthodox teachings, genuine mystical experiences tend always to bring vastly deepened understanding of them to the extent that anything in opposition to those teachings would surely cause questions to be raised about the authenticity of the experience.

IV. Is the Experience Life-Enhancing and Does It Foster Integration in One's Life?

Some years ago, while I was still working as a pastoral counselor, a woman who had recently moved to the

East Coast from California came to see me as a client. She explained that she wanted some help from me in coming to understand her "visions," which she reported as frequent and disturbing. She described seeing horrible scenes of devastation from natural disasters, fires, floods, and earthquakes, as well as some associated with wars, and was greatly distressed and puzzled as to what God was telling her or what she might be being called on to do in response to these things. Someone whom she had consulted about these experiences previously had suggested that, perhaps, God merely meant for her to pray for those caught in such painful situations. Perhaps that was so, though I saw a different possibility. Since it is highly uncharacteristic for authentic mystical experiences to cause such confusion and distress, I had to wonder whether these experiences were, in fact, not "visions" but rather "images." Visions generally, though not always, seem to involve images but not all images are, in fact, visions.

All of our minds create images pretty much all of the time, but most of the time, we are aware that that is the case though at times there can be confusion about this. As psychiatrist Gerald May has said, "We must remember . . . that the philosophical line between reality and illusion is a very shaky one. Because our minds continually create images of reality through our senses and conditioning, it would be true to say that all experience is at least somewhat psychologically contrived. Similarly, since God's grace cannot be destroyed even by our most extreme psychological distortions, it is just as true to say that all experience, no matter how crazy it might appear, holds at least something of God's truth."[6] Perhaps the images of devastation that she was suffering with were more a reflection of her own inner turmoil and devastation than they were of any outside reality, and in this situation, perhaps also God's grace was present, as May suggests it can be, through the way in which her compassion was aroused by what she was seeing. Perhaps, too, someday she might be able to apply that compassion to herself in her own pain and pray, not only for others in pain, but also for herself and begin, then, to move toward healing. Comparing these experiences to the overwhelming sense of joy, peace, and goodness that come in the wake of genuine mystical experiences, we must conclude that this is one example of an experience thought by the subject to be mystical but which failed to meet the criterion of being life-enhancing and integrative for the person, and the authenticity of which, therefore, ought to be questioned.

V. Have the Experiences In Question Been Transformative for the Persons Reporting Them?

The first way we generally see the transformative effect of genuine mystical experiences in a person's life is through the deepening and enlivening of faith, hope, and love spoken of by several persons above. In the wake of such experiences, people often make remarks like, "Everything has changed. Everything looks the same and, externally I guess—no, I know—that nothing has changed; yet, for me, everything has changed radically." Values may shift in that some things that were of utmost importance before may no longer be so, and other things may emerge to take their place in one's hierarchy of values.

When we speak of mystical experiences as being transformative in the lives of those people who have them, we often imagine dramatic changes apparent to all the world, and in fact, such things do, indeed, happen some of the time. For example, a successful businessman may divest himself of his company, go to medical school, and move to a poor country to provide medical care for those who have none; a woman from so-called high society may become a social worker to care for and help drug addicted teens in the inner city or a celebrity may leave the world behind to enter a monastery. However, most of the transformations that follow mystical experiences are of a different nature, are what I think of as "'soft" transformations that aren't directly observable but that permeate and change the person's being over time in truly major ways. Once again, Gerald May has not only researched this issue in depth but has also described these subtle but important transformations so remarkably well and with such perfect nuance that I will make no attempt to cull his main points but will quote him directly and at length to make his thoughts available in his own words for the benefit of readers:

"Someone describes a vision, an encounter with the Divine," May began. "Yet, Is this 'real' or is it an illusion contrived by ego?" People interested in spirituality and psychology have always been concerned with differentiating authentic spiritual experience from psychological symptoms. I have collected eight qualities that may help in reflecting upon these differences. . . . Further, our experiences cannot be judged on the basis of their content alone. We must look at how these experiences are integrated in the larger picture of life, in community, and over time.

1. ***Meaningful integration.*** Authentic spiritual experiences do not exist as isolated "highs." They occur within the context of real life and are integrated in a way that is meaningful for both individual and community. Authentic experiences may contain a perfect end-in-itself quality, but they still have meaning and impact on life.

2. ***Bearing good fruit.*** Authentic spiritual experiences lead to good effects for individual and community. Classically, this includes deepened faith, hope, trust, compassion, creativity and love. Authentic experiences do not lead to privatism or destructiveness.

3. ***Decreased self-preoccupation.*** Authentic experiences lead people to feel more identified with and open to the rest of humanity and the world. Experiences that lead to feeling more special or

better than other people, or to self-absorption, are probably not authentic.

4. **Self-knowledge.** Authentic experiences lead to a greater knowledge of oneself. Signs of repression, denial or shutting out of self-awareness indicate a lack of authenticity.

5. **Humility.** Authentic experiences lead to a particular kind of humility, one that painfully recognizes more of one's human inadequacy yet at the same time increasingly realizes one's own preciousness and worth as a child of God. It is a humility that is combined with dignity. This is in contrast to experiences that lead either to arrogance or devaluing of oneself.

6. **Openness to differences.** By deepening trust in the power and goodness of God, authentic experiences lead to less defensiveness about one's own faith and increased respect for and openness to dialogue with people of differing faiths. Authentic experiences may lead to a desire to share the truth, but they do not result in defensive or aggressive clinging to one's own understanding.

7. **Open-endedness.** Authentic spiritual experiences contain a quality of further invitation: deepening yearning, inspired energy, continued growth and healing. In contrast, experiences that communicate a sense of "having arrived" are cause for suspicion.

8. **Ordinariness.** Although authentic experiences may initially be accompanied by celebration and

*enthusiasm or by fear and trepidation, their inte-
gration brings a quality of wondrous appreciation
of the ordinary; life is holy, and the miraculous
presence of grace flows through all of it. Experiences that lead to a strong separation of the holy
from the mundane must be questioned.*

May sums up his observations by saying, *"If there
is one basic factor that distinguishes authentic from
inauthentic experience, it can be found in a paraphrase
of John of the Cross: in the end, all of us -— and all of
our experiences—must be judged on the basis of one
thing, and that is love."*[7]

When the other criteria we have considered are met
and we also see these "soft" transformations in the lives
of people who report having had experiences of God's
immediate presence, we then have ample evidence
to conclude that their experiences are highly likely to
be authentic.

A CASE FOR THE
ACCEPTANCE OF MYSTERY

What you or any given reader will take away from this
book will ultimately depend on whether or not you
accept and believe in the concept of "spirit" and/
or a dimension of reality that is nonmaterial or, at the
least, whether your mind may be open to such a possibility. Many of us do so believe, though we readily

admit, as has been said before, that, when speaking of spiritual realities, we are in a subject area impossible to discuss with any objective clarity. The reason for this is simple: we have no language that is anywhere close to adequate to describe our experiences and understandings of that ineffable world. In view of that, we try to be extremely careful of the words that we do choose and, most of all, profoundly respectful of the depth of the mystery here, open to discover rather than quick to dogmatically pronounce on these things as though any of us already knows all there is to know about them.

But many others of us, also, do not believe in "spirit" or reality of any kind beyond that which can be tested and measured in a laboratory. On the surface, this appears to be an engagingly uncomplicated way to approach life because it seems to promise that all of our beliefs about reality can ultimately be provable, if, in fact, they are not solidly proven already. It promises to allow us to settle into a comfortable security that we already know, or can come to know through our own capabilities, everything that is really important to know about reality with no need to struggle with anything as odd and frustrating as the idea of "mystery." But that never seems to work for very long because for every blazingly brilliant new scientific discovery that is made and that expands the horizons of our knowledge, we immediately run into, not more security about our knowledge, but ever and ever more questions! So might it, perhaps, be unreasonable for us to hope that the day will come when we will ever know everything about everything there is to know? The question is completely absurd, of course. But to acknowledge that fact means that we are deluding ourselves if we believe that we will ever be able to escape "mystery" or someday live in a world where there are no more intriguing unknowns. (And actually, when you think about it, would we even want to live in such a world? Wouldn't that be more than a little boring? And what would we do with all of the creative potential of our minds if we had no puzzles to puzzle over, no questions begging for investigation?)

The fact is that our lives, our world, our cosmos are all immersed in and penetrated by mystery. It is right for us to rejoice in what we know and to enjoy every minute of our search for more knowledge, but we ought not to let our joy in knowledge lead us to deny the fact that there is always much, much more to learn. Perhaps it is unlikely that such a thing might happen, given that the very search for knowledge is, itself, one of the most invigorating and valuable enterprises that we humans can undertake. And for all of the frustrations involved, the search for that knowledge leads us into what can seem, at times, to be almost unlimited creativity and joy. Do we not feel most fully human and most joyfully alive when we are so engaged? So these words are not meant in any way to suggest that we slow down, let alone leave off, the search for answers to every question we can possibly conceive. That would be unthinkable! It is, however, an argument in favor of all of us living with at least a modicum of intellectual modesty about the limits of our knowledge and understanding, particularly regarding those experienced realities that are not amenable to being weighed, measured, tested, and "proved." In other words, it is an invitation to take the idea of "mystery" as a reality as seriously as we take the idea of "knowledge." It's really perfectly fine that we don't already know everything—that gives us fascinating things to do with our time and our lives!

We know a great deal about the origin and development of the cosmos today, thanks to the world's scientists. (And we are so comfortable with this information now that it is easy to forget that as recently as forty-five years ago, most scientists believed that the universe had no beginning, that its matter was eternal.) We know now that antimatter, dark matter, and black holes exist, but we have only the barest beginnings of understanding about them at this time. Classic physics gives us many elegant descriptions of how our universe works and allows us to chart perfectly the positions and movements of distant stars and planets according to mathematical formulas that have been devised. But when we get down to the subatomic level of matter, the world of quantum mechanics, all bets are off and we are in a whole new world where very little, if anything, can be predicted, let alone charted at this time. To the contrary, scientists are talking to us today about the Heisenberg principle, an uncertainty principle that helps us understand why it is actually physically impossible to figure out both the momentum and precise position of an electron orbiting an atomic nucleus, for example. "What this means, in layman's terms," says one writer, "is that our entire known world is constructed of things that can't ever be known."[8] Even trying to make sense of what the quantum physicists are saying can make us nonscientists feel crazy long before we have any glimmer of understanding as to what they are actually talking about. How can a piece of subatomic matter be both a wave and a particle? What kind of "stuff" are we dealing with that can change just by being observed? We don't yet know how to smash a quark (or any of its fellow subatomic particles) that, so far, have simply disappeared whenever an attempt is made to break them down into even smaller particles. And what is that effort about in the first place? It is an attempt to find the Higgs boson, a hypothetical subatomic fragment that is presently thought to effect the development of mass in the universe. There is hope that the Large Hadron Collider in Switzerland may help solve this problem soon. It may. Or it may not and we could be back to the old drawing board again! (Amazingly, on July 4, 2012, just as this book was on the verge of going into print, scientists announced that they are 99.99999 percent sure they can now confirm that the Higgs boson actually exists as theorized! If true, then we are certainly going to want to be a part of the celebration of this incredible scientific discovery while we wait to hear about all of the new knowledge that will spring from it — as well as all of the new questions that will now arise.) The one thing we do know for sure is that each new discovery like this will bring ever more new, and possibly even more challenging, questions than the ones that have gone before.

We have an amazing and increasingly sophisticated understanding of the human brain and its workings, thanks to the community of neuroscientists, but we still speak haltingly on the connection between "brain" and "mind" and cannot yet define "consciousness" to a level of general satisfaction and agreement. So, we might ask, how might we ever even hope to be able to understand and describe the dynamics of something as ephemeral as mystical experiences to our satisfaction? Such a challenge, however, does not render those experiences unreal nor does it suggest that we ought not try to understand them more fully.

As we do try to come to a greater understanding of mystical experiences, it is important to note that specialists in any field of knowledge or endeavor naturally tend to see any issue that comes up through the eyes of their own specialty. Thus, when the question of mystical experience arises, parapsychologists are apt to say that these are normal human experiences that we cannot yet explain scientifically, while most doctors and medical researchers will argue that these are most assuredly not normal experiences and, therefore, there must be some disease or disorder involved. (I find it interesting that, at the turn of the nineteenth to the twentieth century, the most frequent suspect was some kind of liver malfunction while today temporal lobe epilepsy seems to be the favored diagnosis. We may be tempted to chuckle, or be irritated as William James was, at the earlier "liver theory," though the idea that mystical experience has some connection with the brain's temporal lobes is, at least, understandable. Indeed, we do know that the physiological site where mystical experiences seem to register primarily is within the brain's temporal lobes, which are also vulnerable to the effects of epilepsy.) Neuroscientists are likely to say that there is nothing more going on than some particularly exciting neural activity and/or a rush of endorphins in the brain that is being misinterpreted, while psychotherapists may be interested in the subject's personality structure—is there any evidence of narcissism, of wanting to be "special" and the center of attention, or a history of histrionic and overly dramatic fantasies that may be causing the subject to self-create these events? Sociologists and anthropologists may want to ask questions about the person's extended family or ethnic group to see if there have been any outside influences encouraging the subject to report such experiences. People who believe in reincarnation and do "past lives" work may identify such experiences as flashbacks of joy from a previous life, while astrologers might attribute the experience to a particularly fortuitous alignment of stars or planets.

It is important to acknowledge openly that most, if not all, of these conjectures raised by people from various fields of interest and expertise are perfectly possible. It is absolutely possible that a severe physical illness can produce experiences that bear some resemblance, sometimes even a strong resemblance, to authentic mystical experiences. We know for sure that certain severe mental illnesses are characterized by strange delusions and/or hallucinations that can, on occasion, have spiritual subject matter, and we know that sometimes people fabricate stories of personal experiences of God for their own ends. It is important also to note that, throughout history, spiritual masters in all of the great religious traditions of the world have not been strangers to all of these various things that could falsely be taken for mystical experiences and have, over the centuries, taken with the greatest seriousness the task of separating the authentic from the false. To do otherwise would have been to betray truth and become a party to deceit, which has always been outside the bounds of all of the great religious traditions. And so today people of faith work to follow in their footsteps, refusing to be dazzled by just any wondrous story but using wisdom and the traditional tools of discernment to separate the real from the unreal.

A new and different kind of challenge to the reality of mystical experiences is being made today, however, and that is the challenge coming from many neuroscientists who, while not questioning the subjective experience of those who report such experiences, do not accept the objective reality of the experiences reported on the grounds that whatever is experienced is simply the result of activity in the brain and does not signify anything beyond that. A part of the brilliant work of the neuroscientific community in recent years has been to use brain imaging in studies with experienced meditators as subjects to pinpoint the exact locations in the brain where there is enhanced activity during prayer and meditation. This has led some to conclude that the brain activity itself is the cause of whatever spiritual experience arises. According to Professor David Robinson of Oxford University, this conclusion is an example of faulty reasoning and comes from mixing up the ideas of correlation and cause—the fact that two things correlate with each other does not prove that either one is the cause of the other.[9] One eminent neuroscientist who is a writer as well, commented once in an interview in what seems to be a statement of consummate common sense, "If a human being is going to experience anything, it's going to be in the brain somewhere." With that in mind, it stands to reason, does it not, that if human beings do, indeed, have mystical experiences, they most likely are being experienced somehow through normal physiological channels in our brains and bodies? Still we must remember that the manner in which these events are experienced is a different issue than what is their ultimate source or cause.

The underlying issue here is widespread dedication to the belief that nothing exists except various types of matter and that whatever exists begins and ends with matter. This is a belief that can neither be proved nor disproved; but when stated as an unquestioned "given" by people well respected in our world, as scientists are, it has the power to convince many of us that it must be the absolute truth, the final word, when, in fact, it is but one belief or perspective among others. The Dalai Lama, that great student of, lover of, and advocate for science, has spoken of this with simple eloquence in his book, The Universe in a Single Atom, from which I quote at some length here. He says:

> I have noticed that many people hold an assumption that the scientific view of the world should be the basis for all knowledge and all that is knowable. This is scientific materialism. Although I am not aware of a school of thought that explicitly propounds this notion, it seems to be a common presupposition. . . . Underlying this view is the assumption that, in the final analysis, matter, as it can be described by physics and as it is governed by the laws of physics, is all there is. Accordingly, this view would uphold that psychology can be reduced to biology, biology to chemistry, and chemistry to physics. My concern here is not so much to argue with this reductionist position (although I myself do not share it) but to draw attention to a vitally important point: that these ideas do not constitute scientific knowledge; rather they represent a philosophical, in fact, a metaphysical position. The view that all aspects of reality can be reduced to matter and its various particles is, to my mind, as much a metaphysical position as the

view that an organizing intelligence created and controls reality. . . . In this view many dimensions of the full reality of what it is to be human—art, ethics, spirituality, goodness, beauty and above all, consciousness—either are reduced to the chemical reactions of firing neurons or are seen as a matter of purely imaginary constructs. The danger then is that human beings may be reduced to nothing more than biological machines. . . . The problem is not with the empirical data of science but with the contention that these data alone constitute the legitimate ground for developing a comprehensive world view or an adequate means for responding to the world's problems. There is more to human existence and to reality itself than current science can ever give us access to.[10]

Or, to put it in the more familiar words of one of the great writers of Western culture, William Shakespeare, "There are more things in heaven and earth than are dreamt of in your philosophy."

And that is precisely the message of the "cloud of witnesses" who share their stories with you in this book: that life is, indeed, permeated with mystery and that there is ever so much more to reality than any of us can ever know on our own, that a Divine Reality exists, and that that Reality is alive and powerful. This Reality is intimately connected to us in this world and, on occasion of this Spirit's own choosing, touches and enfolds us with such bright beams of Radiant Love that we are borne so completely into that Love that ever afterward our primary desire is to live in that Love and, ultimately, to carry as much of that Love as we can bear out beyond ourselves to all people, to all sentient beings, and indeed to all of Creation so that, in the end, all is one in Love.

And now their stories — each one an invitation to consider the greatest Mystery of all.

PART TWO
The Stories

The one who hears the word of God, who

has knowledge from the Most High, sees

the vision of the Almighty in ecstasy

with eyes unveiled. I see a figure, but

not really.

I behold him, but not near.

—*The Book of Numbers*

Note: In the case of contributing writers who prefer to remain anonymous and whose work appears under a pseudonym, a few facts in their biographical information have been altered to protect their confidentiality. An asterisk following an author's name indicates a pseudonym.

The Best of Times,
the Worst of Times—and Ecstasy

Joan Sant'Ambrogio

The event that I am going to tell you about happened on the evening of August 5, 1964, around 8:30 or 9:00 o'clock, I believe.

For almost two years before this, I had been living in Africa, in Lagos, Nigeria, with my husband, Ed, who was a foreign service officer on duty there for the Voice of America, and our four sons. Although Ed's tour wouldn't be over until the early spring of 1965, we were planning for me to return home to the States with the boys in the previous August since our eldest, Tom, had been accepted into the Benedictine prep school, where his father had been a member of the first graduating class, and he would need to be at home to start school in September. The plan was that Ed would take his allowed thirty days of rest and recuperation leave as we were going, and we planned to visit Egypt and Greece, then camp across southern Europe to Algeciras in Spain where the boys and I would board a ship to sail home and Ed would return to Lagos to finish his tour. At the last minute Ed wasn't able to get away for the first leg of the trip, so the boys and I took off on our own for Egypt and Greece.

We had the most wonderful time; we visited the pyramids and the Sphinx, the ruins at Saqqara, the Egyptian Museum, then we flew to Athens to visit the Parthenon and Agora, the ancient amphitheater where a performance was being rehearsed, the Greek Museum, the marketplace, and we even took a day's boat trip to some of the islands nearby where there were ancient temple ruins. Tom wanted to see Marathon, so I rented a car and we drove there. After lunch at a little outdoor taverna, we headed south to follow the coast road to Cape Sounion, but the road ended up running out in miles of olive groves. We were lost! So we stopped to swim in the Aegean Sea for a while and then got on the road again, looking quizzically out of the car window at every intersection and, following the smiles and pointing fingers and arms of the country folk we came across, finally made our way back to Athens. Then on to Rome where, when we deplaned, Ed was standing, waiting for us at the bottom of the stairs with a gloriously happy smile on his face. It was certainly one of the happiest times in our family's life.

Tom and his two next eldest brothers all wanted to see Pompeii, so after a day in Rome, we headed south to Naples, where we stopped to buy camping gear, and then on to Sorrento. We checked into a beautiful small campground in a grove of lemon trees by a rocky ravine that led down to the sea, got set up, and had a late lunch. Ed had always liked to go for a short walk, say around the block, to see the immediate environs when we checked in at any stop while traveling, and Tom, now a thoroughly reliable nearly thirteen- year-old, had begun to enjoy doing that, too. After lunch he asked if he could do just that, so we said "Sure," knowing that he would not go far, and I climbed into the car with our three-year-old to take a nap.

I woke up suddenly two hours later, having heard a clear call of "Mom!" in my sleep. When I saw how long I had slept, my first question was, "Where is Tom? Is he back?" since he would never have been gone more than fifteen or twenty minutes. He was not back and I knew immediately that something was very wrong. Ed hadn't realized how much time had gone by, so he went searching for him immediately. He asked the men who were managing the campground if they had seen him or would help search. It took some hours with no success when finally an old man, who lived on the other side of the ravine and had heard that a child was missing, came and said that he had seen a boy sleeping on the sandy bottom of the ravine where there was a vineyard. Now it was night.

I waited on a bench there in the dark with my other little ones, utterly terrified and trying not to know what I think I already did know on some level. The men got some lanterns and went down with Ed, who picked Tom up and carried him up the steps cut in the rock; an ambulance came and took Tom to the nearest medical facility, a little maternity clinic close by. When I arrived, there I noticed that there were five pale blue bows and two pink ones hanging over the door, for the five little boys and two girls who had been born there that day. We waited in the small lobby praying and praying for Tom's life, and soon a kind, young doctor came to tell us that yes, Tom was dead. He had apparently decided to try to climb back up the rocky side of the ravine instead of using the steps he had walked down, slipped, and fell back down. He had some internal injuries, the doctor said, but would have lived had there not been a rock where he landed. The back of his head had, evidently, hit the rock; he suffered a basal fracture and had died instantly.

The clinic staff was so kind; they gave us a room to stay there for the night. I didn't want to see Tom's body—I wanted to remember him alive, so happy and walking down the entrance path just going for a short walk. Ed did, and, although I was actually (and amazingly) able to sleep a little bit that night, Ed stayed up all night going back and forth from sitting with Tom and talking with the doctor, to being with the boys and me in our room. (How he and this wonderfully kind young doctor managed to understand each other is still something of a mystery to me since neither understood or spoke the other's language. It seems that some combination of almost forgotten altar boy's Latin and gestures worked.)

The next morning, a funeral director was called, arrangements made to have Tom's body sent home. We went back to the campground where one of the men, with tears in his eyes, thrust the most enormous bouquet of flowers I have ever seen into my arms. We packed up the camping gear and left for Naples, on our way back to Rome and then home to bury our precious child. The day before, as we had been driving south, we had passed Monte Casino, which I had pointed out to Tom and explained that that was where St. Benedict had founded the order of monks who would be teaching him. This day, as we passed Monte Casino again, my child was dead. But that wasn't the worst of it. I had been taught the Catholicism of the 1930s and '40s that said that only saints go straight to heaven. The rest of us all go to Purgatory where (it was still being taught and preached at that time along with all of the terrifying Medieval imagery still in use) we suffer all the tortures of the damned except that we know that we will be able to be in heaven some day. In those hours and days I was completely unable to question that, so I was living every minute with the thought that my precious, beautiful, and supremely good child was suffering in exactly that way. As I write this now, I have no idea how I was able to keep breathing in the face of the horror of such an idea.

So to Rome and home. When we arrived at JFK airport in New York and were clearing customs, the agent, noting our official passports, said warmly, "Welcome home." What can one say? Home with totally broken hearts. All any of us could manage was a simple "thank you" for his kindness.

At home our families and friends embraced us with all of their love and support, which helped us get through the week until Tom could be buried in Arlington Cemetery. The night before his funeral I wanted to go to confession; a few things were niggling at my conscience, none having to do with Tom, but I wanted to be at my child's funeral Mass with an unclouded mind and heart. I drove out to the Shrine of the Immaculate Conception in northeast Washington, where there would be a priest hearing confessions in the evening in the beautiful lower level crypt church. I have always loved the crypt church—it is usually dark, but cozy and beautiful, with magnificent mosaics everywhere. The mosaics have bits of gold in them that glisten in the candlelight. It has always felt to me like a truly holy place.

I prayed for a while, went to confession, and then walked up to one of the front pews and knelt to say the prayers that were my penance. As I was praying, I suddenly saw (interiorly, not with my physical eyes) bright, bright rays of golden light coming toward me from the tabernacle on the altar, narrow right at the tabernacle door but spreading out as they came toward me until I was totally immersed in the light. At the same time, I experienced an immense, inexpressible LOVE being poured out freely over and through my whole being, so beautiful that I moved into what I can only describe as a state of total ecstasy. My mind said to me immediately, "It's the "Spirit of Jesus." It only lasted for some few seconds, but as I knelt there in complete awe, somehow I came to know that that Love was what my child had gone into. As I got up to leave minutes later, I had tears in my eyes, the first ones shed since Tom had died. But they weren't tears of grief but tears of joy, even of bliss, coming from the unutterable beauty that I had experienced and the assurance that my son was not suffering the tortures of the damned, but was with God, enfolded in God's love.

Tom was buried. Ed went back to Africa to finish his tour, and I and my other children settled in at home. Finally, that state of initial shock wore off and the tears came, oceans and oceans of tears for months, till the worst of my grief was finally spent, though echoes of it have always remained within me on some level. "Can a mother forget the child of her womb?" Isaiah asked. No, never. I have held that experience of the presence of the risen Jesus deep in my heart ever since but never told anyone for years and years. I still have told only a few people. It has always seemed so holy to me that it has felt as though it needs to be held close and protected. I can only write about it now because the desire to help others come to understand more fully the utter, unimaginable immensity of God's love has overtaken any desire to simply hold and cherish this for myself alone.

ॐ ∽

Joan Sant'Ambrogio is a retired marriage and family counselor in her eighties, a Roman Catholic laywoman. She is a voracious reader with a broad range of interests and has done serious studies in philosophy, world literature, theology, music, art, history, and, as a child and young woman, classical ballet. She has had a lifelong interest in archaeology and says that one of her few regrets in life is that she waited too long to go on a dig somewhere as a volunteer, since she is too hampered by arthritis to do so now. She is a widow, has three adult children and two grandchildren. She lives on a small horse farm in the northern Shenandoah Valley in Virginia. Her immediate and extended families and friends are a deeply cherished part of her life.

Jesus Touched Me

Donna Acquaviva

This story is one I've told few people. While I believe in giving witness and thanks when God intervenes in my life, too many people would have greeted it with silent derision or worse, loud derision. So, keeping in mind what Christ said about pearls and swine, I've held this one in my heart and pondered it for many years— until now.

I'd had nine pregnancies and I know stomach pain, but this was different. For one thing, it didn't come and go like labor. It stayed—and stayed—and *stayed*. And it got worse by the minute. Finally, doubled over and almost unable to talk, I asked my teenage daughter to get me to a hospital.

The ER doctors said it was pelvic inflammatory disease, caused by a birth control device I'd foolishly left in far too long and hadn't gotten checked. By the time I was admitted, I was on 30,000 milligrams of antibiotics an hour and nearly unconscious from pain and exhaustion.

A few hours later, a nurse came in to take my vitals, and as she put her hands on my wrist she called another nurse: "We've lost her. I can't get a pulse."

I could hear her (it's true that hearing is the last thing to go, so be careful what you say around dying people) but I couldn't open my eyes, nor could I talk. All I could do was lie there and hope she was wrong.

Well, there was lots of fuss and lots of poking and lots of voices around my bed, and finally I could open my eyes, and finally, I could talk. And when three—count 'em— three doctors came in to tell me that they'd probably be able to save my life but they couldn't save my damaged female organs and they'd have to take them out, right away I had an answer.

Which was, "Wait. Give me three days." The two men and a woman looked at each other and back at me, and one said, "Ms. Acquaviva, we don't know if you realize how sick you are. This can't wait."

"Please," I said. "Give me three days."

"You don't understand," the woman doctor said. "We're giving you the strongest antibiotics we have, and as much as we can—and they're not working. You are so damaged that if you don't get the surgery now, you'll need it in the near future. And later it will be harder on you than it is now."

"Please. Three days," was all I said. They looked annoyed, even angry, but they shrugged and walked out, leaving me with my thoughts. Frankly, at that moment, I had no idea what I was going to do. I simply knew that it was going to involve God.

It was a Catholic hospital, so there was a crucifix across the wall from my bed. I gazed at it and closed my eyes, knowing that I would be guided. Soon I was imaging the sick part of my body. It was gray and lifeless. I concentrated. In my mind it slowly turned pink and healthy and was soon throbbing with life. I held that image for a long, long time.

Then I opened my eyes again and looked again at Christ on the cross, and I decided to talk to him quite frankly. There was no time for tip-toeing around the subject, for the patience that usually is a requisite part of prayer and the spiritual life, for contemplating in silence, and for waiting. This called for action.

"Dear Jesus," I prayed. "When you walked this earth, and someone asked you for healing, you refused no one. You cured the Roman soldier's daughter, you cured the Samaritan woman, you cured everyone who asked you. Well, I know you are still with us on this earth, and I'm your daughter and I need healing. I know you want to heal me. I know you *can* heal me. So I'm asking. Please, please heal me."

Then I told Jesus all that he already knew: that I had seven children who still needed their mom, that I was only thirty-nine years old and still had a lot of living to do and much I wanted to learn, that I had a job with a nonprofit that I loved and wanted to keep, and which I needed to get back to as soon as possible. Nonprofits are notoriously understaffed, among other things, and it was work that God had gently drawn me to.

Then I began the cycle all over again. I imagined my insides all healthy and pink and I talked to Jesus about healing as though he were right in the room. Except for interruptions by medical procedures, meals, and my beloved family at visiting hours, I did this for three days, barely taking time to sleep.

On the third day I felt a presence next to my bed, a strong presence, a silent presence. Another nurse, another blood drawing, what? I opened my eyes. It was Jesus.

I am writing this on the feast of the Transfiguration, and I can only describe the Christ the way Scripture does on that day. "His face shone like the sun, and his clothes were dazzling white." In fact, his face was so bright that I could not see his features—but there was no doubt about who it was. I knew.

He said nothing, but I felt incredible peace and love emanating from him. He was so close I could touch him, but something told me not to do that. Then he reached out, and I felt his gentle touch on my arm. It was over so quickly that I barely felt it. Then he was gone.

I closed my eyes again and lay there meditating on what had just happened. My heart was full and my spirit soaring, but physically I felt no different. All I could say was, "I love you" and "Thank you" over and over again.

The next day the three doctors marched in. Wasting no time in conversation, they closed the curtains around my bed with a swish, and then set about examining me. One by one they straightened up, looked at each other, and looked at me. "Ms. Acquaviva," one of them said, "there is no sign of infection. We no longer see a need for surgery. You'll be able to go home tomorrow."

I always thought it was strange that they didn't ask me what I'd done during those three days. And I often wondered what I'd have told them if they had. Doctors in those days were not real big on miracles.

I just know what happened to me was a miracle. And I'm still saying "I love you" and "Thank you." Over and over and over again.

ৡ৯

Donna Acquaviva, a trained spiritual director, is a professional writer and teacher of writing and a freelance editor. She and her second husband, also a former writer/editor, live in Roanoke, Virginia, where they are active as lay ministers in the church. In addition to her ministry as a spiritual director, Donna is a liturgical dancer, potter, reader to the blind, and hospice volunteer. She and her husband have eleven children, twenty-one grandchildren, and five "greats."

Will No One Help Me?

*Annalee Morris**

I was in my early twenties and married to an abusive husband. After several years of abuse, I was giving up. I had counseled with an evangelical minister who advised me to go home and submit to my husband and pray for him. I had counseled with a mainline minister who wanted to know what I had done to bring on my husband's behavior. Either way, the Church's representative focused not on helping me but on my husband, and I was ready to give up. It was midnight and I was alone, my husband having gone away on a business trip. I drew a pentagram within a circle and lit candles—if the Church was eager to discard me, I was going to give myself over to evil, to Satan. I began praying to Satan, to whatever forces rule this world, to come and take me and show me how to survive and thrive in a world where women are beaten up and men don't care.

Then I heard steps coming down the hall, hard-soled heels clicking on the hard floor. But just as the footsteps got to the door of the room I was in, a bright light

* Pseudonym

appeared before me, and the steps stopped. Jesus stood before me in the light, which was bright but not harsh at all. His eyes are what I remember—so deep and dark, filled with love and kindness, knowing and seeing all of my faults and loving me anyway. His love is so deep, so encompassing, so warm and kind; it flooded me and soaked into each atom of my being.

After a moment he said, *"You may give up on yourself, but you cannot give yourself away. You are mine. You gave yourself to me in baptism. And if you don't love yourself enough to think you are worth fighting for, I do. I did not create you for anyone to beat up or destroy. You do not owe that to anyone. You may give it if you wish, but you do not owe it to anyone. I love you, and if you were the only person in all of history who believed in me, then I would go to the cross all over again just for you."* And I knew it was true, he would have died just for me and only me. And I knew it was true for each and every person ever born—he would do what he did for each of us, and it doesn't make it less special, but even more precious somehow.

Whoever it was whose steps I had heard coming to the door turned and walked away as I fell into the arms of Jesus and wept. Gradually I gathered the strength to leave that marriage, and have now been married for more than thirty years to a wonderful man.

৵৵

Annalee Morris asks that no personal information about her be shared.

What Kind of God Would Do This to Us?

Betty Voight

When I was almost five years old my little brother, age three, died suddenly of meningitis. His death rocked the foundation of my family and left us all, each in our own way, bereft. We moved to my grandparents' farm to get away from the awful memories, but, of course, they followed us. I began to question inside myself, what kind of "God" snatched little brothers from families like this? My parents' grief left me feeling very alone and worried that they no longer loved me.

Then one day when I was about eight or nine years old I experienced this "God," although I had no name or words for this experience at the time. While playing in the woods by a lovely little stream the world around me suddenly became so alive—everything was glowing! I know that the physical reality didn't change but something happened so that my ability to see—to really see the incredible beauty of this place changed. I don't know what happened or how but it was like, for a moment or an hour, I was in heaven right here on earth and now I knew, I really knew that Someone had ordered this gorgeous world—and it was good! Something shifted inside of me after that experience and I was able to see the beauty and goodness of life even in the midst of sorrow and confusion.

છે જી

When I was fifteen my congregation sent me to church camp. I don't know why, but I was like a sponge soaking up water as I heard the Word of God preached and taught that week. I was actually quite a normal teenager, interested in the boys who were there.

Then, at some point in the week, I heard a word from God spoken in my own ear with these words, "*I want to use your life!*" I answered with a resounding, "Yes! You may use me, I am yours!" I am now sixty-six years old and I still remember these words as though it was yesterday. All of my life I have believed this was God speaking directly to me, calling me. My "yes" has been the guiding force throughout my life.

I did meet a boy at camp that year, too, who became my husband seven years later. We were holding hands one night during the chapel service when I heard the preacher say, "If anyone present wants to give their life to Jesus Christ, please stand up." I stood. But it seemed that it wasn't really me doing that standing up. I remember that I was standing and yet it was as though I had no other option. Someone forced me up.

When I came home from camp I spent many hours in my room crying tears of joy. My mother thought that something awful had happened to me at camp, but I would not tell her. What happened was too precious and I was afraid she would not understand. I told no one about this experience of hearing God's voice until I was forty years old.

≈ ≈

Around the age of forty-five I was led to a spiritual director. It was a time in my life when I was actively seeking God (or more likely, God was actively seeking me). After years of what seemed like working for God in the world, I wanted to get back to that intimate, loving relationship I had had with him as a child. This spiritual director suggested that use my imagination and invite Jesus to come and sit with me while I pray. I followed her suggestion. Each morning, as I came to prayer, I closed my eyes and, in my imagination, saw Jesus enter the room. I gave him a hug and put him in a large rocking chair opposite of where I sat, then I went about my prayer. I knew he was there but paid little attention to him other than to be aware of his presence.

One day Jesus got up from that rocking chair! I did not do this with my imagination. He did it—and he came and sat very close to me. I was so startled! Then he refused to stay seated beside me and, before I even had time to reflect on this, he merged into my body. It all happened so fast and was over just as quickly as it began. I have always believed that he was trying to tell me that he was within me and that I didn't need to keep him outside anymore. It has taken me years to live into this truth.

❧

Betty Voight lives in southwest Pennsylvania with David, her husband of forty-five years. They have two grown children and two granddaughters. She says that, on their lovely rural property, they have a hermitage, which is a self-contained cabin for personal retreat. She is a lifelong member of the Presbyterian Church U.S.A., though, at this point in her life, she thinks of herself as more "universal," open to the Presence of God in all people and all of the major religious faiths. She describes her work of service to the world as helping people find the truth of God deep within themselves through prayer, inner healing, and holy listening.

Eyes to See, Ears to Hear

*Deborah Bazemore**

It was twenty years ago that I saw Jesus Christ on the streets of Washington, D.C.

I was participating in a workshop led by the Wellspring mission group of the Church of the Saviour, an ecumenical church established by Gordon and Mary Cosby in Washington, D.C., in 1947. Wellspring's mission is no less than to renew the church of Jesus Christ, "an only slightly presumptuous goal," as expressed by one of our facilitators. Prior to going into the city, we had spent parts of two days at Wellspring's retreat center in Maryland, where we experienced intimate worship, seminars to challenge the mind and heart, and extended periods of silence. We were beginning to grasp the deeper implications of God's call, to understand the meaning of spiritual gifts, to observe firsthand the strength of a highly disciplined community. We had prepared ourselves beforehand by reflecting on assigned readings. Although most of us were longtime members of the Body of Christ, we were discontented with the Church as we knew it. We were ready for renewal!

* Pseudonym

Part of Wellspring's initial workshop experience is to take a trip into Washington's inner city, to talk with those called to a "particular area of pain in the world."

The Adams Morgan/Mt. Pleasant area in the city's northwest is the site of many Church of the Saviour missions. As we listened to the registered nurse at The Family Place, a community center for parents and young children, I was amazed by the statistics we heard: statistics reflecting poverty, inadequate nutrition, poor housing, lack of medical care. I was deeply moved by the stories of young mothers from Central America, some pregnant, some with young children, who had walked across the country to our nation's capital, hoping to find help.

I was overwhelmed by the level of commitment and caring expertise shown by paid staff and volunteers. I was heartened by the data published by the local hospital showing a definite decrease in the infant mortality rate since The Family Place had begun providing medical care, as well as counseling, companioning, and resourcing. These folks were clearly making a vital difference in the lives of some of the city's weakest, most vulnerable residents.

As we left the mission and walked out into the bright July sunshine, a kind of hush came over us. All of us were profoundly moved; we needed time and space to process what we had experienced. As we stood there on Columbia Road, I was stunned to see Jesus Christ himself standing in the midst of the street vendors, gazing with loving compassion at the people around him. There was no doubt at all in my mind that this was Jesus of Nazareth. His image was larger than life. He wore a long, flowing robe of horizontal stripes, with variegated shades of brown. He seemed perfectly at ease among his people, entirely at home there in the inner city.

The vision lasted only a few seconds and I am quite certain that no one else saw it. It seemed to have particular significance for me alone. And, as the years have passed, I have discovered deeper layers of its meaning. Gordon Self has commented that, like the Samaritan woman, whose "brief exchange with Jesus challenged her to draw deeper from the well of her faith," we often refer to these watershed moments throughout our lives, continuing to unpack meaning. The clear message that I have come to over the years seems to be centered around one word: compassion.

My husband, the Rev. Bill Bazemore, and I have been married for fifty-two years, and most of those years have focused on ministry with the poor. Serving the marginalized has always been Bill's "call." He is truly a man of deep compassion, leading with the heart. I have been a faithful companion in ministry but have served more out of my head than my heart. Studying the Myers-Briggs Type Indicator and the Enneagram has enabled me to see and appreciate our different personality characteristics, our different approaches to ministry. Like the apostle Paul before his encounter with Jesus on the road, I served God out of a deep conviction and passion, but failed to realize that something was lacking. I was blind, and God graciously taught me to see more fully, more completely. My spirit needed the quality of compassion to become more human, to become more whole, to become fully who I was created to be.

Henri Nouwen has been an important mentor for me. In the book he authored with Donald McNeill and Douglas Morrison, Compassion: A Reflection on the Christian Life, he takes a critical look at the concept of compassion. The word, he explains, "is derived from the Latin pati and cum " which together means to suffer with." Compassion asks us to go where it hurts, to enter into places of pain, to share in brokenness, fear, confusion, and anguish. "Compassion challenges us to cry out with those in misery, to mourn with those who are lonely, to weep with those in tears. It requires us to be weak with the weak, vulnerable with the vulnerable, and powerless with the powerless. Compassion means full immersion in the condition of being human." He is quick to admit that compassion, understood as suffering with, is something we tend to resist. It is not among our most natural responses. We are pain avoiders and we consider anyone who feels attracted to suffering abnormal, or at the least, very unusual.

Over the years, as I have reflected on Scripture, the compassion that Jesus showed to those at society's margins has always struck a deep chord within my spirit. His raising from the dead the widow of Naim's only son, his boldness in touching and healing those with leprosy, his weeping at the death of his dear friend and soul brother, Lazarus—these and other stories have been compelling and have given direction to my prayer to become more compassionate. Because of my dramatic encounter with Jesus on the streets of Washington, D.C., I have found myself praying for "a heart of flesh" in place of a sometimes "stony" heart. Although I have certainly not reached the level of compassionate living described by Henri Nouwen, I believe that I am on the right road!

Deborah Bazemore lives with her husband, Bill, a retired Presbyterian minister, in a small town in southeastern Ohio. They have shared life and ministry for fifty-five years. Although some of their ministries have been traditional church pastorates, most of those years have focused on the spiritual and physical needs of the poor. They are the founders of a Sunday evening alternative worshiping community in their area, which celebrated its thirtieth anniversary in 2009. Deborah spent fifteen years developing a comprehensive volunteer services program for her town's schools. In retirement she is involved with adult literacy, leads a small Bible study group for women, and offers spiritual direction. Bill and Deborah are blessed to have three grown children, six grandchildren, and one great-grandchild.

The Stations of the Cross: Jesus Falls for the Second Time

Thomas Ball

One beautiful fall afternoon a few years ago, having arrived quite early for a late-afternoon class session in the Spiritual Direction Internship program at Manresa, a Jesuit retreat house in Bloomfield Hills, Michigan, I decided to enjoy the lovely grounds. Coming upon the Stations of the Cross, I slowly meandered along, looking at the half-sized figures mounted at eye level in large coral formations. At one station, as I stood gazing, I thought to myself, "I'm a Protestant boy, born and bred. I wonder what a Catholic would see in these figures. I know what they are, but I'll bet a Catholic would perceive depth and meaning far beyond what I do." A bit later, as I paused to face the station where Jesus falls for the second time, I saw that the figure of Jesus was down on one knee, the cross over his shoulder, and his face was turned right at eye level with the viewer. As I stood there, my vision began to darken from the outside edges, black swirling clouds moving in until all I could see was directly ahead and the eyes of the Jesus figure were staring directly, intently at me. As we locked eyes, suddenly I began sobbing—deep, wracking sobs. "I'm sorry! I'm sorry! I'm so sorry, Jesus. I did that. I caused that. That is my fault. Oh, Jesus, I am sorry, I'm sorry!" This went on for five minutes or so. Then my vision cleared and I went on my way, pondering what had just happened.

It was later in the Spiritual Direction training program that I learned that Ignatius Loyola's second week of his Spiritual Exercises calls for asking God to gift us with an understanding of the depth of our sin.

The next time I walked the Stations of the Cross at Manresa I stood before that figure again. The head of Jesus? It looks down at the ground.

☙ ❧

Thomas Ball founded the Department of Communications at Spring Arbor University and was department head until two years before he retired. He now serves as Graduate Coordinator for an online master's program there and also teaches Counseling Research, Human Sexuality, and Sexual Abuse Recovery in a master's program in counseling. He provides spiritual direction for adult survivors of childhood sexual abuse, many of whom have developed dissociative identity disorder as a way of coping with their pain. He wrote a chapter on prayer for inner healing of memories for the book Ritual Abuse in the 21st Century, published in 2008, as well as the foreword for the book Fire and Water also published in 2008. He lives in Michigan and recently purchased a Big Saur 22 Mosquito and joined a gun club to learn how to target shoot. His wife died a few years ago. He has one adult son who lives near him, four grandchildren, and two great-grandchildren, and he was recently remarried.

An Experience of Prayer Before an Icon of Jesus

Mary Crummer

I have been coming to Shalem gatherings yearly since 1981. Here are some experiences of God that I have had during these gatherings. I was in my fifties at the time.

On one occasion I was in a silent session sitting with the icon of Jesus. While I focused on the icon, I saw it begin to flash and change into a different human face about every second. The faces were of young, old, middle-aged, men, women, children, and black, white, Asian, Native American, Latin people, people wearing current dress and some of an earlier time. I opened and closed my eyes and the icon didn't stop but kept on going. At least a hundred faces appeared. I was in awe. The meaning seems pretty clear—that all humanity is contained in God and God is contained in all humanity. I hope to be able to keep this in mind as I deal with my fellow human beings in the future.

At another time, I was again sitting in silence before an icon. With icons, I am often drawn into discursive prayer, which is a much different form of prayer than is usual for me. I was talking away in my mind like a black-clad matron in an old Italian movie, talking to a statue of Mary. I was abjectly apologizing to Jesus for forgetting him so often as I go about my life, and with great emotional declarations I was promising to dwell in him if he would dwell in me. I heard a voice that I knew to be internal, though it was as close to an externally audible voice as I have ever heard in prayer. A male voice with a noticeably Jewish accent said, *"I thought that was the deal we already had going."* I laughed out loud! The incident reminded me that God has a sense of humor about me, and not to take myself so seriously

What keeps me coming back to these gatherings over the years is the feeling that I am totally in love with the people here. What I mean by that is, when I meditate with them, often my heart seems to physically open and I feel such tenderness. Maybe that is all that this spiritual stuff is about—being able to relax into being in love with people, having an open heart of appreciation for each soul, without wanting anything from them.

Mary Crummer is an Episcopalian active in her church, and she has also attended Buddhist gatherings. Dialogue between Christians and Buddhists has been a longtime passion for her, and she says that people who can listen and try to understand the other from both traditions have had tremendous influence on her. She is a psychologist trained in Gestalt therapy and lives in Gainesville, Florida.

Words from Jesus When the Answer to Prayer Was No

*Julia Bradford**

I had been married to my husband, Tim, the love of my life, for fourteen wonderful years when a tragedy struck our family, the death of one of our beloved children. The youngest of our three little girls was killed in an automobile accident as she was being carpooled to preschool. Although neither my husband or I could have predicted it at the time, that traumatic event ended our marriage. Although everything looked the same from the outside, Tim was never himself again. He went through all of the motions, but it was as if he were dead inside. I wanted for us to hold each other and cry together, but he couldn't stand to hear our daughter's name and always said, "I don't want to talk about it." I found out much later that he had tried to talk about our child's death with his beloved father, who was a wonderfully good and loving man and very religious. His dad had said to him, "I don't want to hear it. I'm glad she's dead because she is in heaven with God where she is meant to be." I learned that he had also tried to talk with his mother about his grief. Her response was, "Think about me. I lost my mother and father and my

* Pseudonym

78

sister all in one year." I don't know if he ever tried to talk to anyone else about it or not. It would be easy to understand, I think, if he had not.

After some months of being unusually quiet, he returned to what looked like his "old self," an outgoing, seemingly happy-go-lucky guy who was so playful that he brought smiles and laughter into everyone's life. From the outside no one would have known there was anything wrong. But he had pulled completely away from me and our other children emotionally. It was almost like a steel door inside of him somewhere had slammed shut. Oh yes, he continued to initiate, and be one of the most enthusiastic players, in lawn games on summer evenings, go to the girls' soccer games, and take them to the pool in the summer, but that was it. It was as though his heart had simply died. Needless to say, I was completely heartbroken. I tried everything I knew to do to try to draw him back to us. We had always talked about everything with each other, which is why we had always been so close, I'm sure. But that was gone. He would only talk about mundane things now. If I reached out and put my arms around him, he would push them away, not unkindly, but with just one word: "Don't." All I could figure out was that, possibly, he, having had to go back to work immediately after our daughter's funeral, had really not had the chance to grieve as I had. And, since I loved him so much, I promised myself—and God—that I would give him whatever time he needed, that I would not pressure him in any way or try to draw him back to me until I saw some sign that he was moving back toward me again.

That sign came two years later. I had gone to bed early and was asleep when he came to bed much later. I was awakened in the wee small hours by a gentle kiss on my cheek from Tim. I turned to reach out for him but there was that word again, "Don't."

Some months later, after Tim had returned home from an assignment overseas, he and I were sitting in the study one morning reading the paper and having our morning coffee. At one point I looked up to see him sitting there with tears streaming down his face.

"What is it, honey?" I asked. He said, just very simply, "I'm sorry for the way things are." "I am, too," I responded, and then as gently as I could say it, "Don't you think we need some professional help?" He agreed.

We found a psychiatrist of our own faith who specialized in marriage and family therapy and began to see him weekly. I remember that, in our first session, our therapist asked Tim how many tears he had left inside over our child's death. His answer? "Oceans of tears." We were compulsively faithful to our appointments for more than a year, at which point it had begun to seem as though it might be best for Tim to have that time alone, so, willing to return at any time, I stopped, leaving the time for him.

He continued faithfully for several more years. But he also started drinking more and more heavily and coming home later and later after work after stopping off at a bar with some of his work buddies. He was faithful to his therapy but nothing was improving for us in any way. We both worked at keeping the wheels of family life in motion, but that is all that was there. It was frightening and lonely, and I prayed and prayed for him and for us every day.

After a few years, he gave up on therapy, saying, in a surprisingly curt tone of voice, a voice I had never heard before, "I'm not going to change, not one iota." The drinking continued and worsened and I began to see signs of a meanness in him that had never been there before. I had no idea of what the fullness of the problem might be. Is it that he had somehow "decided" on some level not ever to love again as he had loved our child so as to never be hurt so terribly again? Did this have anything to do with the fact that he had had so many losses growing up that this one was the final straw? I had no way of knowing, but it seemed as if it might be even more than that. One day I said to him, "It seems like not only can you not let yourself love any-more, but you can't allow yourself to be loved either." His answer was, "I can't say you're wrong." As more time went by, it began to look like living with me and our daughters, who all loved him so dearly, was heaping something like coals of guilt on his head. One day I asked him, "Do you think you would be happier living alone?" "Maybe," he answered.

So he found an apartment and we worked together to get it set up and furnished and he moved out. After a while he did seem calmer and somewhat more at peace. He was home for most holidays and we had lunch together from time to time. Several years later, at lunch one day, he said that he thought he might like to move back home after he came back from a short vacation. How could I describe the elation I felt? Finally! At last! I was so indescribably happy; it looked like our long nightmare of pain could be coming to an end. But the vacation came and went and then six more weeks with nothing said about coming home. When I asked about it, he said, "I can't. I just can't."

I think the fact that he "could not" do this frightened him, so he went back into therapy, doubling his time. And, in the meantime, I continued to pray my heart out for him to be healed of whatever it was that was hurting him so very, very deeply.

A few more years had gone by when one Sunday at Mass, after I had received Communion and was begging Jesus, whom I had just received sacramentally, to help and heal Tim, I heard a soft male voice within me say, not unkindly, simply, but with authority, *"My love is enough for you."* "I know that, Lord," I responded, "but can't I have some of that love through him?" Silence.

I understood that Jesus was telling me directly, in as kind a way as possible, that my prayers and hopes for us were never going to be fulfilled. I held those words in my mind and heart for some days and then slowly began to accept that it was really and finally over for us. Some months later, sitting on the lawn in front of a simple lodge where I was on retreat, in tears, I was able to take my wedding ring off. I know that many people suspect that those who report hearing words from God are really just making them up and "hearing what they want to hear," they will say. But those words I heard, actually not the words themselves but what they portended, were the last thing that I would ever have wanted to hear. But there they were.

In time, as my grief wore itself out, I could look back at those words and see them for what they really were— a promise that, whatever happened, I would never be alone and without love, God's love, in and through my brother, Jesus, who had spoken them to me. And that love has, indeed, always been far, far more than "enough" for me. Now, in my old age, I can only say that, truly, "My cup runneth over" with that Love.

A few years later, Tim died suddenly from a massive heart attack. He waited so long to call for help that he wasn't even able to hang up the phone before he was gone.

శ్రీ ⚬ॐ

Julia Bradford is a life long Christian, Presbyterian in her childhood and Roman Catholic as an adult, who credits the deep faith and trust in God of her mother and grandmother for helping her to learn trust in God, too. She has always been active in volunteer work for the Church wherever she has been. Julia says that she comes from a family of avid gardeners and loves beautiful gardens but thinks that, alas, she seems to have missed the gene that makes all of the hard work of creating one fun. She has two grown daughters, one son-in-law, and two grandchildren and lives on the East Coast.

Worrying About the Challenge of Caregiving

Marlene Anderson

I had been serving as the pastor of Grace Lutheran Church in Sioux Falls, SouthDakota for more than seventeen years when, in 2000, I first took a "leave from call" and then later retirement to journey back home to northern Minnesota to care for my aging mother in her last years. I was sixty; she was ninety-three.

Full-time caregiving was a new experience for me. By this time my mother was living in an apartment in Warren, Minnesota, thirty miles from the farm where my parents had lived for fifty-five years. My father had died in 1995 at the age of ninety-nine. My mother had served as his caregiver after he suffered a broken hip at the age of ninety-five.

Now she needed some assistance because of osteoarthritis as well as other health problems. I was delighted to have some time with my mother; I also found out, as many others have before me, that full-time caregiving can stretch us to our limits and be utterly exhausting. At one point when I was particularly weary, my sister came to stay with our mother for a little while, which provided a chance for me to spend some quiet time in my own apartment at the end of the hall. My first night there, in my tiredness and frustration, my prayer rather quickly changed from pious talk to God to honesty and, finally, more accurately stated, to demands! After giving God a piece of my mind about how things were, I settled into bed anticipating a good, and unbroken, night's rest.

Within a minute or two I was sitting bolt upright in my bed! My eyes went to my "icon" corner and my fears and prayers followed. My fear was now very clear to me. What if I collapsed and couldn't take care of my mother? What if my mother and I were forsaken by God? What if, in embarking on this ministry of caregiving, so unknown to me, I was abandoned?

My eyes fastened on the icon of Jesus with Mary, his mother. It is the Vladimir Mother of God, sometimes referred to as the "Mother of God of Tenderness." In that moment it seemed to me as though Jesus stepped out of the icon and said directly to me, *"Marlene, I took care of my mother from the cross. I will take care of your mother."*

In the five remaining years of caregiving for my mother, that word of promise came to me again and again. I understood that my mother was safe in the love of Jesus and so was I. God kept reminding me along the way to *"Rest more fully. Sink more deeply into my love."* Enough strength would be given, perhaps not an excess amount of strength, but enough!

My mother died in May 2005 at the age of ninety-eight.

ॐ ॐ

Summer came. Every year our county held its County Fair in Warren in July, and a beautiful fireworks display was always included in the schedule of events. I had discovered that the best place to watch the fireworks in all their glory was from the cemetery at the edge of town.

That July I again made my way to the cemetery, but for some reason this time I found myself walking out to the middle of the graveyard where there was a large granite cross. I stopped there. The display began at dusk. The brilliant lights shooting through the sky some-how seemed to bring heaven and earth together. I felt a great oneness with God and with all of creation, including loved ones who had died, there that night. I felt surrounded by "a cloud of witnesses" and, drawn up into that cloud, I felt especially close to my mother. It made for quite a celebration!

So Jesus was, indeed, present with me during those caregiving years and yes, he did take care of my mother, too.

The icon remains in a prominent place in my prayer space.

ॐ ॐ

Marlene Anderson is a former preschool and elementary teacher, parish worker, Christian Education Director and inner-city program coordinator who later attended Luther Seminary in St. Paul and was ordained to the ministry in 1982. She spent four years in Nome, Alaska, and four years in Papua, New Guinea, in global mission work. She is currently sharing in A Sabbath Place ministry with friends in St. Paul, Minnesota, where she works in spiritual direction, prayer ministry, Sabbath-keeping, and hospitality and with peace and justice issues.

A Surprise on the Feast of the Transfiguration

Lisa Cole

On the Feast of the Transfiguration, August 6, 1991, we celebrated our regular Thursday healing service at my church at noontime. As the priest started his homily, I found myself on a green hillside behind the three disciples, Peter, James, and John, standing in front of Jesus. Although all were partially veiled in a translucent cloud, I knew who these men were. Then I heard Jesus' voice very clearly when he said to me, *"Follow me!"*

The Lord, the disciples, and the hillside melted before me. The message remained.

Well, I have followed him and I do—I have since become an ordained deacon in the Episcopal Church, working with and raising up others as we serve the poor, the needy, the hungry, the sick and dying in our community, and carry the Good News of God's Kingdom wherever we go.

೭⊷⊷

Lisa Cole is seventy-one years old and has been married to an architect since 1959. They have two children and four granddaughters whom she thoroughly adores. She is an ordained deacon of the Episcopal Church, USA, and serves as an associate chaplain in the Pastoral Care Department of a local hospital. She is also an artist and works in the areas of design and wearable art. She enjoys creating her own fabrics and is fond of creating collages and assemblages and seeing beyond the surfaces and outlines and printing them. She and her husband live in a small city in mid-southern Michigan in a home that her husband designed and that she loves. She also likes to swim, walk, and ride the bus.

Another very special thing about Lisa is that she has lived with type I diabetes since 1947. That makes her one of a handful of diabetic survivors of sixty years plus—one of about one hundred in the world.

God with Me in the Convent,
God with Me in the World

Inez A. Bing

I grew up Roman Catholic and completed twelve years of parochial school education. Just after graduation from high school, at the tender age of seventeen, I entered the convent to become a Sister of Mercy. My initial experience upon entering was that I had "died and gone to heaven." It was everything that I had hoped it would be. I belonged to a community in which I felt not only a wonderful connection with kindred spirits, but also very much like I had come home. It was a place where I felt welcomed and loved, and I simply delighted in being there. My desire to enter the convent stemmed from a deep inner desire to love and serve God, and this seemed like the best way to meet that goal. I could picture no other.

After three years of training as a postulant and then a novice, I was assigned to a local convent to teach seventy-seven first-graders. My dream had come true— to be a nun and also to be a teacher with my own classroom.

I was somewhat surprised when, in about three years, I began to become disillusioned. I had grown up with the idea that nuns were just the other side of perfect, and that to be a "good person," I needed to be a nun. I believed that God had called me to this "higher" way of being in order to be free of the things of the world. And now I was seeing religious life as it really was. The nuns were all too human, with all their foibles; they weren't the perfect beings I had imagined.

And so, during the summer of 1968, I became aware that my spirits were drooping badly. I no longer felt the joy of serving the Lord that had been there in the beginning. "But this is what I've always wanted," I told myself. "How can this be?" I certainly had no active desire to leave the convent, as many of my young associates had done before me. I was so happy to be a part of this religious community. Or was I? And if I really was happy here, why was I so depressed? After all, wasn't I one of God's "chosen ones"? And then, what did that really mean?

But there I was, now lost in confusion and discontent. I didn't want to face what I was feeling and sought the help of an older, wiser sister to help me understand what was going on with me. "Maybe you are being called to serve God in some different way," she said. I was feeling quite guilty as this was what I had always thought I wanted. "How could I turn my back on God?" I asked myself. I didn't understand; I didn't know; I simply had no idea what to do.

One evening, after night prayers, I crawled into bed to struggle again with the idea of whether or not I was to stay in the convent or go home. Mint green walls surrounded me in this very small room that held only a bed, a dresser, a desk and chair, and a corner sink. I lay there having a conversation with God about my sad state of affairs, still so confused, painfully blue, and desperately seeking guidance. As I lay there, my eyes began to notice over in the corner of the room, just above the doorway this bright light that simply shone in the dark. I was fully awake and knew well that I wasn't dreaming. I just stared at this light and, as I did, I heard a voice clear and loud that said, *"Inez, why can't you just wake up and realize that you don't belong here any more?"* Simple, complete, and to the point! To say that I was surprised is to put it mildly, but I knew clearly from whence the voice came. I knew that it would pretty much have taken God himself to help me accept the decision that was trying to be made. My eyes filled up with tears and, at the same time, I felt this deep, deep inner peace at hearing God tell me what it was that I must do. From that moment on, there was no more distress, discontent, or despair. God was calling me beyond the convent walls, and now I had God's permission to go.

I didn't tell anyone about that night for many, many years, but after that night, I was able to begin to make plans to leave the world that had safely enfolded me as I grew from the naïve seventeen-year-old to a twenty-four-year-old now ready to face the world with an inner strength I had developed within those convent walls.

God loves us in all sorts of ways and often calls us on to wholeness when we're not even looking nor expecting it. I have always known that that moment of hearing God speak to me so clearly in the confines of the silence was a divine gift. Sometimes God uses very direct ways to get our attention and other times not. How grateful I am, was, and will always be to hear the voice of God when God chooses to speak to me.

ॐ ॐ

In the harrowing months after the death of my son, Michael, who was killed in a car accident at the tender age of twenty, I was struggling to understand who God was in my life now and just how He was responding to my needs.

Actually, on this particular day, I was feeling quite angry with God as I walked around the lake at a local park. Feeling quite sad and depressed, I began asking God, "Why do I always have to ask you for what I want and what I need? You must be seeing how much I'm struggling and what a difficult time I'm having these days and nights. You're supposed to know everything. Why can't you just give me what I need so desperately before I ask? Why do you let me suffer so much?" And after laying out all of my frustrations in such rantings and ravings, I heard God say to me, tenderly but explicitly, *"If I give you what you need without your asking me directly, you won't know where it comes from."* I was completely taken aback, realizing instantly the truth of what God was saying to me.

When God speaks, there is no doubt of the source. I was asking direct questions of God and, even though I seldom hear directly from God, this was one of those moments when I did and a tremendous peace came over me as I understood. God doesn't want to be a mind-reader. He wants to be asked and desires to give us the opportunity to know him as present, even as he responds to our need.

಄ ಄

It was eighteen months after my son Michael died in a car accident. My husband, son Christopher, and I were returning from a short vacation with friends in the Bahamas. I was in the window seat in the plane, feeling quite depressed, lost, and sad. While reading some inspirational sort of book with the hope of receiving some comfort, I turned my head and began to gaze out of the window. I desperately wanted relief from the depth of the grief and pain that lay within me.

As I searched the clouds below, trying to hold back the overwhelming emotions that felt like they might consume me, I noticed a light that was shining on the coffee-colored clouds below. I couldn't see and didn't know what was the source of that light. I simply kept staring at it, mesmerized by it in a sense, as tears started to fall from the corners of my eyes. So I just sat there with and in my pain and suffering, simply communicating wordlessly with the light upon the clouds. And then I heard the soft breath of a warm, comforting voice say to me, *"Inez, I am always with you."* Even as I write this, some fifteen years later, it still brings tears to my eyes, as I remember the beautiful love that I experienced surrounding me then. My pain didn't go away, but I felt deeply comforted. I knew in that moment that, regardless of its source, the light on the clouds was for me. God was reassuring me that I wasn't alone, that I would never be alone, that God was always with me no matter what life dealt.

క్రా ⋘

Inez A. Bing, sixty-four years old, lives in Pennsylvania with her husband of thirty-nine years. She raised two sons, Michael and Christopher. She is a retired guidance counselor and teacher and currently companions others as a grief counselor and spiritual director. Inez enjoys her involvement in things of a spiritual nature, whether it is reading, studying, or creative expression. She also enjoys singing, music, traveling, photography, yoga, and having lunch with friends, as well as walking on beaches where she likes to collect rocks, shells, and sea-glass.

An Amazing and Enlightening Retreat Experience

Barbara Kane

The retreat center was cool and comfortable in spite of the heat of the August day some years ago. The building was massive, built of stone and exuding a feeling of sturdiness and timelessness. It seemed as though it must have been there on that spot for years. A former seminary for young men, it was now a spiritual center for lay people and vowed religious persons to remove themselves from daily concerns and concentrate on the concerns of the spirit for a while. I was there for a weeklong directed retreat and was spending most of my time in silent reflection. One of my favorite walks was around to the back of the retreat house where there was a small cemetery. In the cemetery, members of the religious order that had been based there in years past were buried in a semicircle before a large stone cross, all with the same small marker with only a name and date. All were equal in death, even though I presumed that might not have been the case in life.

One day as I was completing my stroll around the grounds, I sat down on a bench on the lawn in a shady spot and began to write in my journal. In a few moments

I closed my eyes and, all of a sudden, I saw myself and hundreds of other people in a huge stadium. We were all on the field, dressed in white robes, and hanging on crosses. No one appeared to be suffering or in pain, but we were all helplessly attached each to our own cross. There was no one sitting in the seats in the stadium, but one man, also dressed in a white robe, was wandering among the crosses. As he came close by I could see that it was Jesus in his resurrected glory. I asked why we had been crucified and Jesus told me that we had done that to ourselves. The man hanging on the cross next to mine was tied fast by his possessions and his need to acquire more, Jesus said. He challenged me to discover what there was about my life that was keeping me tied to my cross. I asked Jesus why he was not with us and he said that his work was complete—the rest of us still had to figure out what had us crucified and fix it before we could join him down off the cross.

At that point, my awareness shifted back to the physical world again. The day was still very warm, the birds chatting back and forth among the trees, the sun brilliant in the sky, and the bench hard against my back. A very, very peaceful feeling had settled over me as I pondered the words of Jesus. Just what was it that was keeping me tied to that cross instead of being free? Was it my need to control, my tendency to judge others, my inability to love as unconditionally as I would like, my stinginess of spirit with some people, or my need to always be right?

I have spent many years trying to fully understand this experience and its meaning for me personally. I may spend as many years as I have left still working away at getting myself down from that cross of my own making. But I know that I will before I stroll with Jesus into the next part of my life, after my death.

৵৹

Barbara Kane is a seventy-three- year-old retired secondary school teacher who says that she has spent a lot of time in the past thirteen years studying and listening and praying. She is a graduate of the Education for Parish Service program at Trinity University in Washington, D.C., as well as a Group Spiritual Direction program. She continues to facilitate groups in Pennsylvania and the D.C. area. She and her husband now have nine grandchildren, who with their parents live close by, so they continue to enjoy an active family life. At present she is learning to play the dulcimer.

Trouble with Jesus the Man, and Christ Sophia

Lyta Seddig

Before I tell you the story of an experience I had in May 2006, I would like to provide a little background about my prayer life: In the past I have had difficulty relating to the person and presence of Jesus while I am in prayer. Contrariwise, I have had little difficulty with the more transcendent or "invisible" aspects of the Holy—Creator, Holy Spirit whose presence I often sense when giving and receiving spiritual direction as well as in other unexpected moments, and Christ (theologically, cosmically, while officiating at the Eucharist) or even the Jesus of biblical times (a foundation for my justice-focused ministries). But when it came to having a prayer relationship with Jesus, I encountered a wall.

So at that time in May, when I was sixty-two years old, on Sunday morning, I was nearing the end of the week-long retreat I had been leading in northeastern Pennsylvania. The theme of the retreat was Christ-Sophia. I had first introduced the group to the Sophia (Wisdom) of the Hebrew Scriptures and then to Christ-Sophia, the Logos of the Gospels. One of our morning activities was to portray the story of Christ-Sophia walking on water. Then, to help integrate our time together, we went out to walk the new outdoor labyrinth. I waited for everyone else to enter the labyrinth and then finally entered it myself, walking slowly and not expecting anything out of the ordinary. As I came closer to the center of the labyrinth, I began to feel a sense of Presence. I wasn't quite sure what this was, but it was very strong. I remember somehow looking around but barely moving my head for fear that it might go away, carefully moving my eyes to the right and then to the left. Then I was suddenly aware that the Presence was that of Sophia, and she was right there walking beside me, relating to me as "sister." She was warm and smiling, even a bit playful. I experienced her presence as affirming, encouraging and empowering me. I cannot say whether or not I actually saw her with either physical or spiritual eyes, but I know without doubt that she was there. And as she was there beside me, I had a sense of her seeing within, or somehow even being within me, loving me, forgiving me, freeing me, co-creating with me—a sense of the fullness of life, a very deep and powerful experience!

I don't know how or when her Presence ended. I became aware of time again and of needing to leave the labyrinth as I was the last one there. I remember that my walking was joyful and lighthearted. As we walked away from the labyrinth, one of the retreatants looked at me, sensed that something special had happened, and encouraged me to take some time by myself.

After lunch the retreat ended with a Eucharistic Celebration of Sophia in All Things. In the days following the retreat, in my quiet times, when I was journaling and especially when I was reminded of Isaiah 43:4: "Because you are precious in my sight and honored and I love you," I had a sense of Sophia somehow being with me. I had never heard "honored" before, and I was in awe because my prayer life previously had had so much a sense of aloneness and flatness, and it was so different now because of her nearness. It is hard to describe the profound joy of this experience!

Two weeks later, when relating all of this to my spiritual director along with my response of, "Who am I to deserve this?" and, "How do I deal with this theologically?" I had yet another strong sense of Presence. My director sat with me in the silence and then gently asked what was going on inside of me. I described a sense of warmth and fullness in my heart and across my chest, almost a burning. And then I was struck with the profound experience of knowing God's yearning for me was so strong that God would even send to feminist-me, the feminine Sophia-Christ. My response was tears of overwhelming thankfulness and gratitude. My director's words were, "Sit with it. Pray with it. Be with it."

However it came about, in both experiences, I have come to appreciate that the mystery that prayer can be was taking place. It has been said that we are prayed. We don't pray. Only God prays in us. I, indeed, was helped by grace to step back and let prayer be. Could I understand this logically? No. But it has been profound simply, though not without difficulty, to rest in the awareness that "only the Holy prays" and to watch where that has taken me in my relationship with Sophia-Christ. Indeed, since then, my experience of the person and presence of Jesus—as well as Sophia—in my prayer life has been opened, is being strengthened, and is deepening.

అం గ

Lyta Seddig is an ordained Presbyterian minister in the Reformed tradition, a wife, the mother of adult daughters, and friend of many. Prior to attending seminary she had cofounded the Family Planning Service of Crawford County (PA) and been a rape crisis counselor for what later became Women's Services. She trained with the Marie Fortune programs regarding domestic violence and religious issues, and child abuse and clergy misconduct and soon found herself doing lectures and workshops throughout the Synod. She has also been a chaplain at the State Correctional Institution for Women at Cambridge Springs, pastor-in-residence at the Presbyterian Peacemaking Conference in Montreat, North Carolina, and is in her eighth year as Protestant Chaplain at Mercyhurst College in Erie, Pennsylvania.

"Here I Am. Don't Pull Away."

Sue Morris

Since 1995, when, as a social action director for the Catholic diocese of Springfield, Illinois, I was invited to experience a Living Stones Pilgrimage to the Holy Land, I have led eight such pilgrimages for other groups. On one of the pilgrimages I was leading, our group visited Mother Teresa's Home for Children with Multiple Handicaps in Gaza City one day.

The Sisters of Charity invited us into a large room where there was soft classical music playing, and children from the ages of two to seven were lying on the floor on large mattresses. Only one of the children was able to sit up. Immediately the members of our group got down on the floor and began interacting with the children. Since I was the "experienced" leader I stood out of the way to the side, allowing each pilgrim to identify with one of the children.

Then I noticed that there was a boy about the age of seven at the far edge of the room who had no one to play with him. I went over and before I knelt down on the floor, I felt myself wanting to reject him and back away because of his condition. Jusef seemed to be blind and mentally handicapped. He had mucus running down his face and, when he swallowed, saliva ran down his cheeks and chin from his drooling. I was repulsed.

As I stood there not wanting to be with him, I told myself to get over it and I began to play with him. As he and I held hands while playing with a ball, I heard a clear voice from within him say, *"Here I am."* Somehow I knew immediately that it was the voice of Jesus. I had almost missed him by refusing to be present to and share attention and care with this poor little boy.

As we played, I began to gag at a very foul odor (he had probably dirtied his diapers) and I decided to get up and leave. Jusef took hold of my hand as I tried to leave. As I began to stand up, Jusef pulled my hand to his chest and, again, I heard the voice, *"Do not pull away."*

Never before had I experienced Jesus' presence in his anawim, his "little ones," who, because of my prejudices, I had pushed to the fringes of the acceptable. I realized in those moments that, throughout my whole life, I had regarded those people living with disabilities as "less than." As I left Gaza, as I left the Holy Land, I knew Jesus' presence in the poor and persons who lived with disabilities as I had never before experienced it. But that was not the only gift that came to me through Jusef. Another was yet to come.

Later that same year, I was diagnosed with Parkinson's disease. My father had had Parkinson's also, which helped me to face where my disease could lead me, yet several years into dealing with the realities of the disease in my life, I was still busy giving retreats throughout the country, as I had been for years. At one point I was invited to give the keynote address on spirituality and justice at a major event, and I couldn't help thinking, here I was, a thoroughly capable presenter who was highly respected, loving my life of being able to share God's presence with others through talks, retreats, and pilgrimages—and I had Parkinson's disease, too.

As I prepared for this presentation, I became apprehensive about whether my Parkinson's symptoms might get in the way. As I sat silently praying, the realization came to me that, in the final stages of my disease, I would likely be like Jusef, drooling, unable to talk very well, and messing my pants. I will probably be very disabled and dependent and no longer the competent and graceful presenter who rejoices in witnessing to the Lord. As I sobbed and grieved for all that would probably be lost, I suddenly realized that Jusef had taught me that, even then, God's presence might be made known through me as it was made known to me through him.

I know that because of that day in Gaza when Jusef allowed me to enter into the world of the broken and there find Jesus truly present.

ॐ ॐ

Sue Morris is a seventy-year-old Roman Catholic laywoman, married to her husband, Jim, for fifty years, the mother of six children and grandmother of eighteen. After her children were in school she taught religion in Catholic high schools for eleven years and then worked for her diocese in the Office of Social Concerns and, finally, moved to spending many years of work as a retreat leader and spiritual director.

I Saw Jesus in the Room

Anne Love

I was one of a group of nine women who had been meeting every other Friday for the past nine months in a Contemplative Living class. It had become a close group as we engaged in centering prayer, sharing our stories and being guided by the group leaders who were teaching us different aspects of contemplative living.

It was our last session and we were participating in a closing ritual. We were sitting in a circle as usual when suddenly I saw Jesus standing in the middle of the circle. He began to move around the circle, placing his hands on the sides of each person's head, calling them by name and saying, *"(Name), you are my beloved child in whom I am well pleased."* When he had completed the circle, he raised his hands in benediction and said, *"Go in peace to love and serve the world."*

When I told the group about what I had seen, one of the leaders said that she had planned a closing benediction but now, of course, it was no longer needed.

Anne Love is a licensed clinical social worker who has a private practice of psychotherapy in Atlanta, Georgia, working primarily with adults. She also has a master's degree in Christian Education from Colgate Theological Seminary and worked as a Director of Christian Education for various Presbyterian churches for a number of years. One of her favorite experiences was working with the students of William and Mary College in Williamsburg, Virginia, some years ago. She is active at Mary and Martha's Place in Atlanta, attends the Shambhala Meditation Center there, also, and is a great book lover.

An Unexpected Blessing on Christmas Eve

Margery Larrabee

When I lived in Washington, D.C., I routinely attended an early morning service at the Methodist church near me as well as going to Quaker Meeting later in the morning. At Christmastime, I attended an adult discussion group at the Methodist church, which focused on the Christmas story. At that time I was very moved and the meaning of the story was expanded and deepened for me. As I walked home I was still very much caught up in the essence of the story.

When I arrived home, I opened the front door and walked into the very large, open living room that I saw was utterly filled with an unusual light. The room was also filled with a very large sense of Presence. I remember just standing there, caught up in this sense of something "Other" and momentarily embraced by Spirit.

I don't know how long I stood still, but I had a very strong sense of being lovingly embraced. A feeling washed over me that I was deeply loved, and being so deeply loved, how could I not go forth and express that love to others as well. This became a very strong and clear intention in my life.

This experience, along with some others, contributed to my commitment to offer programs and experiences that could inspire and assist others on their spiritual journeys. That Christmas experience remains very vivid in my mind to this day and continues to inspire me.

ॐ ॐ

Margery Larrabee lives in Medford, New Jersey, and is a Quaker. Over the years, much of her work has been focused on programs aimed at helping people develop spiritual friendships. She is the author of a pamphlet on that subject entitled "There Is a Hunger: Mutual Spiritual Friendships." She sees spiritual friendships as a gentle and loving bulwark against self-deception, denial, pretense, and escape as well as a powerful tool to facilitate one's authentic spiritual growth.

The Face of Jesus

Dana Castle

I was fifty-one years old at the time and this is the story of a prayer experience that I had at home. While I was sitting in silence, the face of Jesus appeared before me and, as I concentrated on his face, his eyes, he was gazing deeply into mine. I consciously allowed him to see all within, hiding nothing—became vulnerable to him. Then, slowly his face came forward, melted into my face, and turned around so that no longer was I looking out of my eyes alone. Jesus was looking out through my eyes.

This is a prayer experience that continues to challenge me daily. The revelation was that from then on, I was to see with the eyes of Jesus. It had to do with intentional awareness, compassion, mercy, and thoughtfulness, especially as a spiritual director.

ಶಿ ೀ

Dana Castle is in her early sixties, the mother of two sons and grandmother of five, who describes herself as a "cradle Episcopalian" who has been deeply involved in parish life since having a personal conversion experience in

1979. She spent some time as a member of a Roman Catholic Charismatic Healing Prayer Group where people began to come to her to discuss their spiritual lives. As she was finishing a master's degree in English in her fifties, she began to feel a nagging sense that God was asking her to do something, but she was, at first, unclear what this was about, despite having worked with a group at church to help with her discernment. Finally, at the suggestion of a niece, she began to see a spiritual director, who helped her discern clearly that, in fact, that was the path she was being called to follow, herself. She completed her training for this ministry and has been a spiritual director since 1994, for a time on the staff of St. Martin's Episcopal Church in Williamsburg, Virginia, and continues her association with and service to the church, although no longer on the staff.

Laughter in a Quiet Church

Mary Consiglio

I am a Roman Catholic and one morning after daily Mass, when others had gone, I was alone in the church, praying. In addition to saying my thanksgiving, I was recounting to God all of my failures and sins, telling God about my unworthiness. In the midst of this sad litany about myself, I "heard" laughter. Laughter! I was appalled and incensed and told God so. "Here I am baring my soul to you, telling you all about the worst things about me, my very worst parts, and your response is laughter?" Then I heard, *"It will always be like this."* Pause. *"Just come closer. Come closer."*

There was so much comfort in knowing that, just as I am, missing the mark regularly, that I am invited to draw nearer to that Great Love who knows me completely. Whenever I hear the story in Matthew of the weeds and the wheat, I feel that I understand it deeply, and I relax and trust that God will, indeed, take care of all the weeds one day if I just continue to come closer. This drawing nearer over the years has changed my prayer, and now just practicing Simple Presence to God keeps me close.

ֆ ֆ

Mary Consiglio and her husband of many years, Gene, have three grown children and seven grandchildren. Mary is an avid reader and usually has three books going at a time. The couple have a small place on the Elk River where they enjoy spending time sailing and jet skiing. Mary says that she "drives the jet ski like a little old lady, which is what I am!" She also enjoys painting small watercolor note cards for friends. She and Gene love to go to daily Mass several times a week and then out for coffee afterward with friends they meet there. They live in a small university town in Delaware, which they both love, and have been members of their parish for forty-two years.

The Gate to Heaven Is Everywhere

Robert Close

In 1979 I attended a four-day basic retreat at the Shalom Mountain Retreat and Study Center near Livingston Manor, New York. Toward the end of our time, on Sunday morning, we were told to bring something to put on the altar to represent what the retreat had meant for us.

I left the meditation room and went outside to walk the grounds, looking for some symbol, some icon, something that would speak of what this time had meant—something to represent the sacred. The first thing I saw was a small rock and I almost picked it up. It could speak of what the time had meant for me. Second, I saw a flower, a tiny flower, green with two blue bells, and this, too, could speak for me. I was looking and I was seeing. Then I saw a candle that had been used the previous night, then a bird feeder, and then, far off, an old, red tractor. Then I really don't know how to explain what happened next because, all of a sudden, everything I looked at—everything—was sacred. Everything I saw was HOLY. I started to cry and ended up sobbing, tears of ineffable joy, tears of recognition of the sacredness of all life because of God's Presence everywhere and in all things, tears of a deep gladness, a release, a breakthrough. My body was almost contorting itself with tears and, at the same time, I was filled with laughter and joy. I knew I could bring anything and put it on the altar and it would be all right.

Later as we gathered, I came with no one thing to put on the altar. In a halting way I told the group what had happened, the tears still with me, and somehow they understood.

The grace of that moment, this glimpse into the world permeated by God's presence, has stayed with me in some way forming and informing my life ever since that day. I don't live at that peak level all of the time, of course, but somehow that glimpse has stayed with me in ways that I do not fully understand, in ways that cannot be languaged.

My reaction was a deep awareness that everything I may have studied was true! It's all true! But in such a different way—not, certainly, in the dry way one might think; this was no academic exercise. Not "churchy," but confirming of all the things church is to be about, though more incarnational, more intimate, more real, more inexpressible, more experiential and grounding.

Results: sitting loose to the institutional "stuff" of organized religion, but ever more aware and open to the moment-by-moment mystery of God's presence in our midst. Here and now.

"The gate to heaven is everywhere."

৵ ৵

Robert Close describes himself as an "earthy mystic," a compassionate cel-
ebrant of life and seeker/lover of the Mystery. He has been a Presbyterian
minister for forty years and is still going strong and loving his work on the
Eastern Shore of Virginia. He says that he is happily married beyond his
ability to express and is the father of two delightful daughters. As a child of
the church, aware of both its glory and shame, he is a believer in deep ecu-
menicity and is open to people of all faiths or none and is committed to the
way of justice and peace. He says that he is one broken and blessed human
being, still enjoying the dance of life, still awe/wakening.

I Don't Know What to Pray for Right Now

Karen Johnson

The story that I will tell took place in the spring of 1970 when I was twenty-six years old and my firstborn was about six months old. She had been born with a medical problem that required several surgeries and seventeen months of on again, off again hospitalizations before it was finally corrected. The particular event I am writing about occurred after one of those surgeries when she was especially weak and fragile. We were in the old Children's Hospital in Washington, D.C. It was probably the second or third day post-op. She was hooked up to a variety of pumps, drains, IVs, and other medical equipment. Each time blood was drawn or other uncomfortable procedures happened, she struggled and cried. There came a point when I thought she could not survive one more assault on her little body. She did not seem to have enough energy left even to cry. It was the middle of the night. I heard the hematologist's cart come down the hall, stop outside Susan's door, and I knew another stick in the foot was about to happen. Susan was asleep.

I had darkened the room and knew that when the door opened, a stream of light would pierce the peacefulness and probably awaken her. So I positioned myself in such a way that blocked the sharp light. I found myself leaning over her crib shielding her from its intrusion. I felt a surge of concern that she just might not be able to survive all of this. I had never prayed out loud anything other than a community kind of prayer. But I found myself saying out loud, over and over, "Lord, give her peace. Just give her peace."

The hematologist came in. I kept praying. Aloud. In my heart of hearts I suddenly wondered if I might actually be praying for my baby's death, since I was not sure how else she might have peace. I kept on praying. Suddenly something came over me that I can only describe as a deep, deep peace that told me that whether she lived or died, she and I and the whole created order were held in the tenderest of hands. God's hands.

The hematologist drew the blood. Susan did not wake up or struggle or cry. She just slept peacefully throughout.

That experience has stayed with me ever since and has been absolutely formative in my life, gifting me with the peace that we say "passes understanding" in many times of trial. It is a touchstone I return to, a story I sometimes tell, and in my life a treasure whose riches continue to unfold.

அ~ஷ்

Karen Johnson grew up in the Congregational Church in New England, spent some years as a Methodist, and ultimately found her way into the Episcopal Church. She is a graduate of Yale Divinity School and was ordained to the priesthood in the Episcopal Church in 1980. She was the first woman rector in the Diocese of Washington, D.C., and was twice named one of the top ten Episcopal preachers in the United States. She is the mother of three children whom she says "went to seminary with me" at the ages of three, six, and eight. Since her retirement she has been associated with Dayspring Church, one of the small faith communities of the ecumenical Church of the Saviour in the Washington area.

Karen's baby daughter, Susan, lived.

Home from Vietnam and Overwhelmed

Joseph A. Burkart Jr.

A series of events constellated for me in April of 1969. I had returned to college after three years in the US Navy. A major adjustment in itself, I also returned to a culture that had changed so radically from 1964, when I had graduated from high school. I realized that 1964 was about the tail end of an old paradigm of belief in the credibility of our institutions. Three years in the Navy, Vietnam, and a slight movement in maturity changed all of that for me. But I was not prepared for how a complete climate change in energy and attitude had permeated this country in the four years that I was living in a bubble.

I remember feeling as if I was an orphan in the universe. This was compounded by the fact that my mother had died just the month before, in March, my fiancée had been killed in a plane crash in Florida, my brother was deeply into drugs and alcohol and was living on the street and my father had retreated into an emotional cave, emotionally inaccessible to anyone.

My mother's last words to me were, "Please take care of your brother." These words haunted me and, since returning to college that April, I was torn between shoulds, trying to be present to my father and brother and attempting to salvage the semester of college work from which copious time was lost and much work needed to be turned in.

One thing I had to finish was a paper on Duns Scotus for a Medieval Religion course. Scotus supposedly died in a trance, and I was convinced this must have been because he read his own writing. What dry stuff; my enthusiasm for working on this paper was nil.

It was a luxurious afternoon in Maine but I forced myself to head up to my room and an appointment with the typewriter. I needed to start writing, but what I really wanted to do was sit in the grass and stare at Johnson Pond.

Things take on an odd obliqueness at this point. Something like being in the middle of a permeable membrane—on either side there promises clarity but, being in the middle where everything seemed to be moving, it was like pure process and not quite in focus.

I felt the bottom falling out; whatever connected the parts of my sense of self had been hit with some solvent that eroded any connective tissue between them. All the events of the past few months, supercharged by the events of the last three years, seemed to be contained in an Exocet missile that had just found its target, dead center in the heart of my being.

I remember sitting at the typewriter with the blank page in it and coming apart inside. A totally spontaneous cry for help erupted from deep inside of me. It was nothing that I had any control over, and I remember it as perhaps the most pure emotion I have ever experienced, no mixed feelings or agenda at all.

Within a millisecond, a deep and incredibly profound peace entered in, like nothing that I had ever experienced before. It infused my heart and stomach area. Something let go inside and I sat there, knowing that the tasks facing me were still to be done, and yet, something inside had shifted significantly.

I wrote for a while and then, being unable to keep myself from being outside where I could revel in the sensuous beauty of the day and the "green flame of spring" as Whitman called it, I walked around the campus, greeting friends, sitting and talking with people I ordinarily didn't like but who now seemed almost precious in my eyes. The protests against the war in Vietnam were escalating, the war becoming increasingly unmanageable and toxic.

Nothing really had changed on the outside. My external life remained as it had been three hours earlier; papers to finish, exams to take, books to read, and the difficulties at home compounding themselves. Yet the lens through which I viewed all of this and the world around me had shifted dramatically. Hope, benevolence, and charity seemed to overpower the insurmountable circumstances of my personal life.

The intensity of this experience remained for three days or so and then waned somewhat over the following weeks. But the memory, the taste, the penetration of it in my being has never completely gone away.

Having grown up in a family that viewed religion or the church as suspect, if not totally irrelevant, I had no familiar category in which to understand what had happened. As time passed I wondered whether I had experienced a psychotic break of some sort, so I got myself into therapy to "come to terms with the truth." After two years with nothing concluded, I still wrestled with the ambiguity of it all.

I am now sixty-three and, having followed my heart's hunger, with numerous side trips, I am aware that nothing of my motives and actions were devoid of the influence of that experience. From flying as a bush pilot in Maine, to ordination as a United Church of Christ minister, to becoming a psychologist, a Camaldolese Benedictine Oblate and many times a jerk, those things were all woven together with a connective tissue taprooted in this event of my early twenties.

I suppose the validity and the quantum mechanics of any experience can be argued endlessly. What really is the essence of it all, I think, is the transformational quality the experience has on one's life and the resilience and longevity of that experience as one progresses through life and ages. When I see to what extent that has been the case in my own life, I can say, today, that what happened to me on that long-ago April day is that I was touched and transformed in some way by God's presence and love.

What seems so evident now, some forty years later, is that transformational experience is not something that catapults one to some sort of spiritual/psychological plateau on which we then traverse softly. It is quite the opposite, being something that instills a hunger in us so deep that our life, consciously and unconsciously, seeks to incarnate it for the remainder of our days. And this incarnation takes us into areas we choose and don't choose, fraught with peril, epiphany, and ecstasy.

❧ ❧

Joseph A. "Tony" Burkart Jr., a psychologist and ordained minister of the United Church of Christ, lives on a small farm in what he calls the "backwoods" of Maine. He much enjoys the plowing and planting, wood chopping and fire building that goes with farm life. He is professor of spirituality and psychotherapy at the Graduate Theological Foundation in South Bend, Indiana and an adjunct professor at the University of Notre Dame. He has recently retired from his private practice as a psychotherapist and also as a psychologist with his local school system. He and his wife, Donna, have one son, Grey, who is married, and was a graduate student on the West Coast for a time; he and his wife have since returned to live in their home state of Maine.

I Am God's Home?

Eileen Metzger

I grew up in the Roman Catholic tradition, spent a few years exploring mainline Protestantism in my early twenties, then settled into a home among the Mennonites. Because of their peace position and their emphasis on community, and because I could see their commitment to living out what they believe, I cast my lot with the one Mennonite congregation in my city at that time and was anabaptized (re-baptized) in 1983 at the age of twenty-seven. I have been there ever since.

I grew up with the guilt-ridden childhood that seems so typical of many Catholic children of my generation or older. I had a mother who taught me that anger was wrong and expressing it was sinful, and a father who ignored me unless I did something he felt needed correction. Then he was right there to reprimand me. Over the years of my growing up, I grew to hate myself, having been taught that I had to be good to get to heaven, and knowing that I couldn't ever seem to stop "sinning."

At the age of seventeen I attended a Catholic retreat where I had an amazing experience. I sensed the presence of God hovering above us in the room as various young people spoke of the presence of God in their lives. Since this was in a Christian context, I interpreted this presence in the room to be Jesus. This was the first time I actually experienced the reality of God for myself. It was not so much that I felt loved as that something mysterious was happening to my spirit, something I was not fully conscious of and, therefore, something that I could not accurately describe. My inner reaction was to feel as if I had been hugged.

I graduated from high school and, after twelve years of Catholic education, the last four in an all-girls' school, I had my first exposure to public school and boys my age at a local community college. There I met the man who was to be my husband. Thom was the first Protestant I had ever gotten to know well, and his familiarity with the Bible impressed me. I resolved to read the whole Bible.

It was an amazing discovery to me to find, at the age of eighteen, that the Bible says, "If you confess with your lips that Jesus is Lord and believe in your heart that God raised him from the dead, you will be saved" (Romans 10:19). Not may be saved, or might be if you do enough good and don't commit too many sins. You will be saved. A huge burden was lifted from my shoulders and I began to draw near to this Jesus and even to love him, since I could now trust that I wouldn't be judged and condemned. I began to invite and pursue a personal relationship with this Jesus, through prayer and devotional reading of the Bible.

Then when I was in my early forties, I had an experience of God that changed everything for me. One Saturday in December I sat at the breakfast table reading Henri Nouwen's book, Return of the Prodigal Son. At one place in this book, Nouwen wrote, "I am God's home." I stopped right there. I looked out the kitchen window, pondering how this could be true—that the Creator of the universe could be "at home" within me.

Staring out of the window I noticed the Christmas cards I had stuck behind the plants on the window sill and thought, "Oh, I want to put those up around the window frame like I always do. And I want to make Christmas cookies, and I still have some gifts to buy." And then I said to myself, "NO!" and bringing myself back to the book, I said, "This is more important." And, in that moment, I felt a big *"YES !"* from God. I began to cry, and I cried for forty-five minutes. I would stop for a few seconds and think I was done, and then I would start all over again.

From that point on, for the first time in my life, I was able to really love myself. Not because God loves me and so I should too, as if it were a duty. But because I—am—God's —Home. I AM GOD'S HOME! Because God finds me worthy to inhabit. Because God likes me and is glad when I choose to spend time with God. Maybe even because I'm lovable.

Although it seemed inexplicable to me at the time, it was also from this point on that I lost the ability to pray to Jesus. Jesus had been like a big brother to me ever since my conversion experience at the age of seventeen. Because God the Father was too scary, too much like the disciplinarian who was my earthly father, I had turned to Jesus, the one who saves. But on that December day, Jesus disappeared for me. It was like I dialed his number and was told, "There's nobody here by that name." Jesus seemed not to be part of God anymore, and I bitterly mourned the loss. I spent several years wondering if I had lost my faith, although I prayed daily and felt the mysterious presence of the Creator with me always. I felt like a hypocrite sitting in church next to my friends who all believed what the Bible says about Jesus when I no longer could. I wondered if I could even call myself a Christian. I didn't know who Jesus was. Son of God? Aren't we all children of God? God incarnate? What does that even mean? Was God more concentrated in Jesus than in other humans? Good person only, but totally human? That didn't quite make sense either. The Jesus portrayed in the Gospels was not like any other person who ever lived. But what did I believe about the authority of Scripture? Everything was suddenly up for grabs.

I began to read about other traditions. I was impressed with the life and example of Hasidic Jews, Buddhist monks, Sufi musicians, Hindu holy ones. I came to believe that any one of these wisdom traditions would lead to the same end—union with Ultimate Reality, the One Consciousness that is the source of all that is. For a while I considered whether I should join some other faith tradition, and I even tried out a few congregations. But, in the end, I couldn't see starting all over in another tradition when I had come so far on the Christian journey. I determined that I would continue the Christian path and see if I couldn't get to the desired end, union with God, in the faith I'd been born and raised in. Then, about three years after the "I am God's home" experience, I was telling someone about this disappearance of Jesus from my life, and he asked me, "Why would God do that?" Without stopping to think about it, out of my mouth came the words, "It was time for a new image of God." After I said it I realized that Jesus was my big brother when I needed a big brother, but I had grown beyond that need. It was time for me to trust the Creator of the universe in all God's mystery and power. I no longer needed to be afraid that God was like my earthly father, as I had at seventeen. By middle age I was ready for a bigger picture, less clear but truer to God's nature.

A decade later, I continue to look for and be open to new ways of understanding who Jesus was or is. But the authors I feel most drawn to—Thomas Merton, William Johnston, Henri Nouwen, Carlo Coretto, Henri Le Saux, Thich Nhat Hanh, Beatrice Bruteau, Parker Palmer, Robert Kennedy, Sue Monk Kidd—write about the Source of all Being and how we can become more aware of and attentive to this Oneness. My reading, meditation, and prayer have led me to believe that religious traditions like Christianity, Hinduism, Islam are like clothing on the body of God. They make for different appearances, but it is the person underneath that is important.

On occasion I am prompted to talk to Jesus directly, but usually the God I perceive is less defined, less limited to human form than that. Whether Jesus was God incarnate, I don't know. But I know from my own experience that God is always available if I slow down and pay attention. When I do, I begin to notice the beauty all around me, I begin to smile, and I feel at peace. So I follow this way, which may well be The Way.

భ్యా

Eileen Metzger is fifty-three years old, is married, and lives in Rochester, New York. She is an experienced spiritual director. She enjoys long walks in nature and reading children's books and is a member of the Mennonite community.

More than Wrapped in Love

Marcy Keefe-Slager

I was in the convent, a Roman Catholic sister, at the time of the experience I want to share with you.

But first, a little background: At the ripe old age of fourteen, I had entered the prep school of a Franciscan community of sisters and, after graduation, had entered the community myself. Through the next thirty years I was initiated into an intense spirituality, received an excellent education, and entered into ministry. Daily I was growing in my relationship with God. Especially after the Second Vatican Council, my concept of God changed from the harsh God of childhood to the One who is warm and loving, caring and compassionate and ever so present.

Most welcome after the Council was a new approach to spirituality that provided us with the option of making an annual directed retreat that provided daily one-on-one conversations with a spiritual director. I found these opportunities to be quite profound and fruitful. One retreat experience stands out from all the rest.

My director, in our first conference, was quite specific in directing me to start each hour of meditation with a prayer asking God to show me how much God loved me. She had no idea what a difficult challenge she was giving me. Who was I to make such a bold request of God? That meant saying that prayer five times a day— one for each hour of meditation. I didn't have that kind of courage. Maybe I was holding on more than I realized to those childhood images of the exacting, judging God who had been interested only in recording things I did wrong. I just couldn't do it. I didn't do it.

The next day, upon learning that I hadn't followed her directions, my director became truly directive— gentle yet firm. She insisted that I pray as she had specified. I still flinch at the memories of how difficult it was to muster up the courage to make such a direct request of God. With the help of the Spirit, I cautiously, tentatively began to start each meditation as I had been told.

On day seven of this eight-day retreat, I chose to go to a tiny chapel at the far reaches of the retreat house. Why there, I don't know. That was where I was led by the Spirit. Which of the five hours it might have been, I have no idea. Somehow sitting on the floor helped me to get into the spirit of prayer, so I sat on a cushion at the side of the chapel with the altar to my right. The altar was white, with lots of gold trim—of the more traditional style of church architecture. It seems there was a tall extension above the altar, certainly with a crucifix, and probably statues. The space was filled with light. By that time in the retreat I could more easily begin my prayer with the request that God show me how much God loves me. Surely, I had my Bible and a scripture passage, as was the way I went to prayer, but I don't remember the particular passage. Those are the only details that I remember.

My heart skips a beat even as I attempt to tell the story. How does one find words to give the slightest hint of the ecstasy of being lovingly embraced by God? Now that I am a laywoman and married, the closest comparison I can make is to the intimate, holy moments of married love. Yet, even the most ecstatic moments of physical embrace are only a tiny, tiny spark of the love I felt that day. I was more than wrapped in love. I was totally absorbed, warmly embraced, loved beyond question. Though I was in prayer for at least an hour, it felt like only a moment. Not for one moment did I then, nor have I since, ever questioned that God loves me. I know that God answered my prayer—and way beyond my wildest imagination. I KNOW that God is the God of LOVE!

Thirty-plus years have come and gone. How wonderful it would be to have another such experience. Until that day, I live with a deep knowing that God is present and that God loves me and is forever faithful. If God loves me and is true to me, then God has that same love for everyone.

God continues to affirm and validate that I am precious in God's eyes. Once, while meditating on the Parable of the Pearl, God gave me another surprise message. As I prayed to deepen my awareness that Jesus is my Pearl of Great Price, I heard the words, not with physical ears but internally, *"And so are you!"* Treasuring that message, I find it most important that I treasure and care for the gift that I am—the one God made me to be. Then, in turn, I need to respect and revere the dignity of each of my brothers and sisters in God's Kingdom.

જેન્જી

When I left the convent after having lived a relatively sheltered life for thirty years, I found myself having some problems adjusting to such a new way of life. A couple of years into the process I made a retreat in the hope of enabling the birth of the new person I thought I needed to become. In total desperation one day I cried out loud, "God, I don't know how to do this!" Almost immediately I heard a strong Divine Voice say, *"Be attentive!"* Just those two words—*"Be attentive!"* And thus began my journey into greater awareness—the need to be more attentive to God's constant presence.

Soon after that retreat, I invited a gray and white cat into my life. After searching for the right name for him for more than a week, one day, as he was doing his best to get my attention, I shouted, "Toby! Stop that!"

(Of course, it's futile to shout at a cat.) But why did I call him "Toby," short for Tobias?

The answer to that question came while I was on retreat as a part of a spiritual direction training program. On one Sunday we were to be silent throughout the day and to be "at the beck and call of the Spirit," available to be led as the Spirit willed. As I basked in the calm and tranquility of the day, God's Spirit nudged me to read the book of Tobit. As the story unfolded, Tobit counseled his son, Tobias, as he sent him to a far country: "My son, be mindful of the Lord." "Be mindful of the Lord!" Aha! So my feline friend, Toby, had a bigger job than dispelling some of my loneliness. He became my live-in symbol of mindfulness and a constant reminder to "Be attentive!"

As I have increasingly practiced attentiveness, it has led to many of what I like to call "God sightings"— those concrete events that broaden my awareness and help me see God in myriad places in everyday life: in the growing love in my marriage, in a whole gamut of interactions in my ministry, in everyday challenges and celebrations. In short, it becomes more and more the norm to see God everywhere, in all things. I am far, far more aware of God's presence now than when I was younger.

My journey continues. I know my God will continue to be with me, and I will always strive to be more aware and attentive so that God's presence and love, fidelity, compassion, and peace will radiate through me for the growth of God's Kingdom.

ॐ ॐ

Marcy Keefe-Slager was born on February 6, 1940, in an old brick house up a muddy lane to poor farm parents. She is seventy-two years old now. She lives in Jackson, Michigan, where she moved to accept a position as chaplain at a local hospital. Since her retirement she serves as a spiritual director and does some adjunct teaching in the Formation Program of the Lansing Catholic Diocese. Her husband of seventeen years, Harvey, grew up on Long Island, New York; he has a son who lives in England and a daughter who lives in Colorado and they have two granddaughters in Colorado as well. Marcy and Harv worship together in the Catholic Church.

I Was Sure My Life Was Over

A. Nelson Granade Jr.

I want to tell you about an experience I had during my separation and subsequent divorce a few years ago, neither of which were my choice. Trying to pastor a congregation, be a pastor, and hold a family together was more than I could handle, especially since I was also writing a book.

After my ex-wife moved out, but before my congregation knew, I took a ride into the Blue Ridge Mountains to sit along the New River. I was furious with my situation! To top it off, I felt that I needed to preach that coming Sunday. As much as I didn't want to leave, it seemed like it would be easier to go ahead and go home rather than to miss a Sunday and have to come back the next week. So I sat for a while longer on the bank of the river with the sun shining, the birds singing, and the river flowing.

These beautiful aspects of nature, which usually give me peace, seemed to infuriate me that day. I cried out to God, "Don't you know that my world has come to an end?" and "How can the river keep flowing, the birds keep singing and the sun shining?" I wanted God to bring it all to an end. Though not in words, God spoke to me. God told me "Look."

The river was still flowing, the sun was still shining, and the birds were still singing. I was not the center of the universe, and, though I felt as if my life were over, life was going on all around me.

Through my tears that Sunday, I shared that my wife had left and my world felt like it was over. I also shared my experience at the river and how God had reassured me that I still had a life because my life was in the hands of God—the giver of all life. It was the shortest sermon I ever preached, but many still say it was the most effective I have ever preached.

It is now two years later and I still have difficult days. When they get hard, God sends someone to remind me that the river is still flowing, the sun is still shining, the birds are still singing —and there is life to be lived.

∾ ∾

A. Nelson Granade Jr. is an ordained Baptist minister and has been pastor of the First Baptist Church in North Wilkesboro, North Carolina, since 1994. He had previously pastored several other congregations after his ordination in 1986. He has been active in many different ways in leadership positions both within his denomination and within the community. He is the author of Lending Your Leadership: Redefining the Pastor's Place in Community, published by the Alban Institute (2005) and the recent Only a Preacher, published by Duke University (2009). He has two children, JD, age seventeen, and Emily, age sixteen. He enjoys hiking, kayaking, and watching movies as well as serving as an assistant scout master.

Intellectuals Don't Have Visions of Jesus

Kit Wallingford

For fifty-plus years, as far as I can recall, the words "experience of God" had no meaning for me. Then in the mid-1990s, something started happening. One afternoon, after I had sat in a room for several hours talking with four other people, I wondered, "What was that?" It turned out that the others experienced whatever it was, too. Not too long afterward one of them referred to our time together; "the Kingdom of God" was in that room. "Oh," I thought, "is that what it was?"

Then one day I was walking along a sidewalk lined with trees. I heard the leaves over my head rustling and rustling and I looked up and knew with certainty that God was there. Gradually I began to—perhaps the most accurate verb is sense—God's presence. My lifelong faithful Episcopalian churchgoing had offered me a taste of this presence in its liturgy and music, but I had not known the term, and I think all my life I had associated what I experienced with church rather than with God.

When Jesus first showed himself to me, in August of 1998, I didn't pay much attention. His appearance seemed dramatic and stylized, and I think I was embarrassed even though I was all alone. At that time I considered myself an intellectual and everybody knows that intellectuals don't have visions of Jesus! But there he was, plain as day. As I drove down the highway in the Texas panhandle, he was shimmering in the air in front of me, and, although I couldn't see his face or his body clearly, there was no question about it. It was Jesus all right. I wrote in my journal that this experience didn't seem to have a great effect on me, probably because I was aware of being fiercely drawn to God at that time and, therefore, even more fiercely resisting that pull. That interpretation still seems true to me.

As part of this attraction and resistance to God, I had been struggling hard to discern whether or not I was called to the ministry of spiritual direction and, shortly thereafter, whether I was called to ordained ministry. My life for several years felt so intense that each day seemed to contain within it enough experience for a year. I begged for God to leave me alone. Then, of course, I took it back immediately.

Jesus came to me several more times in the next few years, often when I was in distress. These varied experiences were notably different from the first one, less "dramatic," I would say. Often it seemed as though I could summon him by calling up an image I received at a Quiet Day. The presenter on that day, Sister C, contrasted the smoke and confusion and chaos of Satan with Jesus, quiet, alone on a plain. I saw him clearly there, his presence and his stillness very important and reassuring to me. But usually I played no conscious role in imaging him; he just showed up. Once I saw him sitting across the room, with his head bowed. I wrote in my journal that I was surprised to see him! A couple of times he appeared wearing robes. Several times I saw his face clearly, right in front of mine. Once I saw mainly his mouth, contorted in pain.

Now, for the first time since I began writing, I am feeling what I feared about accepting the invitation to write for this book. I am afraid of being presumptuous. These sentences about Jesus sound so matter-of-fact. Here, let me quote from my journal: 4/19/2000: "Flicker of Jesus' face head on, right in front of me." That's all I wrote on that occasion, though sometimes I wrote more. Sometimes I spoke of the giftedness of what happened. Sometimes the journal entries are a simple recording of what happened, sometimes prayer, sometimes the two feathering into one another.

These experiences of Jesus do not stand out from the texture of my life as a whole at that time. Sometimes I experienced deep emotion, sometimes not, and always, as I moved on from the experience, it took its place modestly in the story of my ongoing spiritual awakening.

During this period, God, much less restrained than Jesus, was another story altogether. God engulfed me in presence/Presence and I hardly knew from one moment to the next whether my tears came from joy or anguish or fear. This presence, as so many have described before me, has a tangible quality to it. In my journal I described it variously as simply presence or, to pick a random sampling, a whirling, a circling, a dark place where I know God is. A drenching. A widening circle reaching out into the world. A kind of light. In May of 2001 I tried harder to put the sensation into words: "As has been true in the past, when my life gets difficult, my dear Lord comes to me. Yesterday God came to me but I will never have the words to express how. It was like a wave, but not liquid. A wave of . . . I don't know. A wave of sensation? A density of the air?" Again and again, I was simply in God: the words of Scripture, "Abide in me as I abide in you" (John 15:4), were not so much a command as a description of the way things were, not so much words spoken just by Jesus but by the whole Holy One, whoever that is, whatever words we want to use to describe the Holy.

God in me/me in God: this was going on/ongoing, underlying my life with my husband, Rufus, our children, Halley and John, as they married, as their families began to expand. I was in God through friends old and new. Since my childhood, I had found in the printed word a connection with people who helped me to know that I was not a space alien, that there were actually other people like me out there. Increasingly, I knew it was God who was coming to me through those people. I was in God through liturgy and ministry at Palmer Memorial

Episcopal Church, through contemplative prayer at Shalem. I wept with gratitude.

After the millennium it seemed that my experiences of God were becoming less intense. "This is not a complaint," I wrote. "I'm just trying to describe what happens to me, what it's like. How God-ness happens to/for me." I was wrong, though. As the years went by I spoke of my "greedy" desire for God and my knowledge of God's desire for me. I spoke of my sweet love for God; I wrote/whispered, "You, Lord, You, You."

It is so hard to describe the different ways God came to me. In November of 2000 I wrote this: "God is close. He's a 'he,' these days, like a dandy—I can't see him but I know he's dancing, maybe with a cane, and flirting a little—or maybe that is me doing those things." I liked that—still do. Then, during a period of a few months, a male voice spoke in my ear several times, *"Kit."* Just my name, nothing else, but rather insistent. I'm quite sure that it was God calling me.

God came to see me as a visible "person" only once, and I really, really loved that God experience. For one thing, Jesus was there, too. (How that is possible I have no idea.) It happened in August 2000, in Colorado, and I was in the middle of writing something that was giving me a lot of trouble. I felt burdened. God and Jesus appeared on either side of me, their shoulders to mine, and started walking me up the stairs toward my computer. Stalwart companions, right there with me. I did not feel any sense of, "All right now, come on, you have to do this thing." I had more a sense of, "We are here with you, shoulder to shoulder, as you go to continue your work." Only later did I notice and feel surprise that God had shown up as a human being, and a man at that!

Today I continue to know that I live in God and God in me. The experience of God has changed for me. It is . . . softer now. Perhaps I see more clearly that all experiences of God are different manifestations of the Presence that is always with/in us whether we are aware of it or not. God and Jesus haven't come to me as divinities named "God" and "Jesus" recently. The feeling of their shoulders bolstering mine merges in my memory with the recollection of my granddaughters' warm arms against mine as they slept, one on either side of me, on an airplane one afternoon when they were toddlers. Because of the Dear One, all is connected through unbounded Love. I think of webs, filaments, underground roots and pools, streaming with Love.

Always as I write, I am aware of the inadequacy of words. My deepest experiences of God I cannot write about, not only because there are no words for them but also because they are of deep nothing. Perhaps a kind of . . . bordered nothing. I don't know how to describe it.

But this writing seems a way of throwing myself into a pool of unbordered Love we are all washed in, that comes from a stream that flows from the Source.

❧ ❧

Kit Wallingford is an Episcopal priest. She and her husband live in Houston, Texas, where, in her retirement from full-time pastoral ministry, Kit is assisting priest at Palmer Memorial Episcopal Church. Her special interests are leading worship, acting as a spiritual director, teaching, and joining in contemplative prayer. She likes to read, play Sudoku, and hang out in Colorado with her husband, two adult children, and four grandchildren.

Trouble Asking God a Hard Question

*A. Grace**

In my last year of high school, after a lifetime of knowing church and the community as a locus for social life, I found myself at a conference where, for the first time, I met peers who had an active spiritual life. I had never seen this in people my age. I knew it was something I didn't have and knew that I wanted it. Over the next seven years I searched, begged, pleaded with God, put myself in the midst of faithful people—and nothing happened. Then a personal loss plunged me into a depression I labeled "death" and I quit searching, as I focused on going through the motions of daily living at the lowest possible level.

Then came the first Sunday in Lent. My custom, as a member of the choir, was to sing at both Sunday services. At the second service on this Sunday, in the middle of his sermon, the preacher said, for the second time that morning, "See how much God loves you!" And, for the first time in my life, I saw it, heard it, knew it in my heart, soul, mind and body. The world changed in an instant!

* Pseudonym

I no longer felt the pew beneath me, where, in the previous moment and for nine months before, I had felt weighted down. Where I had previously felt that I was slogging my way through a dark swamp, now there was light all around me and I felt buoyant. I felt I was leaping up, floating to the ceiling, laughing and joining the singing that filled the room. Joy exploded within me. The buoyancy lasted for a month, the joy continues still. Now, although I don't align myself theologically or spiritually with those who label themselves "evangelical," I have no hesitation in saying that I was reborn, because that is exactly what I experienced. I was dead, then I was alive.

ৰ্চ ৵৾

For twenty-five years following my rebirth, I threw myself into the life of church, becoming a supreme "doer." I wanted to be a part of everything, and the church became my life. But, with the exception of a twelve-month flirtation with the large charismatic community to which many of my friends belonged, I continued to run from most opportunities to nourish my spiritual life through anything resembling prayer and devotion.

Then came a week in late October when, by now living in a different community in a very different life situation, I found myself becoming more and more restless. At first I had no idea what my problem was. But by Thursday, I realized that had been starving myself spiritually—living off nothing more than an occasional hors d'oeuvre stolen from the kitchen, and that I couldn't go on that way any longer. I spoke with my pastor, who agreed to meet with me for prayer once a week for a month and gave me my denomination's new book of Daily Prayer.

I didn't wait for our first meeting. The discipline of prayer took me completely by surprise. I have never been a disciplined person and was astonished to find the gift of discipline coming through prayer! I did nothing to make this happen. I was seized by a power greater than myself, led by the hand, set before the Scripture, embraced by God's Presence, and for two years I never missed a day. It was during this time that I was given the courage to investigate contemplative prayer, and I knew instantly that I was home. Life has not been the same since.

ॐ ॐ

Some time later, I enrolled for the Group Spiritual Direction program at Shalem. On my way to the first full meeting for the program, I expressed to God my fear that I had nothing to share with the group. I was able to let that fear go without any revelation of what I might say. Our group met in a tiny chapel, where I was the second one to share. I simply started talking and have no memory of what I said. But as I sat in the ensuing silence—all of us with our eyes closed as our group seemed to need to do—I heard a voice over my left shoulder say, *"You did fine."* I turned and saw a figure in the corner. It was clearly a human figure, very bright, with human features but too bright for me to be sure of the details. Something in me knew that it was Jesus, alive and present. I saw in his face an invitation to draw nearer to him. I knew in my body that I had moved—although anyone observing would have seen no motion at all. He held out his hand and I moved closer. He stretched his arm out, inviting me to let him give me more and I moved within it. My approach was like descending a climbing rope, letting go a little, slipping down closer, hanging on, then releasing a little bit again. Finally I settled into his embrace. He held me close, silently stroking my head. I was aware of the feeling of pressure on my skin, the warmth of his body—my body sensing his physical presence. Eventually I came back into the group, which I had never left, of course. Nor did Jesus ever let me go.

～～

A. Grace describes herself as a lover of nature—woods, mountains and meadows, flowers, rugged beaches, secluded lakes, spring, beauty and color, Celtic lands and spirituality, especially Iona, the Pacific Northwest (her native land), choral singing and early music. She is a late-in-life Presbyterian seminary graduate currently looking for a position in a church that embraces diversity, change, and liturgical mystery, preferably in western Washington state or Oregon. A. says she loves solitude, one-on-one conversations with others, and reading, and she has dabbled in liturgical art, poetry, and children's theater. She lives in northern Virginia with her husband; their two grown children live in Seattle.

Was That a Nudge from God?

Gay Doudoroff

For three weeks I had been repeatedly telling God that many of the people on my prayer list were dying and I wondered if my prayers made any difference. My back had been hurting me, as happens occasionally, so on this particular morning I was alone and intent on using a heating pad for relief. I was completely focused on gingerly lying down on the floor by my bed so as to line up the pad with my area of pain. Once prone, I realized that I had nothing to read. Then it occurred to me that I could use the time to pray with my list. I reached up over my head to the night stand and picked up the list. Immediately there was a sensation of a strong concussion against my body, similar to what I imagine it must be like to be hit by a car. I wasn't hurt, but I burst into tears. As I looked at the list in my hand, I saw that each of the names on both sides of the paper had a thin, silky thread tied to it, and that then the threads from all of the names rose in a shimmering column up through the ceiling, through the roof, and as far as I could see into the sky. I seemed somehow to understand that, living or dying, we are always connected to Him.

༃ ༃

My family was visiting my widowed mother for a few weeks. I had long been praying for a change in our never-adequate relationship. Two days before we left to go I had badly burned my mouth on hot coffee, and the night we arrived, I couldn't sleep and was complaining to God that, once again, in spite of my best efforts, nothing seemed any different between the two of us. Then I heard God say to me, inwardly somehow, *"Ask her forgiveness."* I was irate! If anything, I thought she needed to ask for mine! God repeated the request. We were deadlocked for about an hour, with me trying out other options on God, and God resolutely repeating the request. For me, what He wanted me to do was metaphorically on a level with a moth trying to fly to the moon. I finally said, "All right, I will say the words but that is the most I can do." The time came. I got the words out, and, in response, my mother said, "Whatever for?" I said, "For anything I have ever said or done that upset you." Her mouth hung open and she was silent for the first time in my memory. I don't know if she was changed in the long term by this event, but I certainly was. And so I saw, firsthand, the power of forgiveness.

༃ ༃

Gay Doudoroff is sixty-eight years old. Although she started life on the West Coast, she has spent most of her life in the Midwest. She is married and has one child. Though she had a short career as a secondary school teacher, she has had a long vocation as a volunteer in many different capacities, all people oriented. She is a lifelong Episcopalian and a trained spiritual director. Gay says that she has been much blessed by having been able to travel extensively and that she enjoys the arts, on both the production and attendance levels, and that she is never happier than when she is swimming.

A Life-Changing Experience on a Retreat

Louise E. Miller

I was at an early Advent Simple Presence Winter Retreat at Bon Secours Spiritual Center in Marriottsville, Maryland. We had the opportunity to gather several times each day in a circle to practice "simple presence" to God.

Sometimes I got drowsy and dozed a bit, but there were always periods when I was awake and alert. During one such morning, I became aware that something was happening: there was a Presence there that came so quietly, so unobtrusively, that I could easily have missed it. Steady, silent, very present, it continued even when our time ended and participants began to leave the room as noises from others in the hall outside were beginning to be heard. Yet I remained, immobile, aware of the sounds outside, yet even more deeply aware of the Presence. I was astounded that I could be so deeply engaged and simultaneously aware of the external noises and movement without losing my interior stillness!

At some point this experience flowed to an end, leaving me deeply shaken, at an utter loss for words, written or spoken: I jotted something down in my journal for reflection later. I knew my experience would be impossible to speak of to another. How could I possibly do that? This experience was deeply life-changing in some way, but I'm not sure if life-changing is really the most accurate term to use. I felt knocked off my pins, almost numb but very alive. I could not move, could not think, did not want to think. How I managed to go to lunch and eat I have no idea, nor do I remember anything else. Though, on some level, I wanted to tell someone, I knew that it was impossible to speak of and expect another person to receive it with understanding and appreciation. (I tried to do so in a small group in the late afternoon, only to find that my intuition about that had been correct.)

It is almost as though I have lived through this experience again as I have been writing about it; so vivid, so fresh that I have been caught up in it again. Reliving such powerful experiences can be this way, though. I knew with no doubt that it was God present, so profoundly REAL. There was no one else it could be.

This experience was radically different from all of those previous times in my spiritual life. I was profoundly stirred in a way I had never been before. It was so much deeper; I wondered if possibly all of the other moments of awareness in my life that preceded it were simply preparation for this.

Sometime later I came across these words in 2 Corinthians 5:17--18: "If anyone is in Christ, that person is a new creation: the old has passed away: Behold, the new has come."

It seems as though this is what happened to me that day on the winter retreat. In some way that I cannot describe, I became a new person.

ಶ‍ಞ

Louise E. Miller is an Episcopalian living in Baltimore, Maryland, retired from the Baltimore County school system where she taught history and was later a library media department chairperson. After leaving the school system she worked part-time with Listening Hearts Ministries as program coordinator, learning the computer along the way. Reading, travel, walking, music, and laughing (including at herself) nurture her, giving her great joy, as do retreats. Being very active in her parish, Memorial Episcopal Church, she has served in several capacities, both liturgically and organizationally, including pastoral care and healing ministries, and she now does volunteer work with church archives. She completed training for the ministry of spiritual guidance in the summer of 1995 and offers spiritual direction, a rich and important ministry that she says never ceases to inspire and amaze her. She says that she loves to accompany people in their journeys with God and to be aware of how God is working in them. She adds that not only is God full of surprises but God also has a sense of humor, which she sees as a saving Grace for all of us! Louise ends by saying that "Although I am in the category of senior citizen, I really do not know what that label means."

To Mission or Not to Mission?

Donna Acquaviva

My husband, Bob, and I were lifelong journalists—and we were both so hooked that it seemed to be in our very DNA. We even met at a newspaper, I a reporter, he an editor. But one day after we'd been married for eight years, when I was writing for the Washington Post and my husband was editing a national equine magazine out of Virginia, something happened to change all of that.

I'd begun feeling a gentle tug to leave journalism and go into lay ministry. I couldn't explain it, and it wouldn't go away. As the tug became a pull, I knew I had to tell Bob, although I feared he'd be terribly disappointed and even feel a bit abandoned. Every day we drove into work together and came home together and the conversation was always about our work. How would he deal with the fact that the dialogue would not be about our mutual love of writing, but of something quite different? I was scared.

One night on the way home (we always worked late) I took a deep breath, turned to him, and said, "Bob. I've been thinking of leaving journalism for full-time ministry."

And he said, "You, too?"

I couldn't believe my ears. Once again, God had placed us on the same page.

We applied for overseas mission with the Franciscans (we both belong to the Secular Franciscan Order), but while we were waiting to hear from them, we were offered the positions of founding director and deputy director for a brand-new ministry to the elderly, disabled and poor in Shepherdstown, the first of its kind in West Virginia, and a ministry blessed by the good God from its very beginnings.

One day we heard from the Franciscans. They wanted us. When could we start? We were torn. What was God's desire for us? What did he want us to do? We loved our new ministry, but the idea of working in a new land to minister to the people of God in a community of Franciscans drew us like a magnet. How could we choose? Which one was right and which was wrong? If both were right, how do we make the decision? We talked to our spiritual directors, attended daily liturgy, and prayed hard for guidance.

But it didn't come.

One night I was sound asleep in my bed when I awakened with a start and sat straight up. And I heard Someone say, *"Go downstairs and pray."*

My prayer place was in the basement where the only heat was a woodstove, which I didn't know how to make work properly, and it was midwinter. So I slipped into some warm slippers and a fuzzy robe and went downstairs.

Obediently I plopped into my prayer place, lit a candle—and a stick of incense for good measure—and waited. Silence. I waited some more. More silence.

After half an hour I finally spoke to God in a matter-of-fact voice. "OK, you woke me up in the middle of the night, you called me down here, and here I am. And now you're silent. Well, I'm not leaving until you tell me what you want."

The answer wasn't long in coming. The same voice I'd heard in my head when I was awakened spoke again, this time so tenderly it brought tears to my eyes. *"Donna Rose,"* the voice said, using the name only my dear mother and husband call me, *"Don't you know that I will love you no matter what you do?"* Not an answer but a question. That was so like God, I thought.

But joy filled my heart to its brim. I blew out the candle and ran upstairs, leaving a slipper on the stairway like Cinderella. I shook Bob awake. "Bob, Bob," I said in a trembling voice. "Guess what? We don't have to make a choice. God says He'll love us no matter what we do." After Bob recovered from the shock, we talked as though a message from God in the middle of the night were an everyday occurrence. And we made our decision right then and there.

Exhausted but content, we fell asleep in each other's arms. We would stay with the Shepherdstown ministry and do our very best for God. That was really all He asked of us—and it was enough.

&

Donna Acquaviva, a graduate of a two-year spiritual guidance program, is a professional writer and teacher of writing and a freelance editor. She and her second husband, Bob, also a former writer/editor, live in Roanoke, Virginia, where they are active as lay ministers in the church. Donna is a spiritual director, liturgical dancer, potter, reader to the blind, and hospice volunteer. She and her husband have eleven children, twenty-one grand-children, and five "greats."

Behold, I Will Give You a New Heart

Paul Millin

Early in the 1970s, I recognized and named some deep yearnings I was feeling as a hunger for spirituality. During a weekend retreat lead by the Rev. Jack Biersdorf of the Institute for Advanced Pastoral Studies, I was introduced to meditation, which I was grateful to learn and began to practice regularly. Several years later, I returned to IAPS for an advanced workshop, again with Reverend Biersdorf.

As the workshop began, Jack announced that, on the last evening, there would be, for those who wanted it, an offering of healing meditation prayer. "Healing prayer" was something I associated with the more dramatic forms of charismatic Christianity. Usually I would have been very skeptical. However, my experience with meditation and trust in Jack's leadership stirred curiosity.

On the last evening, Jack had us gather in circles around the four people who desired healing prayer. In the center of my group was a woman whose excessive talking I had found increasingly irritating during the week. In this behavior, "Jane," as I will call her, reminded me of my grandmother, which didn't help. So I knew this was going to be a challenge for me.

To begin, Jack invited everyone to meditate with eyes closed for twenty minutes. Then, he asked those of us in the circles, who would be offering healing prayer, to partially open our eyes and begin to focus our attention on the person in the center.

At first, I simply gazed upon Jane. Then, after several minutes, a curious thing happened. Although my eyes were focused on her, in some unexplainable way, I could also see my heart in my chest! This was a totally new experience, yet I was not frightened and stayed with what was happening.

My heart was small and very dark. Then, from somewhere deep within, I heard the words, *"Behold, I will give you a new heart."* As I continued to focus on Jane, I now saw two pincers of light like ice tongs flow toward and gently rest on Jane's temples. Then my heart grew larger; the blood color became a rich red. Shortly, this vision faded and I saw only Jane.

In the follow-up period of sharing what had happened for both those praying and the focus person, I shared this experience. Jane had not sensed anything on her temples. My experience was a beautiful gift, yet unexplainable.

Now, twenty years later, as I write about this experience, a new perspective emerges. Yet it is grounded in my original response of this being a "beautiful spiritual experience." As the connection between Jane and my grandmother emerges more strongly in the telling, the experience may be addressing my strong reaction to both women who were of above-average height and had a large body frame. My reaction to their excessive talking without listening was angry and judgmental. Perhaps the visual and auditory experience was about healing my own hardened and shriveled heart. A gift of a "new heart"; I was the one who had been started on a journey toward healing some old pain from childhood.

Over the thirty years since, I have worked with a pastoral counselor regarding my relationship to my grandmother's "smother" love of silent demand ("Look what I have done for you!") and overprotectiveness. I have slowly come to appreciate how difficult it was for her at age forty-seven, as my father's widowed stepmother, never having had children of her own, to take on the care of her three-year-old grandson. Also, that, in her English Victorian tradition, she was more comfortable expressing affection through cooking and cleaning than in being able to respond to the emotional needs of a child who lost his mother when he was twenty-one months old.

∂∘ ∘∂

Paul Millin, a retired United Church of Christ pastor, says that he delights in offering individual spiritual companioning, retreats, and workshops in spiritual practices. He lives in Lowell, Massachusetts, with his wife, Betty. They have three grown children and two grandchildren. A New Hampshire A-frame on a small pond provides a getaway in the woods where, from a wide deck, he and Betty can enjoy seeing a variety of birds and, occasionally, spot a deer. Paul's evening fishing usually didn't land any small-mouth bass, so he began taking his camera with him as there are beautiful sunsets and a pair of graceful loons in residence there. The family watchword soon became, "Dad catches more pictures than fish!"

Paul enjoys music, particularly jazz and classical, reading mysteries and novels, and "Bill Cosby style" humor that helps us laugh at our human foibles. He and Betty have enjoyed a number of trips abroad, and his discovery of Celtic spirituality has been an important gift of some of those travels.

A Prayer for Healing, Answered

Nancy Yacher

Although I come from a centuries-long line of Quakers, in the 1970s I was a member of the Episcopal Church. This was a time when the Charismatic Renewal was sweeping through Christian churches, the Episcopal Church included, of course, within which, in Lawrence, Kansas, I became a member of a large charismatic fellowship that later came to be called The Mustard Seed. Within this group I became acquainted with the gifts of the Spirit and saw both emotional and physical healings take place. This led in time to my sense of willingness to pray for healing for others as I might be called on to do.

With this background, I dare to describe for you a healing miracle brought about by God that I was graced to be a part of. I was overcome by such awe at the time that I could barely speak of it, and then only with some trembling and rapid heartbeat and those same feelings arise in me again as I remember and begin to write about it now.

A dear friend of mine at the time, a Conservative Jew, who was also a member of our charismatic fellowship, was burdened by brain injuries after having fractured his skull. His right ear had been damaged beyond repair, he could not kneel in church with his eyes closed without losing his balance, and he was suffering from increasing vertigo. He asked me to pray for healing for him.

After having received the Eucharist one night and praying for guidance as to how to help him, I began to pray for his healing. In my mind's eye I saw the ceiling of the Sistine Chapel, the place where the figure of Adam is stretching out his hand to receive the touch of God that brings him to life. The hope in that gesture perfectly imaged my deep and heartfelt reaching out to God in prayer for my friend to be healed. Then I heard the words, *"Since I can create Adam from the dust, why do you think I can't create an inner ear from the broken bones?"* I continued to pray silently for the ear to be re-created. When I had finished, I turned to my friend and whispered into the damaged ear that had no hearing. He heard me! He raced immediately to the telephone to check out his hearing by calling for time and weather. Yes, he really was hearing everything.

Then he called the rector to report what had happened. Soon afterward he went to see an audiologist, who told him that the new ear was the ear of an adolescent, undamaged, whereas his other ear was already showing signs of degeneration and some hearing loss. Today, thirty years later, the re-created ear is the only one with good hearing. Later he discovered that the night blindness from which he had also suffered, as well as some long-term food sensitivities, had also disappeared.

How awesome is the power and love of our God?

సా ⸈

Nancy Yacher is a recently retired former professor of literature at the University of Kansas and a specialist in the work of C.S. Lewis. She still does some teaching about C.S. Lewis occasionally at the large student center at Kansas University. She has two adult sons who are happily married and have five children between them, and she is now married to the friend whose healing she describes in her story above. Eight years ago, she became a member of the Catholic Church, where she says she finds a happy connection again with the mysticism of her Quaker heritage.

"I Love Your Dress"

Kate Finan

A few years ago a prayer group friend invited me to attend a "Blessing of the Father" conference at the Toronto Airport Christian Fellowship. I was excited and remember telling God, as I entered the building in Toronto, that I was leaving my feminist theology at the door as I wanted to enter fully into the experience.

During the evening session the leader of the conference talked about God as a loving father. He acknowledged that many of us may not have had a good relationship with our earthly fathers. He asked how many had problems with their father? Hands shot up from probably half the two thousand people in the room. Almost as an afterthought he invited us to come up to the stage where he would pray for us. I got up and walked down to the stage with the others. We stood all around the stage and in the aisles. Then he began to pray God's love, healing, and forgiveness on us—more and more until I was in tears for my dad and gratitude for God's love.

When his prayer was complete, there was a great silence. Then I heard God say to me, *"And I love your dress!"* At first I did not understand. Within ten seconds it flashed into my head. Usually when I hear what I think is God's voice, I would be tempted to say, "Is that God or is that just me?" This time I had no doubt. This time I knew God the Father was loving me and healing an old hurt that had been affecting me since childhood.

You see, when I was thirteen years old, I was a chubby teenager. My parents wanted me to lose weight and my dad would often say, "Get away from the food." I had been invited to a party on one afternoon. After dressing in my best clothes and looking as good as I was able, I walked through the living room. My dad looked up and said, "Burn that dress!" I was crushed. I knew then that I would never "be enough" or "good enough" for Dad.

And what about that dress? I still wear that dress all these many years later, feeling God's love wrapping around me as the fabric touches my skin. Now I know deeply that I am loved by God—and that is enough.

ᘛᘚ

Kate Finan is sixty-five years old and married and has two grown children, a boy and a girl. She and her husband have three grandchildren who are, she says, "a major joy in our lives." They are members of a Roman Catholic community. For the last sixteen years, Kate has been a daily money manager for the elderly in her local area. She helps them pay their bills, balance their checkbooks, take care of Medicare and secondary insurance issues, organize and file papers, and prepare for tax time. She says that this is both a profession and a ministry. She is a Eucharistic minister, a spiritual director, a longtime member of a charismatic prayer group and the Cursillo movement, which, she says, nourishes her life and gives her opportunities to serve others. Besides playing with her grandchildren— one year old, fifteen months old and three years old—she enjoys photography, pottery making, gardening, ushering at a music center, and any time spent near the water.

What Is God Doing These Days?

Sr. Sharon Kanis

As I was walking one day, I experienced this inner event: I saw an old woman sitting at a loom, weaving with silver threads. She was beautiful and vibrant, and she wore a simple brown robe. She said, *"Don't worry. I am here and my work is being done. Let the powers do as they must.* [By this, I understood her to mean global, political, church, and community leaders who sometimes act in contradiction to God's desires.]*"I am very busy and my work is being done. I am connecting you to one another."* And I saw the people of the world connected through their hearts by a fine silver thread. Then I realized that the thread she was weaving to connect us—was her own silver hair.

❧ ❧

This from a time while I was on retreat:

"Well, God, I sat here for a half hour, full of distraction. I kept going over pictures that I have seen of you standing at the door and knocking. You, Jesus, are dressed in the traditional robe and cape, carrying a staff and knocking persistently on the large oaken door of my heart. I imagine myself inviting you in for a beer."

The image doesn't fit. It doesn't move me at all. Suddenly, I find myself standing at the sink in the "kitchen" of my inner self. There is a knock at the door and I call, "Come in. The door is open." You did.

You are a woman, mid-forties (slightly older than I), dressed in jeans (which I do not wear) and a colorful Guatemalan blouse. Your hair is braided in a long, single strand reaching midway down your back. I know immediately that you are a friend who understands everything, a friend to me, as I have tried to be a friend to others.

We have a cup of coffee together and talk of those we love. I tell you about each person who is dear to me and you receive each story with understanding. Then I begin to tell you of those I do not love well, those who frustrate or annoy me. Somehow, suddenly, I can see them as you see them, and each one is incredibly beautiful and precious. Each one is unimaginably brave, simply for living life each moment. I weep with love.

You thank me for my tears, telling me that I weep on your behalf as well.

The impact of this experience has stayed with me for twenty-five years. It has transformed the way I experience people.

❧ ❧

Sr. Sharon Kanis is a School Sister of Notre Dame in her mid-sixties, a member of her congregation for forty-five years. She was born in Baltimore, Maryland, and has been a teacher/professor in Baltimore for most of her life, teaching high school science, religion, and theology and religious studies on the college level. She says that she loves learning and teaching as well as "sharing our stories" with others. She also serves as a spiritual companion for others and facilitates retreat experiences. Music and the arts are sources of great personal pleasure for her, and she says that she has been much enriched by having had opportunities for travel and meeting people from other cultures.

Learning to Rest in God's Love

Margaret K.

About a decade ago, I sat down to pray somewhat grudgingly. I was armed with the long list of prayer requests I'd agreed to make on other people's behalf, but had the increasingly uncomfortable sense that I was being rude to God in just rattling off a list of names as if I were reading from the phone book. In fact, I had been neglecting these prayers, though I thought they were important, because they seemed so dry and fruitless. This particular day, however, as I began to pray, I seemed to sense a message coming to me, voiceless yet perfectly clear to understand, that I remember now as God telling me, *"I know about these needs, Daughter; they are mine now. What I want now is for us to gaze at each other in love."*

I was puzzled and a little surprised, but I did as God asked. At first, it seemed almost as if I were crawling into a tunnel inside my mind toward God and, there, simply resting in and experiencing the love that we shared. Ah! This seemed to continue to be God's will, and was so lovely for me that I began to do it regularly, gradually coming to see it not as a tunnel, but as an open, dark space deep within me filled with God's incorporeal Presence and a gentle, still, quiet sense of love. This is still by far my most common type of experience of God today.

At some point it occurred to me to wonder to whom I was praying, as the only attributes I could identify were Presence and Love. I described my evolving prayer to a theologian friend, seeking his help in identifying to whom I was praying, realizing that, while I'd been a lifelong, sometimes ardent Christian, if the Presence weren't Christ, I would have to choose it over Christianity, as it was so real and true to me that I could not follow a doctrine that did not include its reality.

In fact, it was this realization that showed me how profoundly this new form of prayer had impacted me. My friend pointed out that Jesus had said, "No one knows the Father except the Son." Thus, I began to understand intellectually that I was, indeed, encountering Christ in the spaciousness of the silence.

Even so, that recognition was only the beginning of the process for me; it took many spiritually rich months to integrate the teachings of Christianity with this powerful awareness of the immediacy of God's presence. It was only a couple of years later that, to my amazement, I encountered numerous books that described my experience, and learned that the type of prayer I was practicing had a name—contemplation. I took the first of these that I read, Merton's little book Meditation and Spiritual Direction, to my spiritual director and said,

"Look! Merton is talking about what I am doing!" It was delightful to know that God had taught this prayer to others, to see the unifying nature of the Holy Spirit.

One day, I sat down to pray and drew the Bible off my shelf to find a lectio divina prompt. Opening the Bible at random to the Gospels, I was distressed to find myself looking at Luke 11, in which Jesus teaches the disciples the Lord's Prayer. "Why, God?" I groaned, "Do you want me to use words again?" God's response, which I experienced only as an urging, seemed to be along the lines of, *"Humor me,"* so I began to pray the Lord's Prayer. I got as far as the word "Our." As I look back now, it seems to me as though that abrupt stop was perhaps triggered by my recognizing the incredible invitation to be a member of God's family, ("Our Father"), but I felt myself being drawn actually into God, swept into what felt like a dynamic whirlwind, God as relationship.

At the time that I first began learning and practicing contemplative prayer, I had been holding God at arm's length for years, afraid that if I were ever to fully give myself to God, God's next action would be, "Ha! Gotcha!" and God would disappear, leaving me heartbroken. All the talk about "dark nights of the soul" only reinforced this fear. So God's hardest, and sweetest, work with me has been to teach me trust. Many times I've thought that I should be keeping notes of the gentle faithfulness God has shown me in teaching me to trust God. The chief of these occurred one day when I sat down to pray, caught up in mental gymnastics involving a complex theological understanding I was devising of the universe as interconnected, and I got the sense, more clearly than at any other time, that God spoke to me, saying, *"Have fun with these ideas if you like, but always know I am right here."*

&∽

Soon after that experience, I had a dream that I was a small child playing on a grassy mountaintop (picture a scene from The Sound of Music) with a cherished family friend, and I was chasing a beautiful butterfly, while the friend laughed beside me. I dashed off after the butterfly, running farther and farther away, and suddenly found myself in a wintry wood on a pond with ice cracking beneath my feet. In panic, I turned to cry out for my friend, imagining him to still be up on the mountain in the spring, and, as I turned, I brushed against him! He was so close, I was not able to turn without bumping into him. *"Always know that I am right here."* I can't number the times that those words have come back to me with their original clarity to remind me of God's faithfulness, of God's reality against which everything else seems ephemeral. I now believe that if I were to experience a dark night, those words would follow me into the darkness.

&∽

In time, God seemed to teach me a new form of intercession in which I would draw a single person into the God-space with me to see what God would do with him or her. It is difficult to explain this, as I have never seen God as having a physical presence. Perhaps what I was seeing was the person for whom I was praying in a new way, as if through God's eyes. I remember one time in particular, however, when I was praying this way for a friend and, during the prayer, saw him cradled in the arms of Mary, who was rocking him tenderly. I was a bit surprised by this as I had never had a particular affinity for Mary, but when I told my friend about it, he explained that that image was very powerful for him, as he had felt abandoned by his mother at an early age, something with which he still struggled.

On another occasion, I was extremely distressed one day, to hear on the news about a young Palestinian suicide bomber who blew up both herself and a young Israeli girl in a grocery store in Tel Aviv. I brought them to God in prayer and suddenly felt myself floating above a vast sea, which I somehow knew was God's grief. I knew somehow that, if I were to touch it or enter it, I would be annihilated but I longed to drink from it, to drink in God. I saw, though, that God is always restrained when interacting with me, that when I long to drink from the ocean of God's grief, it is as if God, instead, offers me a breast, rather than overwhelming me with the flood that is God, and I am caressed by the mists rising from the flood. This led to my writing the following poem, as

I attempted to capture my experience of God at that time:

I am suckled at the gentle veil of God's restraint,
Caressed by mists rising from a fierce flood of love,
Drawn into the spinning joy of God's infinitude
in beams of warmth,
on beams of sacrifice;
Known utterly and so, freed,
so free
So intimately that as I whisper love songs
my lips brush God's, are God's.

సా తా

Margaret K. is forty-nine years old and a lifelong Episcopalian. She is a spiritual director and a leader of contemplative prayer groups and is a member of Shalem's Society for Contemplative Leadership. Professionally, she works as a career counselor for college students. She is married; she and her husband have three college-age children of their own and she is an avid gardener.

Depression and a Personal Pentecost

*Jane Traselton**

I would like to share one of my experiences of the immediate presence of God that took place on September 9, 1970, while I was alone in my former home.

First, a little background: I had had my sixth child a little less than two years before this event took place. It had been a difficult pregnancy healthwise, including a period when I had mononucleosis that lingered after the baby was born. Despite my deep love for this baby, I felt like I was carrying the weight of the world on my shoulders and I descended into a postpartum depression, which had not happened to me after any of my other children had been born.

On that Wednesday morning in September I felt a tremendous urge to get up and go to Mass, although most days I could hardly drag myself out of bed to get the older children fed and ready for school. But, somehow on this morning, I felt energetic enough to go to our parish church, which I had not been able to do for a long time.

* Pseudonym

One of the readings at Mass really stood out for me on that morning: "The Spirit of the Lord is upon me. He has anointed me to bring good news to the poor, to bring liberty to the captives and new sight to the blind; to free the oppressed and announce the Lord's year of mercy" (Luke 4:18–19).

After I returned home I felt an overwhelming sense of joy. I rushed into the dining room feeling a wonderful Presence enveloping me and I knelt down and threw up my arms in praise and surrender to God, all of my burdens lifted. (You should know that some time previously I had been introduced to the Charismatic Renewal by my eldest daughter and had attended one of her prayer meetings with her where hands were being dramatically raised in prayer and I had said to myself on that occasion that, being a rather formal prayer, never, never, never would I do that.) Then I found myself singing my heart out, not in words but with joyful sounds and syllables just spilling out all over each other.[1] I danced and sang all over the house. My husband was so happy when he came home to see how wonderful I was feeling!

The peace, joy, and love that filled my being that day lasted for many years and changed my life. I had been the "captive" who was liberated, the "oppressed" who was set free, and the "blind" who could now see!

---

1   This is ecstatic speech, usually referred to as "speaking in tongues."

In His mercy, God had set me free from all of the suffering I had been through! I had so much energy that, with new zeal, I could spread His word.

I have had "crosses" to bear since then, but I believe that is part of my spiritual journey and my purification, and I have learned during these dark times. For example, I now have far more trust in God and am more aware of His presence within me and without. I seek to become less self-centered and I feel more compassion for others. I also have a new understanding of the role of suffering in our lives and learning to "let go and let God" take care of many things I have previously held onto too tightly.

I now spend more time with the contemplative prayer practice known as Centering prayer, and I also have a spiritual director to companion me on my journey. I still have much to learn and do not always feel joy, but when I am tempted to doubt my faith, I recall this wonderful experience that I have shared with you and then my faith in a loving, merciful God is completely renewed.

⋙ ⋘

Jane Traselton is a seventy-four-year-old Roman Catholic laywoman who has received a spiritual director's certificate from the Haden Institute in North Carolina. She presently facilitates group spiritual direction gatherings for women around her own age and appreciates what she gains from others in the group as well. She and her husband are the parents of six children and grandparents of eleven. They now live in the country just over an hour's distance from most of their children, and they recently celebrated the fiftieth anniversary of their marriage.

No Words, No Time

Kathryn J. Campbell

There are no words for the most important things. Joseph Campbell said that somewhere. But I can tell you about the place. The Wildlife Management Area teems with life and light. The end of the small lake, made from a stream in what used to be prairie, is filled with reeds and cattails. The water in between them reveals the green-filled depths of the cove. Small frogs plop into the water. Light dances on the ripples of the lake. The breeze blows small waves onto the shore. Red-winged blackbirds chirr their warnings. Along the banks a thick growth of young trees reach for the sun. On the other side of the trees butterflies check out the wildflowers that wave in the breeze alongside the tall grasses.

I walked there often. And stood. And drank it in. At least a couple of times a week I needed to get away from cement and schedules, machines and manicured grass to visit this place, in order to keep my cool and be a decent person.

So when I was on a three-month sabbatical at age sixty in the verdant late spring and early summer, the gift was to go earlier and stay longer than usual. After days of sabbatical tasks and sociability I knew I needed to get to the lake. I was up and out the door early to keep my rendezvous. I walked, and sat, and stared at the water and the butterflies and the birds and the weeds in the water. My whole insides were caressed by incredible beauty and wonder that words simply cannot tell, no matter how many exclamation points follow.

I closed my eyes and was gone. It seemed wanton, reckless to do it in a public place where anyone might come along, though my intellect claimed no one could tell by looking what was happening to me. What that was, I do not know, cannot say. I wanted to dissolve into . . . whatever had me. For a moment I felt poised between dissolution into that bliss and going toward people. I did not know. I had no will. I had to say, "As you will." How long I sat on that old log on the dusty ground a few feet from the lake I do not know. A few minutes. Many minutes. There was no time.

Writing about it now feels like prayer. It was of God, that much is clear. It was intense. It was overpowering and awe-inspiring. It filled all of the empty places and left me, at that moment, with nothing to accomplish, nothing to achieve, nothing to want. It was a great gift—a gift that demanded its way with me. Yet it is more accurate to say that I longed to honor the gift by returning to such a place often, where I could praise God for the wonder and beauty of the world. The longing was so great that I knew I would shirk duties and leave tasks undone in order to respond.

Around that time I read in a newsletter on spirituality these words from Thomas Merton: "What longings of our hearts really represent a personal gift which we alone can make to God? If there is some gift which we alone can give, then almost certainly God asks that gift from us." I had to admit that I didn't think many other people wanted to leave their tasks just to bask in wonder and respond in praise—though, of course, I don't know because who talks about such desires? This did seem to be a gift I was called to offer. And to receive.

When I returned from sabbatical to the large church where I was an associate minister I struggled with incorporating that call into my routine of board and committee meetings, paperwork, e-mails, phone calls, hospital calls, worship. I struggled with whether this was simply a private joy, for I cannot comprehend what it might mean to God. But I could not deny that when I honored the call to revel in the beauty and wonder of Creation and to praise our Creator for it, I was more grounded, more content, more patient with and attentive to others, less distracted, less irritable, and more was accomplished in my ministry at the church. In retirement, with a much more relaxed schedule, the calls and the gifts continue.

The ways of the Holy One continue to surprise and delight me—and sometimes make me laugh out loud!

ﳢﳢ

Kathryn J. Campbell is a lifelong Congregationalist (now United Church of Christ), was born an Easterner but now lives in the Midwest. She says that some of her early memories include crawling through long grass, the pond on her uncle's farm next door, and an empty animal pen in the middle of a mysterious woods. A significant fact of her life is that her mother died when she was six years old. The church was always important to her, more, she says, for the community of people who remembered her mother than for any sense of God, who seemed very distant, or for any joy or mystery in worship. After a time away from church in her twenties, she returned, wanting the church community for her small daughter. She says that in time God drew her closer until, when her three children were nearly grown, she discerned a call to ordained ministry in the United Church of Christ. She has served small, rural congregations in Missouri and a large, multi-staff congregation in Lincoln, Nebraska. She has been divorced, is remarried, and is blessed by a grandchild.

I Wasn't Looking for Trouble

Anne Marie Regina*

I am the eldest child from a boisterous, churchgoing Catholic family. Growing up, my Irish and German heritage manifested itself in liquor-infused celebrations involving fine china and party dresses balanced with nun-inspired discipline and a relentless work ethic. There were definite rules growing up. It was the sort of family where you colored inside the lines, didn't ask questions, and didn't dare disappoint with a bad report card or a note home from Sister.

It is hard to say if my parents were happily married; there was little affection between them and I have a sense that there was a lot unspoken in their relationship. Cocktail hour fueled their conversation. Entertaining frequent guests kept them distracted. On the surface, everything was fine as long as no one dated a non-Catholic or non-Caucasian, had sex before marriage, or voted Democratic.

I loved church as a child—the stained-glass windows, incense, and hymns. It was predictable and soothing. As a family, we never missed Sunday Mass. My dad's rule

* Pseudonym

was that, as long as we were there before the gospel, it "counted" and we left straight from the communion rail like docile novices to meet him outside where he'd have the car running so we could beat the crowd out of the parking lot. We made all of the regular Holy Days, including the Feast of the Assumption that would inconveniently fall during summer vacation, leaving us scrambling for a weekday Mass in a strange city. For good luck we even celebrated the Feast Days. I distinctly remember the feel of the unlit candles placed across my throat for a special blessing from St. Blaise on his feast day.

In adulthood, some young man commented on my devotion to the Blessed Mother, which, at the time, struck me as an odd pickup line. But in grade school I did love the ghostly way my glow-in-the-dark rosary looked, hanging from the bedpost. I often prayed two rosaries, lickety-split on my knees beside my bed, trying to erase all the evil inside of me. I remember being quite proud when, as the shortest girl in my class, I was asked to wear my First Communion dress a second time to crown the statue of Mary in our school yard one year. I was a child desperate to believe in something. There were odd chunks of time lost to my memory, which I would not understand for many years, but I knew that God was everywhere. God was an imaginary friend to me, full of miracles and magic—what with water into wine, angels making babies, and all that rising from the dead.

As one might predict, that kind of faith does not survive the rigors of adolescence. At twelve years old, I couldn't find the rosary anymore but I knew how to make Dad's very dry martini and Mom's frothy scotch sour. When I turned eighteen (and not a day before), I was invited to join in the evening cocktail hour that often lasted until well past eight. I helped uncork the champagne for the mimosas with which the family toasted Christmas morning. I rolled in the kegs for our raucous teen parties. The family made eager pilgrimages to the New Hampshire tax-free liquor store on the way to our summer place in Maine. As the child with the shortest legs, it was my fate to tuck the case of libations under my feet. I knew better than to complain. By senior year of high school I was a few tenths of a point off valedictorian status, but I also kept a pilfered bottle of vodka in my bedroom closet for those mornings when I just couldn't breathe. I considered it a compliment when adults marveled that I could drink like my father.

God would make guest appearances in those years, usually during Holy Week, but I had better things to do on most Sunday mornings. Besides, I was liberally outraged about church teachings against gays, birth control, and women priests. The virgin birth became a quaint folktale rather than a miracle. I simply lost the ability to suspend my disbelief. Then, one summer afternoon, I remember lying in the grass looking up at the sky, probably recuperating from a long night out, and suddenly realizing that there was no God. It was like freedom blowing through my brain! I could stop worrying about collecting jewels for my crown in heaven. I could relax because there wasn't a God up there keeping a punitive checklist of my venial infractions. I felt liberated from trying to live up to impossible expectations. I didn't have to struggle mightily to be "good" anymore. I could just live.

And live I did, on the outskirts of the theater world in New York City after college. I worked hard with assorted jobs—hanging stage lights, doing temp work for the Audubon Society, role playing job applicants for AT&T, and, of course, waiting tables. I got my union cards from bit parts on soap operas. I did summer stock. But the grind of late nights, wine tastings, and invitations to share drugs with exotic men started to wear me down.

Looking back I think that must have been when the angels started to gather. (Before she died my grandmother told me that she specially asked angels to watch over me as a child, and in that she may have succeeded.) In any given restaurant in New York City one finds a mix of charming, inebriated waiters, anal retentive tipplers, and usually one or two converts talking up AA. I wound up working at such a place at just the right time. There is a special bond that develops among a team standing valiantly between hungry people and the surly staff cooking their food. I heard things—not that I listened, not that I asked, not that it had anything to do with me—but I heard things about the disease of alcoholism. I also had a longtime friend who came from his own sodden family who passed along a book about children whose parents drank. My parents' drinking had grown more pathetic over the years, less festive and more morose. Visits to see my parents now included trips to the hospital, my mother's late-night crying jags, and the ever-present sense of drama. So it was easy for me to head off to Adult Children of Alcoholics meetings and sit in a classroom and listen to stories that seemed somehow familiar—after which I would leave and meet my own friends at a bar.

I'm always slightly embarrassed by sobriety stories; the German ancestry part of me doesn't like all the fuss. But for me the moment was so dramatic, so crystalline, that I have to admit that it was nothing short of a visit from God. I was sitting on the floor in the living room of my studio apartment. I was sobbing, probably over another romance gone bad. I may even have been to an ACOA meeting that night. I was reading the stupid book that my stupid friend had given me about alcoholic families and—the—world—stopped. There was a flash of clarity so sharp, so above and beyond any of my previous thinking that it is hard to describe. My brain actually felt something click into place. Then there was a feeling like a waterfall of cool water quelling my tears, bringing me to a calm, steady center. In that moment I just knew I had to stop drinking. It was unequivocal and it was definitely not something that came from me. It was God. From that instant on, for about a year, this angry atheist self felt God almost physically like a wind at my back. I had no volition; it was like being shot out of one of the water slides at a theme park. I was in the flow of Something Much Greater than Myself.

I never spoke but I went to AA meetings religiously every day, never doubting the stories told by the former prostitute, drug dealer, homeless man, or former movie star. We were all telling the same story of hell and redemption. I won an award that included some money, enough to leave restaurant work. I got a sponsor, started therapy, rearranged my friendships. I struggled with going home for holidays, since even without saying anything about it, my not drinking was an affront to the status quo. But I was walking a path I could not turn away from and part of my soul was starting to heal.

I wasn't looking for trouble and wasn't particularly interested in digging into the past. But as I crested eighteen months sober, the real miracle happened. I'd been "working the program" and doing whatever was recommended. I had even started to pray again. (It is one thing to know that God is at work in one's life; it is quite another to actually engage God in conversation!) Prayer in my twenties reminded me of the gullible child with the glow-in-the-dark rosary that I once was, the child who prayed with earnest desperation. But I'd always been good at following the rules, and there are steps about surrender, about prayer. So I kept repeating the Serenity Prayer with the tenacity of a drowning person paddling to shore.

I got swept into the memories of my childhood sexual abuse mid-afternoon one Friday on the Long Island

Railroad. This was long before Roseanne was on the cover of People magazine with her story, before there were organizations decrying false memory syndrome. I was blindsided by the knowledge. My boyfriends had grown accustomed to my telling them I was on the ceiling, disembodied, looking down at myself with them. I had always attributed my rather profound sexual anxieties to too many lectures by the nuns while I was growing up. I thought I was just Catholic! But, in an instant, my world changed and everything I thought I knew about myself vanished. Very like before, it was a flash of insight, recognition of a deeper truth of which there was no doubt. It was a gift come unbidden.

I do not know how I got off that train and to the safety of my apartment. I was being flooded with memories and sensations and horror and realizations all at once. I just know that, once again, it was not all me. I also know that it was God who was behind the phone message from a long lost friend on my answering machine that day. I had not spoken to her in a very long time but, as God would have it, she was now a clinical psychologist with a specialty in working with survivors. And, when I phoned her in the small hours of the morning, she heard the panic in my voice and said, "Can you stay where you are? I'll be right there." This friend Amtraked to me from D.C. within hours and sat beside me while my life spilled apart. She was my no-nonsense angel. I happened to be between jobs at the time, so when she suggested that I come to D.C. and stay with her, I just went.

For me, this second experience of God was very similar to the first. There was a moment of life-changing insight that swelled over me suddenly and without warning. But this time, the presence of God was more profound. One part of my brain was in agony trying to grasp the conspiracy between my parents about events that had happened years before. The very year I crowned the statue of Mary, actually. At the same time, somewhere inside me there was a calm, silent, bright place that stood still. Everything slowed down like I was living in a tunnel and, again, the same sense of God as wind behind me pushing me forward. I wasn't capable of rational thought at the time, but there was an angel, in the person of my old friend, who said, "Come with me," and I got on a train and was lifted out of my old life.

The aftermath of that day still astonishes me. I was abandoned immediately by my "loving," boisterous family. I was vilified and betrayed. I wound up sleeping on a bare mattress in a house full of strangers the first Christmas after I left New York. My baby sister was lost to me, a tragedy I still mourn. I could not take her with me, so she was left behind in a world of lies and half-truths. It still shocks me to recall how quickly and completely the ranks of family closed against me. It was ten years before my dying grandmother confirmed what I had remembered, and even then, she did nothing to set things right.

But in the midst of the excruciating losses, the blessings rained down on me. I got a waitressing job that provided me with enough money for a competent therapist. I found a home and a man who loved me and a new extended family of friends who supported me on my journey. Years later when I got an e-mail that my father was dead, there was someone to sit with me by the riverside while I mourned. People tell me that I am brave; they say I am resilient. Frankly, I believe these transformations have nothing to do with me at all. Like when Jesus approached the fishermen that he called to be his disciples, I simply had to follow.

I dabble in contemplative prayer now; for me there is too much about God that cannot be captured adequately in traditional prayer words. Spiritually, I still go through periods of anger and outrage and grief. But I never go through doubt. I will celebrate twenty-five years of sobriety in December 2012, and I have a life that feels like a miracle every day. I volunteer with teens living in foster care. I help raise funds for soldiers suffering from post-traumatic stress disorder. I lead a contemplative prayer group at my church. I am a godmother three times over. I laugh. But in my heart I know I am just waiting. Part of me believes that these events are meant to ready me for something else. So I patiently live day to day getting ready for the next time the world stops and God rushes in and I am blown onto the path I am meant to follow.

Anne Marie Regina lives in a condo in Washington, D.C., with a spectacular view of Rock Creek Park and the National Cathedral. She works for a federal agency advising Congress on ways to improve health care programs. She is a fan of Fr. Thomas Keating, Cynthia Bourgeault, and Eckhart Tolle. She attends a liberal Episcopal church where she is a lector and teacher of Rite 13. She recently received an e-mail from the sister she had to leave behind.

Pulled from the Sea

Linda Graebner-Smith

My husband, Rick Graebner, and I had been missionaries in the desert regions of northern Kenya near Ethiopia for two years when the story that I want to tell you happened.

It had been a devastatingly hard two years. We were to be working under the leadership of senior missionaries who were themselves the children of pioneering missionaries from Canada who had been working in down-country Kenya a generation before. They were hardworking and were especially dedicated to practical works for the people they served, like getting fresh, safe water for these northern nomads as well as for their flocks of camels, cattle, sheep, and goats. Rather than learning the Boran language of the Gabbra people, they relied on their fluent Swahili, the predominant down-country trade language of East Africa. Unfortunately, this left them somewhat removed from the tribal culture of the Gabbra, who had come to see them as caring but aloof.

Trouble reared its head almost immediately as Rick and I, young, fresh, and excited to be there, arrived and threw ourselves into the task of learning the language and culture of the Gabbra people. People flocked around us every day as we forged out to engage them and practice our newly learned dialect. We were immediately welcomed by the nomads and were invited to many gatherings and events, to our great delight, although we noticed that this seemed to be beginning to cause an unpleasant rift between us and the veteran missionaries. This rift unfortunately widened and ultimately led to the redirection of money that had been designated by our home faith community for Rick's and my housing to other purposes over which we had no say. It was a difficult and stressful position to be in.

In addition, I had begun to develop some health problems. The hot, dry wind that would sweep fiercely across the sand and volcanic terrain stirred up huge dust devils, called bube by the Gabbra, that kept sand in the air, outside and inside of the house, and breathing this sand on a daily basis led to several bouts of bronchitis/pneumonia for me. Luckily, medical personnel would fly in monthly with antibiotics to treat the infections, but the concentration and strength of the meds was such that all good florae in my system were wiped out, along with the pernicious bacteria—leaving me with dysentery that lingered and lingered through the year, sapping my strength further.

Rick and I were already decidedly discouraged by the time the Africa Inland Mission (AIM) field leadership recommended that we take a week's furlough near

Mombasa and consider reassignment to a different area of the country, not such an extreme hardship area.

And so we found ourselves in a small fishing village near Malindi on the Indian Ocean, staying in a little beach house that belonged to one of the AIM bush pilots. Perhaps this time close to the water would bring new strength to my weary body and a healing to our discouraged hearts.

The first morning there, Rick discovered that two young men in the village had crafted their own catamaran. The hulls had been carved out of tree trunks; then they fashioned the crude vessel with sails. Rick had hired them as tourist guides to take us out to a reef about one-half mile off shore where we could snorkel, swimming among some of the gorgeous tropical fish that inhabited the reef. With fins for our feet and snorkel gear, we climbed in the catamaran, communicating with the Malindi "travel agents" using the minimal Swahili that we knew. It was a sunny morning, with an intense blue sky. The ocean was shimmering in the bright light, and once over the reef, we could see that it was teeming with electric-colored, beautiful, exotic fish. Our guides encouraged us to get in the water and around the reef as far as we wanted and discover all of the coral, manta rays, swaying plant life, and hundreds of fish.

We ventured short distances from the boat a few times. I was timid about how far to go because I had become so weak and worn out from the year of dysentery. Our guides urged us to go farther and not to worry. They would keep a watch out for us and would be ready to come and collect us when we were ready to go back to shore. We relaxed and started to enjoy our discoveries. We ventured farther and farther away from the moored boat, lost in the joy of God's creative diversity. On a deep dive, I noticed that the sand on the bottom of the ocean floor was unusually muddy and worked up and wondered what had changed about our surroundings. I motioned to Rick that we should surface and check things out. When we popped to the surface this time, however, the catamaran was nowhere to be seen! We looked around in all directions, but not even as a speck on the horizon could we see the boat! Then, panicking, turning to look inland toward shore, we realized to our horror that we had been pulled out to sea and were now about two miles from the shoreline. The familiar beach area and village from where we had launched was gone. We were way down toward the end of a major land peninsula that jutted out into the Indian Ocean. Then we heard it. Behind us, sweeping in from the Southeast, was a dark and menacing thunderstorm. Lightning bolts were striking the water. The swells we were now treading had become four-foot waves, then six-foot, and were becoming white caps. We vainly tried to head back toward the shore, swimming on top of the water. That not working, we tried to swim just under the surface using our snorkels to breathe. The splashing waves filled our snorkels with salty spray. Soon it was obvious that we were making absolutely no headway. As we earnestly swam toward the shoreline, we were, instead, being helplessly dragged to open sea.

It hit me then that I was extremely spent from the hour or more of snorkeling. Was it a minute, or perhaps just seconds before I realized I was not strong enough to tread water until we might be discovered there. Certainly, I was not strong enough to make it back to the shore. I suggested to Rick that he swim in, since he did have the strength to make it alone. He could find someone on land and come back out and search for me. At least he would live, even if I perished. He objected impatiently to this suggestion, but agreed that we had no options but to stay there. That is when I prayed fervently and silently to God, "We really do deserve to die here today, Lord. It was foolish to go snorkeling when I had been so sick and worn out. But, if you do wish to save us, Lord, could you help us fairly soon?" From that moment I remember feeling a strange sense of peace and calm. Perhaps I was going to die there. If I did, I was OK with it. I was ready to go and join my maker. As the storm raced toward us from behind, we continued to tread water, quietly, patiently, saying nothing more to each other. About fifteen or twenty minutes passed.

Then, looking off to the right and out to sea, we saw them! Making headway to beat the storm, between the land and us, we noticed a small white fishing boat! Two African men were rowing wildly against the waves, making quick speed across the water toward the shore.

Rick started shouting wildly and raised his body up as high in the water as he could to get their attention. Rick is a big man—about six-foot-three. We could not believe it! Despite the crashing of the waves, the thunder and claps of lightning, they heard him and saw us! They motioned to each other, then in our direction, and turned their tiny fishing boat to come back out to sea to get us. I noticed, as they were pulling closer to our position, that there were letters on the seaward side of the boat that read Rafiki Yesu, which in Swahili means, "Friend Jesus." Wow, with additional relief I thought, "What a blessing that these fishermen are believers, too!" When they pulled up to us, I handed them my snorkeling gear and fins and they each took me by an arm and pulled me into the boat. One of them exclaimed in Swahili, "Choka sana, Mama, choka sana, Mama!" The English equivalent means something like, "Boy, lady, are you tired!" We all agreed. Then we realized that, with the two of them and me situated in the middle between them, the tiny vessel was completely full. There was no room for Rick to join us in the boat. They gave him a rope and suggested that he hold on. With that arrangement, they rowed all of us to shore.

I remember that they helped me out of the boat. Rick then helped them drag the boat up onto the beach. Suddenly, Rick and I came to the realization that we had left all of our money, passports, visas, and belongings with the tourist guides in the catamaran. Even the key to the beach house was in that pouch with his wallet and watch. With minimal Swahili and hand signals he tried to convey to the two fishermen who had saved us that he would leave me there to rest and hike back up the coast to Malindi, to find the tour guides and get our things back. He would come back for me when he found them. Everyone nodded and agreed, as he turned and ran up the shoreline.

I remember the sun pouring down on the beach at that moment. Deciding to lie down, too tired to stand, I felt greatly relieved that I was left in the company of these wonderful and kind fishermen. The last thing I remember is the two of them smiling at me as I closed my eyes and drank in the wonderful warmth of the sun on that beach.

I don't know how much time passed by before the din of shouts and voices woke me from a deep slumber. I sat up to see Rick leading a pack of villagers running toward me from the direction of Malindi. Rick later explained that they had been anxiously gathered together when he ran back along the coast and found them at the launch site. They were worried that the municipal authorities would hold them accountable for our deaths and that they would be judged harshly for abandoning us out at the reef. They claimed that they had waited and waited for us to surface from the reef and had trolled back and forth in the area where we should have been. Hopelessly, they decided to come back to shore and stay ahead of the approaching storm.

When they got close to where I was now standing, Rick asked, "Where are they?" "Where are who?" "The fishermen," he said, breathless from running up the coastline. I looked around. They were nowhere to be seen. They were gone and the little fishing boat was gone. The villagers asked me what they had looked like. I described them: short-statured, muscular, strong men, with very dark, almost blue-black skin, dark, fiery eyes, thick, strong hands—the tiny white boat, shorter than a canoe, wide at the center because of the seats and the oars, with the red letters Rafiki Yesu painted on the left side. The villagers were quite perplexed. This was their world, their territory, their village and lands, and they had seen neither men that looked like that nor a boat of that description. I realized then that the Malindi villagers standing around us were genetically quite different—taller, lean, lighter brown skin, light brown eyes, lips that were straighter and thinner. Then we noticed, looking around on the sand, that the only markings we saw were Rick's footprints running up the shoreline away from me. There were no markings of a boat having been pulled up on the sand, no other footprints leading back to sea or in another direction. The villagers became quiet and mumbled with each other softly in their tribal language.

In the aftermath, I found myself feeling stunned. I remember sitting for hours that night, back at the beach house, wondering about this miraculous, redeeming experience. The next morning, early, there was a knock at the door of the beach house. A neighboring tourist had come to tell us that yesterday morning, one of the other missionary families that was staying in a beach house nearby, had been wading in the water close to the shore. It was a nice family, AIM missionaries like us, about our ages of thirty-three and thirty-four. They had three young children on furlough with them. They were all walking the beach looking for seashells. While they were wading and watching the storm roll in, the mother lost her footing and was pulled under the water by a strong undertow current and drowned.

To this day, I am filled with such an unbelievable sense of gratitude for that miraculous redemption, pulled from the sea. Were those fishermen angels that God sent in answer to my desperate prayer? Why did they save me, why us? Why didn't God save the young woman who had three young children depending on her, instead? This has given me a tremendous sense of God's personal call to me, to be the person that, by His design, He has created me to be. I am unique. I am His. He has preserved my life for His purposes. This knowledge has challenged me ever since. Upon arriving in the States, we elected not to return to the mission field. Since then, I have become a professional business-woman and I believe strongly that I have been called and sent as a lay leader with a compelling call to help other lay people discover God's unique purpose for their lives.

࿓ ࿓

Linda Graebner-Smith is the founder and president of CoCreate Consulting, Inc., a company that recruits leaders and professionals nationwide for a broad range of businesses as well as working with nonprofits and faith-based communities. For more than twenty years she has been active as a lay leader for churches through teaching, administration, preaching, and facilitating change for vital congregations. She is divorced and has been remarried to Fred Smith for more than ten years. She has one daughter, Becky, who is a college student.

Touched by God and the Return of Joy

Avis Vermilye

"I feel ripe for something, yet do nothing. Can't discover what the thing is. I feel fertile merely. It is seed time with me. I have lain fallow long enough."
—Henry David Thoreau

I had this entry from Thoreau's journal tacked over my desk at work. It almost literally jumped off the page, so aptly did it describe my state of being.

Emerging from a long depression and a couple of years of therapy, I was once again able to consider a future for myself but hadn't a clue as to what it might be. I had discovered Quakerism, which had provided an open door to reclaiming the legacy of spirituality I had abandoned as the rebellious daughter of a Methodist preacher. Though I couldn't define it, I felt in some deep place that my future would have to do with the spiritual path and a life of service. Recent reading had led me to consider going to Georgia as a volunteer with a community called Koinonia Partners; I also learned about a fledgling Habitat for Humanity, related somehow to Koinonia. A letter of inquiry had been answered by Habitat's director, Millard Fuller, encouraging me to come and join in. But I had a background and experience in professional theater, had dabbled in crafts, and was drawn to explore my own creativity. There was also the question of money, as I had virtually no reserves to draw on and didn't know whether I could go without the assurance of a job.

Decision making had never been my strong suit; I knew it was time for me to make some kind of commitment, but I felt frozen.

On my lunch hour one day I stepped into a Catholic bookstore, something I would never before have considered. (When I grew up in the 1950s, Catholics were simply beyond the pale!) I was drawn to several bins of record albums and began idly looking through them. I was stopped short by an album cover with a stunning color photograph of brown-robed monks striding joyfully across a vast green landscape. I was enchanted. Album notes described a monastery in Vermont that welcomed guests to come for retreat. It was absurd, but I knew that I had to go there. That notion lodged in my heart, and a day or two later, on an impulse, I managed to reach the monastery by phone. Yes, they accepted women, and yes, I would be most welcome. Not knowing why, I had a feeling that two or three days would not be enough, so I arranged to spend five days at Weston Priory, a Benedictine Monastery in Vermont.

On my arrival, my senses quickened; there was beauty everywhere, a large pond, small garden plots, spectacular views, colorful wildflowers of every color and hue, birdsong, chubby bumblebees on their rounds. I sat on a huge rock beside an elaborate, well-constructed beaver pond, and it was all I could do to keep from shouting, "I'm alive! I'm glad to be alive." I watched the brothers at their various chores, and to my surprised delight, a huge black, rather lumpish Newfoundland dog was romping around the grounds with abandon.

Once the delight of discovery had passed, I was unsure of myself, not knowing what to expect. At the same time, I felt as though I were exactly where I was supposed to be. The first three days felt fragmented, disjointed, as I tried to settle in, acquainting myself with the daily rhythm of work, worship, solitude, community. Conversations with the resident Sister in the women's guest house were not particularly helpful, as she didn't seem to understand my quandary and tried to guide me to the security of a good job with a financially secure future. I flitted from one thing to another, impatient to discover what I had come for, to be "given" what course my life should follow. If I just read this book, or maybe go pray, or write in my journal, maybe I could find the answer. I was always tempted by the compulsion to do something, even if only passive, like reading, which gives the appearance of quiet. Gradually, I quit trying to "hurry up and be quiet." In time, I was able to simply give myself over to the feeling of the place, at least for brief periods.

Unaccustomed to rising before first light, I sleepily attended morning prayer in the chapel. A stunning hand-thrown pottery vase with a bouquet of fresh flowers and a Bible were the sole adornments. The monks wandered in one by one, jeans visible below their robes. The singing of the monks was celestial and went right to the marrow of my bones. I continued the process of surrender, letting myself absorb the healing I was beginning to experience. I was finally, simply there.

But underneath an outward calm was my own version of a Greek chorus: "What doth the Lord require?" "Here I am, Lord, send me!" ("But where?" I wondered.) Rilke's admonition to "live the questions" and Parker Palmer's provocative assertion that the cross is where all our contradictions converge joined in a lively inner conversation.

On the fourth morning, relinquishing as best I could my impatient groping for clarity, I went for a long walk, breathing deeply of the fresh mountain air, stopping to pick up a butterfly wing by the side of the road, and a little farther along a tiny jawbone of some creature, a lizard, perhaps. Walking along holding the fragile wing in one hand, the small predator's bone in the other, and recalling an earlier sight of the Newfoundland proudly displaying the wrong end of a frog dangling from his mouth, I suddenly stopped as though struck by lightning. The polarities in my life had felt like such a struggle, leaving me permanently exhausted and incapable of choice. But in that instant, I felt I had heard God speak to me, wordlessly somehow, letting me know in every fiber of my being that I was loved. God loved me in all my contrariness, loved all the contradictions I kept stumbling over! God really didn't care what direction I took. I was simply to know in my whole being that I was loved. Period. It was a profound revelation, only lasting a second.

A short time later I spied another butterfly, this one very much alive, with brown velvet wings dipped in white, open to bathe in the morning sunshine, then closed, pointing to heaven as in prayer. My eyes filled with tears. I felt a great weight lift. I was ready to take wing again. A chipmunk skittered across the road, tail straight up, and I burst out laughing. I felt free and truly alive for the first time in years. Joy had returned. That brief moment forever changed my life.

I had had insights before, but this was new. For previously I had thought that my life really would be different. Now I understood that while my life wouldn't ever be quite the same, nothing really had changed. I still had decisions to make, still felt torn by competing desires and dreams. The difference was simply that I knew I was loved— unconditionally—and that knowledge became the bedrock for a journey that continues even now.

છે જ

Avis Vermilye says that, if her spiritual journey, intentionally begun in her thirties, was portrayed in visual terms, it would look like a patchwork quilt, since there are elements of prayer, contemplative practice, intentional community, servanthood, faith-based activism, Catholic mysticism, and

Quakerism all there. In the past she has been a volunteer at Koinonia Part-ners, led retreats at various centers, and, with her husband, lived and served in South Africa during the time of the death throes of apartheid. Both on her own and with her husband she has written numerous articles on personal spiritual journeying that have been published in various journals. She lives with her husband, Dyckman, in Taos, New Mexico. Both have grappled with life-threatening illness in recent years, which has led them to explore illness, aging, and diminishment as spiritual practice.

Desperately Trying to Find My Way

Anya Johnson

I, Anya Johnson, am best defined by color.

I throw colors upon myself each morning with gusto. My clothes, my thoughts, my breakfast—then I throw open the door of my house to step into the work world, and the gray cement of monotonous days threatens to dilute the colorful creation God made of me. I have not always understood how to withstand this threat that culture names as vocation, job, work, giftedness, calling. Over months, decades, and now years I have contemplated, studied, researched words, concepts, phrases, books, seminars that consistently dribble into endless nonsense to me without helping me solve anything or learn to keep my colors in a gray cement world.

As of this writing, I still hesitate at the door most mornings; however, today I breathe more evenly because of the tale I shall spill forth on these pages, an extraordinary moment in which two issues converged and moved me forward.

The telling of the tale necessitates a bit of background. I led a rather secluded twenty years on an

Illinois farm that also included eight years of zealousness with a para-church group, a rather insular world for a wide-eyed girl. I woke up to the world in Los Angeles, California, where I reentered school to study fashion design and merchandising. I loved moving from isolated, restrictive thinking to open creative minds. My creative self leaned into the beginning of coloring outside the lines.

Nonetheless, I still floundered, flopping around like a beached whale trying to find some ocean depth in me. Over the next few years, I moved from state to state, job to job, church to church. I also journeyed through thousands of pages, read hundreds of books, attended hours of classes, and still felt like a flop of a creation.

Finally, a few years past, I applied to Shalem's Personal Spiritual Deepening program (PSDP) in an attempt to climb into God's lap for a deeper sense of who I am and who God wants to be in me. I didn't apply with any notions of getting clearer about "vocation." What I was most aware of was just wanting to be able to breathe freely without falling down on gray cement every day. In addition, because of one more move, I had settled into an administrative position and tried on an entirely different denomination in church land. As you can no doubt see, I was something of a restless and rootless wanderer.

The PSDP required two weeklong retreats within the space of a year. The months between the retreats, I fumbled about with contemplative spirituality while simultaneously becoming interested in learning about and practicing healing prayer, a form of intercessory prayer that focuses on inner healing and physical healing.

As the time of the second retreat drew near, I arranged to arrive a day early at the retreat site as I wanted to enter this contemplative time rested. I also decided to exercise, which, unfortunately, led me to injure my hip. I was determined that nothing would distract me from God's intentions for me for the week. Thus, when other retreatants began arriving, I asked two of them to pray over me with healing prayer. As they began praying—one actually singing over me— an image emerged in my mind. Images were new to me that year. I had not known of their existence until I stepped into healing prayer with others, and if someone had told me that this could happen to me through this type of prayer, I think I would not have believed them. Therefore, when I began to experience images, I could not ignore them, as I had not pursued them or even imagined them to be.

During this particular healing prayer time, the image that surfaced showed me on an operating table. I screamed inside my head, "No!" Instantly the image changed and I saw myself lying on the altar at my church. Then I saw Jesus step up to the altar. He pulled me to my feet and then seemed to be dancing a quiet little soft-shoe. The image ended and I laughed. My hip never bothered me again that week.

Several weeks before the retreat, my spiritual director had given me some information about St. Therese of Lisieux in a conversation about (what else?) vocation! This Carmelite nun who lived in the late nineteenth century had numerous ambitions—she wanted to be involved in mission work, found a religious order, and perform great works—and she never attained any of these goals. She died at age twenty-four, leaving these words: "I understood that Love comprised all vocations, that Love was everything, that it embraced all times and places . . . in a word, that it was eternal! Then in the excess of delirious joy, I cried out, 'Oh Jesus, my Love . . . my vocation, at last I have found it. My vocation is LOVE."

The days of the retreat moved along well. I was to meet with my spiritual director, Patience, at the beginning of the day, which would be spent in complete silence but for our meeting. When we sat down together, I immediately got frustrated as she broached the subject of vocation with me—again! I think it's fair to say that she really went after me about it, though in her usual "Patience" kind of way. She must have been feeling something like how I feel with others who bemoan or repeat themselves complaining yet doing nothing to change their situation. She kept pouring out the word gratitude at me, suggesting that I should accept my life as it is instead of lamenting what it is not. (She's right. I know she is. I could feel myself obstinately standing against her. She knew it, too! I can be such a brat.)

After a little time of silence, my resistance began to dissolve and I snapped out of it. In a while, with tears in her eyes, she spoke of Nelson Mandela, telling one of his prison stories. It seems that, when he realized that he could do nothing about his situation, he set about loving those about him—the prison guards, wardens, government officials, many of whom belonged to organizations that the ANC considered the enemy. (I later found this quotation from Mandela himself: "I was in the company of great men. Some of them more qualified, more talented than I am. To sit down with them, to exchange views was one of the most revealing experiences I have had. It enriched your own life. It fortified your morality. It gave you courage to do better than your best.") When my time with Patience was over, I left and went back into the silence of the rest of the day.

As we ate dinner silently that night, I noticed one of the retreatants sitting on a couch nearby silently crying. I felt stirred to go over, lay my hands on her back, and silently pray. I felt incredibly vulnerable to be taking this step in public. Another friend joined me. Then another friend. Holy and strong.

Later all of us converged for a contemplative time in silence. Another surprise awaited me—this time centered on healing prayer. We were divided into groups. The woman I had prayed over was placed in my group. I found myself drawn to praying over her in even more vulnerable ways.

219

When we reentered the larger group for a closing worship time, an image appeared in my mind. I found myself taken back to a time in my childhood that had been deeply hurtful. I saw Jesus enter this childhood scene and redeem the hurt quite powerfully. The next morning I set out on a walk through the surrounding woods. As I voyaged my way back to the cabin, I realized that I could no longer see the path because of the falling leaves. I looked down to see exactly where I was and discovered that I still had the path under my feet. In that same instant I heard the words, *"This is the way, walk in it."* Dumbfounded. Awed. Stunned. I knew I had just heard from God directly. And I knew two other things instantaneously; I knew in my soul, my spirit, my heart that those words pertained to my job and to my church. I also thought that those words were from the Bible, but I had not a clue where they were and had no memory of ever having heard them before. Later that day, I found them in Isaiah:19–21:

> *O people of Zion, who live in Jerusalem, you will weep no more. How gracious he will be when you cry for help!*
> *As soon as he hears, he will answer you. Although the Lord gives you the bread of adversity and the water of affliction, your teachers will be hidden no more; with your own eyes you will see them. Whether you turn to the right or to the left, your ears will hear a voice behind you saying, "This is the way, walk in it."*

I felt as if a hand had reached out to steady me in the crazy circle of my culture's definition of vocation and success.

It's almost the second anniversary of that retreat. I had not actually comprehended fully until I was writing this story in its fullness the extent to which God had been spelled out v-o-c-a-t-i-o-n during that retreat week. I, who had a history of moving job to job and church to church, had clearly heard the message, *"This is the way, walk in it."* I continued to scuffle somewhat in my job and in my church, but I also continued, this time, to "walk in this way." And, amazingly, soon a healing ministry began opening for me within my church, too. Funds miraculously appeared enabling me to travel the country, meeting people and attending seminars to enhance this God-given healing ministry. The dream of returning to a fuller Christian ministry tugged at me. Even so, I still hear the words, "This is the way; walk in it," and I live by them.

So, despite still mundane tasks at work, I have come to see how I short-circuit God by focusing on the job instead of the people. Recently I told God that I want to see my company blessed in spite of the fact that I do not believe whole-heartedly in its mission of commercial development. As I prayed, I sensed the Holy Spirit saying to me, *"It's not about the business, Anya. It's about the people."* I now see glimpses of how I can live in my creativity through my passion for prayer at work. I have begun to walk around the office when possible and pray over the space, the individuals. It is not always easy. Yet I love the people I work with daily who need healing.

Patience's stories about St. Therese of Lisieux and Nelson Mandela run right into Jesus and his "Love your neighbor as yourself." Run right into me.

I, Anya Johnson, am best defined by color.

I throw colors upon myself each morning with gusto.

I open the door of my house each morning to walk out in love.

⇟ ⇠

Anya Johnson is a fifty-nine-year-old Episcopalian who says that she "purposefully lives in busy northern Virginia as she has heard God speak to her about showing others how to live 'at rest' in this fast-paced commuter-oriented, government-driven, economically centered culture." St. James Episcopal Church in Leesburg, Virginia, is her spiritual home, where she is deeply entrenched in healing prayer, the prophetic, leading small groups, and introducing the arts into worship. She says that she particularly loves the integration of art and theology and that one of her deepest dreams is to someday write about the laughter of God, which she believes should be taught and lived as that could change people's concept of God in such a way as to heal their souls from top to bottom. She has a deep love for her family, which includes nine siblings and sixty nieces and nephews.

Dancing with Jesus

Alicia Conklin-Wood

There have been numerous times in my life when I have felt a Holy Presence, that some might call "God." In our normal, everyday world they may seem strange, but they were very real for me, although not at all in what we might call a literal way.

During a very stressful time at home and at work, I made my first eight-day retreat. I had been resisting it, with many excuses as to why I shouldn't go. Fear of the unknown was behind most of it, although time away looked very inviting. When I finally agreed, my spiritual director said she would find the place and make the reservation. The day I arrived, she was there also to check me into my room, acting like a mother hen. Her care and concern was a beautiful entry into God's loving arms, though I could not have described it as such at the time.

The first three days I spent sleeping from the exhaustion of the past year when I had suddenly become senior pastor of a 650-member church in turmoil. Gradually I was able to let go of the church, friends, and family—and then was left with all of my internal family history, and finally, myself. By the third day I felt totally bereft, lonely. I cried my eyes out—until later that morning when I felt a Presence that was beyond describing, and a peace and acceptance and love that I will never forget.

A day or two later I was on one of my daily walks back in the woods when I somehow sensed an invitation from Jesus to join him and Mary Magdalene in a dance. I know this sounds silly but, truly, this is what I experienced. So that is what we did—we danced! After a while Mary Magdalene dropped out and it was only Jesus and me. Around and around we danced, holding hands and laughing with each other. When I suggested inviting my spiritual director and some others into our circle, Jesus thought it was a great idea. We danced and danced. To this day I remember that dancing time and it always makes me laugh with joy. Sometimes, when life is hard and I feel drained, I will take myself back into that memory and be renewed. At the end of that retreat when I returned to my work, I carried our dance with me and Jesus' presence supported me through those hard times. Ahh, what a dance! Truly to dance in this way is to be in the Presence of God.

శ్రా ఆ

I was on retreat another time at this same location. My personal and church situations continued to be more than stressful. On my second evening, again, I had found myself totally bereft. "Scared, lonely, whimpering," I wrote in my journal. I wanted to run away from that place and from all the "demons" and all that was so stressful in my life. Again, from my journal: "Who wants to deal with this mess when you can't get a handle on it? It's easier to skirt the surface like a water bug. O God, save me, from me and the demons within. Let me sleep until it's safe to waken." Later that night, awake, I wanted to push God away. "Fine! Just go away! I don't need You!" I said. "I've always taken care of myself and I'll do it now. I don't need You!" (This despite my real experience of the Divine all of my life.) The feelings continued into the morning—bitter, angry, and lonely. By noon that day, however, I was crying out, "O God, who do you want me to be? What do you want me to do?"

After lunch I slept for a couple of hours and then went for a walk in the cold winter wind. I found two branches to sit on near the pond, close to the water in the sun. It was quietly peaceful, watching the birds skim over the water, the lone banded Canada goose, a few water bugs, underwater grasses waving to each other, wind skimming the surface, and overhead the trees with arms uplifted dancing to the sky. The sun was warm in this sheltered place.

And then a voice spoke within me: *"This is all mine. I want you to enjoy it. Empty the busy places, let go of the hurting places, so you can enjoy my beautiful creation."* I stayed sitting very quietly for another half hour—very still, very peacefully still.

In May 2007 I experienced another, quite different time of Presence. Unexpectedly one night an ambulance was taking my husband to the hospital. He had awakened me, hardly able to breathe. For several hours I watched the emergency room staff work on him, and heard them say once, "We're losing him." A physician's assistant sat with me for a few minutes, asking me if I had a pastor that I would like them to call. About 2:30 a.m., my husband was now more stable and he was taken for a test. I was left alone in the semidark waiting room. There was no one around at that hour. I tried to read my book but could not concentrate. Then I saw a copy of the Bible on a nearby table. Although it was a version I don't even like, and would never normally open, I picked it up and turned to the Psalms, translating automatically into inclusive language and from the King James English to modern language. I was just leafing through them, not staying long on any particular psalm. I still couldn't concentrate. Suddenly I felt a sort of quiet peace come over me—nothing dramatic, no bells or whistles, or even a spoken word—just deep, quiet peace. It felt like what I have called it since, a "sip of peace," but it was enough. I knew then that no matter what the outcome of that night, I would make it through and I would be OK. There is no doubt in my mind that this Presence was the one we call God. Now, a year later, I can still relax into this peace in times of stress.

ळॐ

Alicia Conklin-Wood was one of four children in a military family and grew up in the suburbs of Washington, D.C. She was raised in the Episcopal Church and attended high school at the National Cathedral School for Girls. She says that, even as a child, worship meant a great deal to her and, from a young age, she took the words of the Episcopal liturgy very seriously. After her marriage and the birth of her first child, she and her husband began to attend the Presbyterian Church (U.S.A.). Her young family moved to the Finger Lakes area in New York and lived there for twenty-three years. She was always active in church wherever they were living and ultimately studied at the Colgate Rochester Seminary, was ordained to the ministry in 1986, and began to serve as co-pastor or pastor in several different Presbyterian congregations. She is also a graduate of a two-year spiritual guidance program and, though she is presently retired, she continues to serve as a pastoral associate for spiritual formation at First Presbyterian Church in Lancaster, Pennsylvania.

Synchronicity? Or the Humor, and Graciousness, of God?

*Mira Martinson**

I was in my late thirties, at a time in my life when there were serious difficulties, and I needed God's reassurance that everything would be OK. Although I was not in the habit of putting God to the test—having only done so once before in my life—I became so desperate that I decided to ask God to give me some sign that the difficulties would resolve favorably.

But what would suffice as proof?

One morning I decided to request getting a traffic ticket—not a parking ticket, but a moving violation! That sounds ludicrous but, up to that point in my life, I had not received a ticket for a moving violation and I thought that getting such a ticket would be the proof that could satisfy me. To push the envelope further, I requested that I get the ticket that day. This would be the proof-positive that the difficulties would resolve favorably. (As an aside, I fully understood then—and I understand now—that I could drive in such a way so as to get a ticket, but a police officer would have to be present to witness such driving and I had never even seen a police car along my route to work.)

* Pseudonym

228

That day, I drove to work in my usual fashion, along my usual route. About a half mile from the hospital where I worked, I saw flashing lights in my rear-view mirror. Not sure that the police car was following me, I pulled to the curb of the relatively congested city street and he pulled in behind me. "Thank you, Lord," I said with a smile. The proof that everything would be OK in my life was worth a little ticket. The officer approached the driver's side of the car. I rolled down the window and grinned. I was euphoric. "Good morning, sir!" I said. "Good morning," he said seriously. "May I see your license and registration?" "Of course," I smiled, handing them over. "What have I done?" Without a smile, he said, "Our radar got you at seventy miles an hour in a thirty-mile zone." Immediately, my face dropped. It was impossible that in morning rush-hour traffic I was driving that fast on a city street. I wasn't even sure that my old car would go that fast. As the officer returned to his police car, I was left alone with God.

Pounding the steering wheel, I said to God, "I asked for a ticket, not points. You know that! Even without any previous violations, forty miles over the speed limit is going to get me some big-time points. "What were you thinking?"

The officer returned to my car and, without looking at him, I asked, "How many points am I going to get?" To my surprise he responded, "None." Jerking my head to look at him, I asked, "Why not? Didn't you say that your radar got me going forty miles over the speed limit?" "Unfortunately," he replied, "our radar doesn't seem to be measuring speeds accurately this morning. So I can't give you a ticket for speeding." I breathed a sigh of relief, but as he handed back my license and registration, he added, "But you are getting a ticket for failing to have your seat belt fastened. Please sign here."

I signed the ticket and wished him a good day. As I drove the rest of my journey to the hospital (with seat belt fastened), I thanked God for giving me a break—and my proof. In fact, I chuckled all the way to my office at the hospital, for the joke was surely on me.

And, as I would soon learn, the trouble in my life had already been resolved.

ॐॐ

I had been struggling with the possibility of having a very serious, potentially life-threatening illness. This possibility had hit me like a ton of bricks because I seemed so healthy and I was rarely ill with even a cold. No one knew what I was going through except my doctors.

What bothered me the most was the state of limbo in which I found myself. Was my body healthy or was my body brewing up a major illness, undetectable to myself or my doctors? It wasn't clear and the doctors, although confident, could only say, "Only time will tell."

The ambiguity was almost intolerable. And so, one evening, I asked God to help me understand that I was OK. I didn't ask for a particular sign or for a certain proof. I merely asked that God would help me to settle down and give me some reassurance. The one specific thing that I did ask for was that I receive this reassurance on Ash Wednesday, the following day.

I got up on Ash Wednesday and prayed, "Thank you for what you are about to give me." I went to Mass and received ashes. I felt nothing. I went on to work, alert for any signs that might come my way. Nothing. I went to another Mass at noon. Nothing. I worked all afternoon continuing to be vigilant for anything that might reassure me. Nothing. On the contrary, it was a miserable afternoon, one that was filled with hassles and employee bickering, not peace.

On my way home, I stopped at a chapel and begged for reassurance. But all I felt was emptiness and aridity. With a heavy heart, I went home.

I arrived home and got my mail. I sat in my living room and cried. God and I had enjoyed an intimate relationship at that time in my life and God had been present with me through a series of medical tests. God had already given me so much. Why wouldn't he give me just one more thing, the reassurance that I so needed?

Through my tears, I started to open my mail. One of the items was a small package that contained a book that I had been expecting for well over a month. This book was from a mail-order store in another state that only specialized in rock music books. A major fan of the Beatles, I purchased every book about them. But that evening, I was not in the mood to think about the Beatles, and I left the package unopened.

A couple of hours went by and I decided to go to bed. The package was still on the coffee table, and I finally decided that I should open it to see if the company had sent the correct book. As I opened the package, a green piece of paper flew out and landed on the floor. I assumed it was the invoice and initially ignored it. After I checked that the book was the correct one (it was), I bent to pick up the green piece of paper, which was the only piece of paper in the package.

When I looked at it, I gasped. It was not an invoice. It was a small, published pamphlet containing the testimonial of a woman who had been healed from a serious illness. The illness matched my own. She attributed her healing to God.

I sat on my sofa and cried and cried and cried. They were tears of joy and gratitude. But they were also tears of awe. I was surrounded by not only a sense of the Holy, but also by a sense of overwhelming love.

I was, indeed, well and have been so for twenty years. And I still have the pamphlet that had nothing to do with the book I ordered. But most importantly, on that Ash Wednesday evening, I was also healed.

৵৵

Mira Martinson is a highly educated and widely respected professional woman who has asked that no specific biographical information about her be shared.

Words in My Ear and Questions about God

Marie Raymond *

I have been blessed by many experiences of the immediate presence of God in my life. Certainly nothing like the raptures of Teresa of Avila, but unquestionably real nonetheless. I will share three of these occasions with you.

The first came when I was in my junior year of college in 1977. Before this happened, I had experienced a spiritual awakening, what might be called a "born again" experience. In the aftermath of this awakening I had been taking classes about my faith to update my knowledge. The class dealt with contemporary issues facing the Catholic Church, including the issue of the ordination of women. I particularly enjoyed arguing about this issue with an attractive young man in the class whose views were quite different from mine. One night, while working at my dorm's snack shop, this young man came in and placed an order. We picked up on our discussion from class. As he left, he commented, "Marie, you woman priest!" in jest. Suddenly I heard in my right ear, *"You are to be a priest."* I turned around to

* Pseudonym

234

see who had said this but no one was there. I struggled for years over what this meant. In the blossom of youth and my newfound found faith, I thought that everything was possible and believed that my Church would change to make this possible. I was reluctant to bring up the possibility when even the most hesitant suggestion that this was my call was met with, shall we say, less than approbation. As I came to realize that this would not be an option for me in the Catholic Church, I questioned whether God wanted me to join the Episcopal Church in order to fulfill those words. But I didn't want to do that; the thought did not bring me any sense of peace.

So then I thought that maybe God wanted me to work for change in the Catholic Church, but there was no peace in that for me either. It took me twenty years of struggle to realize that I am a priest, not an ordained priest, not recognized by the Catholic Church, but a priest in the priesthood of believers. I think of myself as being something like Francis of Assisi who heard God say to him, "Rebuild my church," and thought, at first, that God meant for him to rebuild the little ruined chapel of San Damiano, where he had been praying, and coming to understand only years later that God's intention was that he "rebuild" or reform the institutional Church itself.

&ᴥ&

Another experience of God's presence happened after a summer experience in the Dominican Republic, where

I lived and worked with a group of Dominican sisters who were working with base communities in the mountains. It was my first experience in a developing country and of seeing the poverty, the suffering, the huge disparities between life there and what most of us are used to in the United States. I had been strongly affected by the experience and questioned God, "How could you allow this?" I began to wonder, "Is God good or not? If God is good, how can this be?" In the midst of my questioning and agonizing, I dropped out of school and quit my job. At some point during this painful time I came upon a book of selected writings of Teresa of Avila and found some comfort in her words. One night, while I was praying, I experienced myself so completely enveloped in God's compassion that my questions melted away still unanswered. In that experience I came to know God's great compassion for all who suffer and realized that God suffers along with us. For Catholics, this is the mystery that we speak of when we refer to the "Sacred Heart of Jesus."

❧❧

Sometime later while I was serving at an inner-city church in Flint, Michigan, I took part in a healing service as part of our Sunday worship. I was part of a team of five who took turns praying over people for healing. When we planned this, we had no idea what to expect. We thought that maybe a few people would come forward; instead, practically the whole church full of worshipers came forward, each individual with his or her own needs for healing. In the midst of the service, I felt myself lifted up for a moment, caught in another reality, in the middle of the cosmic battle of good and evil—evil in the form of sickness and suffering and good in the presence of God's healing power. This experience lasted only for a moment but it had a very powerful impact on me.

There have been many incidents of not just knowing but experiencing God's presence in prayer, alone and with others, but none so dramatic as these.

කිංෂ

Marie Raymond is fifty-three years old, a divorced mother of adult children. She lives in the Midwest where she works as a chaplain. She is also a spiritual director as well as a writer and teacher. She says that the experiences she has shared here are "the reason I went into ministry and why I've been able to stay in ministry when others have burned out and left."

I Was Lost, Completely Lost

Vivian Hiestand

I found guided meditation through the "est" movement in my Quaker Meeting in my late twenties. By my early forties I was in the midst of a nasty church conflict that shook my religious convictions to their core. I left that congregation and denomination, questioning everything I thought I had learned about God and Christ. I went into what I now recognize as a dark night of the soul. For the first time in my life—and the only time so far—I did not even have a felt sense of the presence of God to sustain me. That presence had been a constant since my awakening in early childhood, a foundation I could count on, though I never heard about such a thing in any mainline church I attended.

Though I had two young sons I barely functioned. I thought only a few days passed, but my husband assures me that it was months I spent in darkness. I couldn't pray, couldn't reason, couldn't read Scripture or inspirational books. I was lost, completely lost. As I sat on the couch one day I thought, "Well, I will behave as if a good God existed, for surely acting with kindness and love will make the world a better place than if I act only selfishly." I used that as my guiding principle for a while, but I was still in the dark, for my actions and words seemed hollow, meaningless, even when well received.

One night, as I sat on the couch watching a television show my boys enjoyed called Christy, I heard a voice deep within me say, *"I'm here."* I came awake within, and the voice spoke again: *"I'm here within you. I have always been here and always will be. Do not seek me elsewhere."* This was not my voice, not the voice of my psyche. Those who have heard will know what I mean when I say that those who practice silence learn the many sounds of their own inner voices, and the unmistakable sound of the Holy. This was the Holy, and I was filled once again with quiet, burbling, living water that I knew I could never lose. I have never again lost that presence, though I have never sought anywhere outside myself again.

৵৵

I was sitting alone in prayer one night when suddenly I was lifted up from myself by two beings, each grabbing me by an elbow and under its corresponding arm. I had a sensation of flying in an upward arc until we breached a barrier of time and space. I have always felt that I could hear "all nature sing" and the "music of the spheres," as the hymn says. Now I was beyond the world, yet in the world. I was a part of all creation, within the world and beyond our created world. I could taste colors and touch aromas; I could swim through music and dance within rocks. I was everywhere in the vast universe at once, with billions and trillions of other conscious beings; I was one with them, we were one consciousness, yet we were each unique individuals; individuality and unity coexisted. I was with God and I was God, at least an indivisible part of the whole. I don't know how long this lasted; I only know that, at some point, I was back in my living room in my prayer chair. From that point on my sense of unity began to grow stronger than my sense of duality, and I began to understand how and why we are designed to enjoy both. Duality brings the sweet gifts of incarnation: delicious food and sweet lovemaking. Unity brings love and kindness, and the ability to share and enjoy the gifts of duality with relationships. This is a joy beyond measure, and a gift beyond price.

↪↩

A final comment: Visions do not hide the material world around me; they appear as a translucent overlay, as if they were appearing on a clear screen that is closer to me than the world I see beyond the vision. Both are real; they just exist in different ways. I am aware that my visions are not of material reality but are a way of seeing truths that cannot be known on a purely material basis.

↪↩

Vivian Hiestand has maintained a contemplative prayer practice for thirty years. She is a graduate of a two-year spiritual direction program and has led workshops, retreats, and classes in various spiritual practices. With her husband, John, she has led Taize services for more than fifteen years. She created and leads an annual ecumenical retreat in the Taize tradition at the Alton L. Collins Retreat Center (UMC) located in the foothills east of Portland, Oregon. She is now in a master of divinity program at the Iliff School of Theology in Denver, Colorado, and hopes to serve as an ordained minister in the United Methodist Church in the future. Vivian and John are the loving parents of their son, Jonathan, who lives in Tulsa, Oklahoma, and their son and daughter-in-law, Jeffrey and Anne Marie, who live in Portland.

For Jews Demand Signs

Leslie Miller

I was born into a nonobservant Jewish family in Chicago and had been attending a Unitarian-Universalist church for fifteen years. But in late 1996, after visiting a Benedictine monastery to write a newspaper story, I suddenly became fascinated with Catholicism and found myself, at age forty, inexplicably drawn to the Catholic Church.

When I returned to my home and my job in suburban Washington, D.C., I continued corresponding with the monastery's abbot, asking a million clueless questions, which he answered patiently and with good humor. I joined a spiritual direction group at the Shalem Institute, trying to discern what to do about this new obsession. Finally, I went through an Inquirers Class at the Catholic parish a few blocks from my house, asking yet more questions. While I began preparing to enter the Church, I still had some lingering internal hesitation. But my experiences the night I was baptized, at the Easter Vigil service in 1998, helped reassure me that God is real and is intimately involved in our lives—and that the Catholic Church was the right path for me to continue to seek him. This was my experience that night.

Those of us being baptized stood in the darkened sanctuary, holding our baptismal candles, as the lectors read the Easter Vigil's many Scripture passages, punctuated by the chanting of psalms. The readings started with the story of Creation, including these words from Genesis:

Then God said, "Let the water under the sky be gathered into a single basin, so that the dry land may appear." And it happened: the water under the sky was gathered into its basin, and the dry land appeared.

Then the congregation sang a responsorial prayer based on Psalm 104:

Lord send out your Spirit, and renew the face of the earth.

Then came more readings, including the story from Exodus about how God led the Jewish people through the desert, appearing as a pillar of cloud by day and a flame by night, helping them to escape the Egyptians' pursuit:

The angel of God, who had been leading Israel's camp, now moved and went around behind them. The column of cloud also, leaving the front, took up its place behind them, so that it came between the camp of the Egyptians and that of Israel. But the cloud now became dark, and thus the night passed without the rival camps coming any closer together all night long.

There were more readings, and more chanted psalms:

You are my inheritance, O Lord . . .
I will praise you, Lord, for you have rescued me . .
Lord, you have the words of everlasting life . . .

Standing in the dark, smoky church, staring at my candle and listening to all the stories and chanted psalms, it seemed that, even as a part of me was there listening and participating, another part had shifted focus to somewhere else, some timeless place where I was alone with the God described in the reading from Isaiah:

The One who has become your husband is
your Maker, his name is the LORD of hosts; your
redeemer is the Holy One of Israel, called God of
all the earth.

I felt that he was walking me through the history of his life with his people and letting me enter into it with him. I was reminded of the experience of visiting a new sweetheart's relatives for the first time—the way they pull out the old photo albums to show you his baby pictures and photos of him growing up surrounded by sisters and brothers and parents and other family. Except this time, it was as if I were being retroactively inserted into the album, too, as if I had been there from the very beginning.

When the priest took the water from the baptismal basin and poured it over my head, I felt that I was right there in Genesis, my body the pristine beach of the new-formed land. For one long, timeless moment, I was there; I could see and hear and feel the new sea splashing, splashing, splashing on my shore.

And looking up at the tall Paschal candle, I felt that I, also, was in the eternal-present of Exodus, walking with the Hebrews through the shadows of the dark desert night. We stared up in wonder at the pillar of flame that was somehow guiding our way.

Later, when I went up to the altar to receive my first communion, the wafer felt alive and pulsing in my hand, like the small hummingbird I had found lying stunned on the ground the week before; I had heard it thump against a glass window pane and saw it fall. I picked it up and held its quivering body in my hand, dripping sugar water on its tiny beak until it finally revived and flew away. Was God calling me, I wondered, to revive and renew the body of Christ? Would he show me how?

I recently celebrated the tenth anniversary of my baptism, and I have not forgotten my experiences that Easter night. I don't talk about them very often, but, like the Virgin Mary did with her experiences, I treasure them and continue to ponder them in my heart, along with several other experiences I have had over the years, when I have spoken from my heart to God and received what seemed to be a clear sign in reply.

While I know that some people are skeptical or suspicious about so-called mystical experiences, I believe they are just God's way of communicating with those who open-heartedly try to listen to his voice. The Bible is full of stories of people's personal experiences of God, as well as his larger-scale signs and wonders. While not everyone needs to get knocked off his horse as Paul did, even he acknowledges (1 Corinthians 1:22) that some of us, though I think not only Jews, sometimes need signs.

May our personal experiences of God continue to strengthen our faith and teach us the many ways in which God communicates with those who listen to him.

ॐॐ

Leslie Miller is a newspaper editor who supervises reporters who cover higher education, religion, and behavior topics. She lives in northern Virginia and attends Our Lady Queen of Peace Catholic Church in Arlington. She spends a lot of time doing volunteer work for the Shalem Institute as well as other nonprofit organizations.

Praying and Singing with Borrowed Words: A Musician's Story

David C. Partington

If I could borrow words to tell the story of a singular, profound experience of God, there are several folks who could help me. I could borrow words from Annie Dillard who tells her memorable story of seeing the light in the trees.

Or I could borrow words from Thomas Kelly when he reminds us that "a new song is put into our mouths." Or I could borrow from Blaise Pascal, who finds language to express the inexpressible: "From about half-past ten in the evening until half-past twelve . . . FIRE . . . God of Abraham, the God of Isaac, the God of Jacob, and not of the philosophers and savants. Certitude. Certitude. Feeling. Joy. Peace."

Or perhaps I should follow the example of the prophet Ezekiel who never does find the exact words but can only say, "It was something like . . ."

The challenge is to find words to tell a story when so many of the words that I must use are overused or freighted with so much baggage that they have the capacity to stop a reader in his or her tracks. If you are that reader, please read on.

Even as a little boy, I had the heart and soul of a musician. As a little boy, I used to sing my heart out to God. I can remember the exact moment and place. I would stand on my bed in the "twins' bedroom" in the Methodist parsonage in Eden, New York, where we lived and just sing. In my high, little-boy soprano I improvised melodies and let them soar. Those were times of unbridled joy.

But there were childhood wounds, too. I was a sensitive child, and a sensitive child with a sensitive heart is easily wounded. As a young boy I heard and witnessed things that a little boy should never hear or witness. I carried the pain of those memories into my adult years and there were times when I wondered if I would ever be free from that pain and free from the anger and free from the disillusionment.

Music stirred my soul and continues to stir my soul. As a young pianist, when my hands touched the keyboard, it was, and still is, like my soul flows through my fingers into the keys of the piano and then, through the music that I play, comes back to strengthen my soul. As an adult I enjoyed a career as a music maker that was more than anything that I ever dreamed of as a child. Long before, I had given up the dream of becoming a concert pianist but found that there was another path for musical fulfillment. As a twenty-seven-year-old musician, I, my wife, and our firstborn son moved to Winston-Salem, North Carolina, where I would enjoy nine years of life as a professional musician. Fresh from earning a master of sacred music degree from the School of Sacred Music at Union Theological Seminary of New York City I and my family arrived, in 1966, at First Presbyterian Church where I would serve as director of music as well as organist and choirmaster.

But there was more. The next year I was invited to become the conductor of the local Singers' Guild, which eventually became part of the Winston-Salem Symphony. With great joy I conducted the Symphony Chorale. I prepared the Chorale to sing Carl Orff's Carmina Burana, Beethoven's Ninth Symphony, the Stravinsky Symphony of Psalms, Leonard Bernstein's Chichester Psalms, the Poulenc Gloria. The list goes on. As the conductor of the Winston-Salem Symphony, I realized a dream of conducting the Bach St. John Passion and Mendelssohn's Elijah. Add to this mix four years of being the choral director of the North Carolina School of the Arts. This was the musical richness that had nourished me as God was leading me to the moment of an amazing gift.

During my ministry at First Presbyterian Church it was the custom of the church to present "Renewal Weekends" from time to time, which I usually attended. In December of 1972 the church had invited Peter Marshall Jr. to conduct the weekend program. By this time I had begun to hear words like "Charismatic movement" and "speaking in tongues" in tones that seemed to carry the implication that you were a second-class Christian if you were not part of this group. At a dinner meeting with

Peter on Thursday night before the weekend program began, Peter asked each of us what our expectations for the weekend were. I surprised myself by answering, "I just want to understand."

I was conducting a concert on Friday night but was at church the next morning to hear Peter speak. He spoke on forgiveness and his words penetrated my heart. I ended up convinced that all those times of waking up at night with the horrible childhood memories could be dealt with only through forgiveness. I went to him, asked for prayer, and described the steps that I planned to take toward forgiveness. Why I said it I do not know, but I also told him that I was no longer uptight about charismatic language—though, I added, "I do not seek those gifts."

From the December Renewal Weekend, my wife and I began to take steps to deepen our spiritual life together. We prayed together. In my prayers I expressed openness to whatever God wanted to do in my life. However, I note that I did have my guard up and fenced the request as I prayed: "I'm open to whatever gift you want to give me but I can guarantee you that you will not get me into a room of people where I will get all revved up and start speaking in tongues!"

On the evening of January 22, 1973, my wife and I were kneeling at our bedside praying together. As we were praying, three words came into my mind. I can only write them out phonetically, but they were something like sabbat rhudi Jerusalem. I was puzzled by those words in that moment and thought, perhaps, that I was being invited to pray them so, in private whispers, I began to speak those words. I borrowed those words to make them part of my prayer. In a very uncharacteristic moment, my wife asked me to tell her what words I was saying. Then she demanded that I speak those words out loud. To be asked to actually speak those nonsensical words out loud was like being asked to dive a thousand feet into a pool of freezing cold water.

But I spoke those words out loud for her. I spoke them again. Now I really need to borrow words. I'll borrow from Ezekiel. What I experienced was something like a physical overtaking of my vocal chords and I began to sing. I sang and sang in a very high voice. Those moments were something like being lost in wonder, love, and praise. My wife tells me that, as I sang, she was flooded with a peace that surpasses all understanding. She tells me that the voice she was hearing was not my voice and that neither before nor after that moment had she ever heard me sing so high and so "angel like."

The time of singing with joy and abandon went on for about thirty minutes. And then it stopped. I remember saying to my wife, "Do you understand what has just happened here?" Now I will borrow from Annie Dillard who said, "It is less like seeing than like being for the first time seen, knocked breathless by a powerful glance. The flood of fire abated, but I'm still spending the power. Gradually the lights went out in the cedar, the colors died, the cells unflamed and disappeared. I was still ringing. I had been my whole life a bell, and never knew until at that moment I was lifted and struck."

As I have reflected on that moment, it has come to seem to me that God may have been saying to me, "David, I want you to sing to me again like you did when you were a little boy." That experience took place thirty-five years ago, but it lingers on in my heart and soul. I think of Thomas Kelly's words, "We sing, yet not we, but the Eternal sings in us. The song is put into our mouths, for the Singer of all songs is singing within us. It is not we that sing; it is the Eternal Song of the Other, who sings in us, who sings unto us, and through us into the world."

I like to think that I am borrowing words from God and then giving them back to God. I trust that God is praying in me and singing in me all the time and, when I make space to give those borrowed words back to God, I "brim my barreled lungs with joy and empty out the song." When I borrow those words, which are never the same, I am edified and sense moments of deep, spiritual intimacy with God.

Praying my borrowed words, for a season I journeyed with folks who were self-identified as "charismatics." In my renewed time of spiritual growth I was grateful for their love, for their friendship, and for their encouragement.

But the story of that glorious moment in our bedroom cost me. The morning after that wondrous moment, I went to the office, and following our morning prayers, I told the ministers and other program and administrative staff about my experience. Some wept for joy. One left the room in absolute bewilderment. A couple of weeks before that moment we had all been joking about the "charismatic folks." Now this story from me—it was all too much. For a season it cost me some friends. However, little by little, over time, folks began to trust that I had, indeed, experienced a profound and authentic moment with God.

I felt compelled to fly to West Palm Beach, Florida, to visit my parents to tell them what had happened. My father was an Episcopal priest. As I look back on this time, I sometimes wonder if, during this time of spiritual euphoria, it might have been better if someone had put me on a slow boat to China! Still, in this time of afterglow I wanted to celebrate the sweet gift of such a moment in my life.

It also cost me my career as a church and community musician, which, amazingly, turned out to be a "good God thing." A few months later, I woke up from a nap in the big Pawley's Island hammock in our yard with a deep conviction that I would be entering Union Theological Seminary in Richmond to study to become a Minister of Word and Sacrament. I had never envisioned such a calling, but somehow I knew this was going to happen. After some days I shared this with my wife. She concurred.

Together we shared this sense of call with our pastor and his wife. They concurred. Then with some trusted elders at our church. They concurred. Things began to fall into place—housing, a place to store our furniture, and different people assured me that finances would not be a problem.

And so it came to be. I completed studies for the ministry, was ordained, and went off to my first assignment at two Presbyterian churches and a Mountain Chapel in West Virginia. During the time that I was there, I connected with an ecumenical group that gathered at Holy Cross Abbey in Berryville, Virginia, once a month to discuss and reflect on various spiritual classics. There I encountered and learned another way of being with God in prayer, the contemplative way. During the three years that I journeyed with the monks and others, I began to introduce more contemplative ways of prayer into my life, though the praying with borrowed words and borrowed melodies continued to be one of God's invitations to me.

In 1982 I accepted a call to found a new church in Lewisville, North Carolina, and also connected with the Shalem Institute for Spiritual Formation to train for the ministry of spiritual direction. Both processes proved to be rich in graces for me.

I must admit, however, that there has been some degree of sadness for me in that, in my gatherings with Contemplative folks, there had seemed to be little understanding of my journey that began in my bed-room all those years before with a mystical moment with God, or any sense of welcome of my experience that night. However, I continued to pray as invited by God and carried, and do carry, that experience and that way of being with God in prayer in a very private and personal way.

Now in my seventieth year and now engaged in some postretirement ministry, I think I have finally learned that I cannot be some other saint. I do not need to be any other saint. I do not need to compare experiences or have my experiences confirmed. I am my own "saint" with invitations from God that have been and are personal invitations to me for moments of intimacy with God for my journey. I trust that, in those moments of prayer, when I pray with "sighs too deep for words" that God uses those prayers for the benefit of others and for the world.

Because they so perfectly describe my own feelings, a few more words borrowed from Annie Dillard to end:

The presence of God:
He picked me up
And swung me like a bell
I saw the trees
On fire, I ran
A hundred prayers of praise.

જે જી

David C. Partington is a retired Presbyterian minister who continues to enjoy ministry as a parish associate for pastoral care at First Presbyterian Church in Greensboro, North Carolina, and also continues his ministries of spiritual direction and retreat leadership. Since his retirement from full-time ministry he has been able to return to the piano and says that a wonderful gift for him has been a new friend with whom he enjoys playing four-hands pieces for the piano. He also now sings regularly with the Chancel Choir at First Presbyterian. David and his wife, Brokie, who celebrated the fiftieth anniversary of their marriage in 2010, are parents of three adult children, John, Willis and Mary. Both sons are married and each has a son, David and Brokie's two grandsons. Their daughter, Mary, sadly suffers a significant developmental disorder and lives close to them in Winston-Salem.

The Daily Round of Life and the Blessing of a Lifetime

Marie Deegan

I married in 1957 at the age of nineteen. My husband, who worked for a large American corporation, was transferred to different offices around the country with some frequency and so we moved a lot. As the years moved along, we had two children, a boy, Bruce, and a girl named Angela.

Ten years later, a year after a move to Jacksonville, Florida, when I was on the cusp of thirty, I began to question the meaning of life. On this one particular day, after my husband had left for work and the children were off to school, I began asking the same question over and over in what I can't say was a dialogue with God—much more a monologue in fact, since I was the one doing all of the talking. As I went about all of the usual household chores, over and over again I kept asking, "Is this what I am here for, is this all? This ceaseless round of chores done today and to be repeated tomorrow? Surely, it must be for something more."

Finally, realizing that the children would soon be home from school with the Cub Scouts expected to arrive shortly afterward, I ceased my monologue and went upstairs to bathe and dress. In the process, just as I looked into the bathroom mirror, I heard a voice within that said, *"Marie, do it for me."* The voice had a clarity and warmth that I immediately understood. It was the most humbling experience and yet elevating at the same time. Immediately, the motivation for my life changed because now I realized that I had a higher calling than I had been aware of, the highest calling there is, in fact—to do everything for God.

Later I realized that this message is what Scripture tells us, but it took this awesome experience of the Holy Spirit's intervention for me to truly understand.

ॐ ॐ

In the summer of 1978, I attended, for the second time, a Christian camp that is held on the campus of St. Leo's College in central Florida. The camp is interdenominational, although it leans somewhat toward the Pentecostal. While there, I received a laying on of hands in prayer that was followed by a profound experience of God's presence that is usually spoken of as being "slain in the Spirit" and that brought with it the gift of speaking in tongues. This was an awesome experience, something like those often described as happening during near-death experiences, I believe. I felt a love enfold me that defies any description in words. Although I knew well that I could not stay in that space, I truly did not want to ever leave. I felt totally embraced in the heart of God.

ல ௭

Marie Deegan is a seventy-two-year-old lifelong Episcopalian who lives in Norfolk, Virginia. She is a member of the Vestry at St. Paul's Episcopal Church, the only pre–Revolutionary War church still remaining there; she reports that there is still a cannon ball embedded in the walls of the church from a bombardment by the British during that war. Professionally, in her earlier years, she worked as a teacher's aide in kindergarten classes for children with disabilities for some time and then later as an administrator in various nursing care facilities.

Marie is a woman of many interests. She loves music—she was once a member of a women's "barbershop" chorus, loves opera and symphonic concerts, and is a member of the Opera Guild. She is also active with the Norfolk Historical Society. She is a graduate of a two-year Shalem program and, throughout her adult life, wherever she was living at the time, she has always been active in lay ministry in the church, both attending and leading Bible study, prayer groups, and other activities. She also loves to travel; she and her husband returned from a round-the-world cruise in the spring of 2011.

Hearing Voices and Being
in Two Places at the Same Time

Francis Geddes

During the summer quarter of 1947, while I was a student at Stanford University, I attended weekly evening discussions on the teachings of Jesus held at the Palo Alto home of Professor Harry Rathbun and his wife, Emilia. They invited Stanford students into their home to discuss the teachings of Jesus as articulated by the New Testament scholar Henry Burton Sharman. Camping out in the Canadian woods during summers with Sharman, they had studied the records regarding Jesus as understood and taught by Sharman. Sharman saw Jesus as primarily a teacher of wisdom, and the Rathbuns, in their own teaching and discussions, presented Jesus as a kind of Jewish Socrates. Harry and Emilia were a dynamic duo and they made Jesus come alive in a way that was quite new for me. When the summer quarter was over, I decided to continue my studies with the Rathbuns for three weeks during my vacation break. They called these three weeks the Sequoia Seminar and it was held at Asilomar, a conference ground on the ocean near Monterey, California.

During that retreat I had a surprising experience that radically changed the direction of my life. One morning, during the first session, Emilia put a challenge to the group: "If you think that you can direct your life more effectively than God can, then go right ahead by yourself. But if you think God can do a better job of directing and guiding your life than you can, then turn it over to God."

I had plenty of evidence that directing my own life was not working well; things were sometimes chaotic. Standing under a pine tree during the break I said to God, "Things have been going badly for me; my girl-friend has tossed me over, I feel like I'm at sea, and I'm ready to turn the whole mess over to you! Take it." I returned to the second part of the morning session and thought no more about it.

In the middle of the second session, Harry Rathbun was describing the way that we find ourselves cut off from God. He told us that it was like living inside of a hard shell that surrounds us completely. The light of God is outside of the shell, he said, always and in every moment seeking to get in, but can find no opening to enter. Then something traumatic happens in our life that strikes a heavy blow to the shell. It cracks, and the light of God moves through that crack and touches the tender center of our heart.

As I sat there, listening intently, I suddenly became aware that I was in two places at once. I was in the room, but, at the same time, I was also in outer space billions of miles away! I heard three beautiful soprano voices singing without words and interweaving magnificent melodies. I was stunned with joy. Waves of profound beauty washed through me. I could hear people in the room speaking softly, but the singing was much louder. That shift in consciousness lasted about forty-five seconds or a minute. Then, just as suddenly, I was no longer in two places at the same time, but back in the room, and the singing stopped. I sat there amazed and grateful for the intense beauty that had moved me so deeply. It was overwhelming.

After a few minutes I began to think about what had happened. The thought came to me, "I just heard voices. Did I experience a psychotic episode?" I was a bit worried, so I talked to a fellow participant, Ray Magee, sharing my experience and question. "You have not had a psychotic episode," he said. "You have just had a classic conversion experience. Read William James's book, The Varieties of Religious Experience, and you will discover that many other people have had very similar experiences."

Later, with much anticipation, I did read James's book and discovered that for hundreds, perhaps thousands, of years, many people in various parts of the world have heard the voice of the Holy in ways similar to my experience, while others had visions with or without an auditory component. James said that our culture had no way to understand or process these kinds of spiritual/visionary experience and therefore simply labeled it as mental illness. It was a comfort to know that I was not alone.

෬෨

Francis Geddes is a retired United Church of Christ minister. He lives with his wife, Virginia, in Santa Rosa, California. Their daughter, Ann, and son, Patrick, and their spouses live in Marin County, California. Francis has served a number of congregations in the San Francisco Bay area during the second half of the twentieth century and was also a spiritual director at the San Francisco Theological Seminary in the late 1990s. He has taught contemplative healing to about nine hundred individuals, in groups of twelve at a time, in West Coast mainline congregations over the past thirty-five years. His forthcoming book, Contemplative Healing: Practicing Healing Within the Congregation, is currently in press.

Rev. Geddes is eighty-six years old and, over the years, has enjoyed photography and backpacking in the high Sierras in California.

A Journey to Get Home to God

Jesse Paladowsky

I am the seventh of seventeen children, from a working-class, midwestern Catholic family. In my teenage years, the tensions of alcoholism and depression brought my family to its knees. My parents fought constantly about money. Teenage brothers and sisters, one at a time, ran away from home. My fifteen-year-old younger sister, Lisa, got pregnant. My eighteen-year-old older brother, Charlie, who was smoking a lot of weed and dropping a lot of LSD, got shot in the back hitchhiking home at 4 a.m. through the ghetto and became crippled. My father's depression and drinking led to the loss of his job. When my family defaulted on the mortgage to our house, we sold our furniture on the front lawn in the middle of January, packed our remaining belongings into a U-Haul truck, and made our way out west for a new start.

As a young boy I felt called to be a priest. Part of this was a real sense of piety. I truly felt a love for God. The Holy One was the only one I could count on amidst the emotional and physical violence of my family. At the same time, religion was a socially sanctioned way to escape from the chaos. Like many devout Catholic mothers, my mother prayed fervently that one of her eight sons would dedicate his life to God. Taking on my mother's dream gave me a special place in her eyes. I dreamed that I could run away to high school seminary and find the safety and sense of validation for which I deeply yearned. That way, I could leave home without being seen as a rebel, without risking the loss of my mother's love and approval.

My childlike faith led me to believe that if I were perfect and saintly, the Creator would look down upon my family and magically remove all of our pain. I embraced what I understood to be the "priestly" role with gusto. My whole identity was wrapped up in the roles of "hero" and "peacemaker" in my family. Because Mom was enamored with the Jesuits, she refused to let me go off to the high school seminary of our diocese. Seminary could wait another four years. So I dedicated myself to getting good grades at the Jesuit high school, being a helper in the family, being validated as a leader by the priests and by peers, and getting elected as an officer of the Student Council.

Inside I was dying. The alcoholic family's code of silence and denial worked in tandem with teenage male conditioning in a toxic way. I was deeply depressed by all that was happening at home. I struggled with a tremendous sense of shame. I had no way to access my own needs and feelings, much less the ability to articulate them or to ask for the help I desperately needed.

When I could no longer play the role and pretend that everything was fine and I could no longer force my brain to spit out answers on college prep exams that had lost all meaning for me, I dropped out of high school. The priest who had been a mentor, Father O'Toole, expressed concern that I would lose the opportunity to attend the college of my choice. I experienced his concern as judgment, as if I were somehow letting him down, rather than as a sense of empathy. I felt extremely lonely and isolated. The all-male environment of a college prep school, even though a good deal of it had been positive for me, was not at all helpful in this time of great turmoil. There was very little room for emotions in this highly intellectual, masculine world. I encountered no one who could help me to begin the process of opening my heart and healing my deep wounds. I was so isolated in my pain that I felt like I was going crazy.

At some level dropping out of high school was the first legitimate action I had ever taken in my life, the first action that was not geared toward pleasing someone else. It was as if my soul, body, mind, and spirit had gone on strike and refused to budge until reality, however painful, could be invited into the room and dealt with in a meaningful way. I have never known how much the Jesuits knew about the breakdown in my family. Even after I dropped out of all my classes except for English and history, they let me continue coming to school, because school was a sanctuary for me, my only place of safety. I have always appreciated that generosity.

This whole time was a death-of-God experience for me. The God of my childhood, with whom I had bargained to save me and my family, was now officially dead. I had no idea who I was outside the roles of "pleaser," "good kid," and "family savior" that I had played my whole life. The deep depression that lingered just under the surface came out full-force at this time.

During spring break senior year my friend, Randy, wanted to go to "the beach." He invited me to hitchhike to California with him. We went from Toledo to Los Angeles to San Francisco and back to Toledo in ten days. We put our sleeping bags down on the side of the interstate and ate leftover toast off of people's plates in truck stops. We went five thousand miles in ten days and spent twelve dollars each. This became a new religion for me. Some people find themselves by joining the military. In a strange way, hitchhiking provided something like that for me. I was free for the first time in my life to live outside of the "pleaser" mode, and I ended up hiking some thirty thousand miles around North America in my late teens and early twenties. I would pump gas or wash dishes for a month or two and then stick out my thumb again and hit the highway. Prior to this time I had always avoided alcohol and marijuana, but in this time of rebellion I became dependent on inebriating substances.

In my midtwenties I started getting scared about the inevitable lows that followed getting high. My inherited tendency toward depression was exacerbated by hangovers. I was also feeling a profound sense of emptiness from the meaningless, menial jobs that occupied my days. My high school buddy, Joe, was attending an alternative arts college that catered to musicians and actors and dancers and mimes and fine artists. It was the only kind of college that would have possibly drawn my interest at that moment. I insisted that any learning that I was engaged in must be connected with my heart as well as my head. I still had some unfinished business from my Jesuit high school days that manifested as a profound skepticism with the pursuit of intellectual knowledge for its own sake. This school seemed right to me and so I enrolled and became a student there.

While in college, I started studying Siddha Yoga with a faculty member who had become a practitioner. Learning to meditate was a very important move. It was my first, small step into an adult spirituality. Meditating gave me a focus and a tool to let go of mind-altering substances. I was able to totally stop smoking marijuana and abusing alcohol. I appreciated that Swami Muktananda's writings said that he was not trying to convert Christians to Hinduism, that the way of Siddha Yoga was universal. The swamis who headed the Ann Arbor ashram were a Jewish couple. I went there for a few extended Christmas retreats. At this point, I was totally alienated from my family, and Christmas was always the hardest and loneliest time of year. To be in a Hindu ashram run by a Jewish couple and to be sitting under a beautifully decorated Christmas tree singing Christmas carols totally tickled my funny bone!

I have never been a morning person, yet the pre-dawn chanting and meditation filled me with a joyous sense of wonder. I loved the beauty of the regal colors, the sweet smell of the incense, and the power-filled rhythmic chanting and drumming that went on for hours. I was transported to a place far beyond my troubles. In spite of Muktananda's words about the universality of the yogic path, there was a part of me that was skeptical. I felt truly thankful for the ways that Siddha Yoga had changed my life for the better, by giving me a spiritual discipline and focus. But I still had feelings of discomfort with meditating in a room that was filled with pictures of Hindu deities. And I felt totally ambivalent about the importance of receiving shaktipat initiation from the guru, which is central to this path. (Shaktipat refers to an inner unfolding of awareness that leads to progressively higher states of consciousness and is explained in Hinduism as resulting from kundalini energy traveling up the spinal column and the opening of the "third eye." It is usually thought to happen through the mediation of a guru or spiritual master. Elizabeth Gilbert writes about this path in her book, Eat, Pray, Love.) It was hard for me to see my way clear to venture to upstate New York and meet Muktananda in person. This was where I drew the line.

I continued to chant and meditate. It provided my daily life with structure and balance. Every few months I visited the ashram for a personal retreat. I really felt torn. On the one hand, I felt great joy, particularly with the powerful music and energetic chanting. At the same time I felt increasingly uncomfortable with the giddiness of the devotees who lived there. "We're like the disciples around Jesus!" I heard one of them say, as a group of men rejoicing over their relationship with a living guru. The part of me that had served peanut butter sandwiches and coffee in the dead of winter to winos on Skid Row as part of an outreach program at the Jesuit high school thought, "Yeah, well, if that's true, what are you doing with it? Didn't Jesus say, 'By their fruits ye shall know them'? "

Four months later I was at the ashram for another personal retreat time. My depression was in one of its periodic full-blown gales. I had seen several different psychotherapists. That was helpful only to a point. I have never tried hard drugs, but I cannot imagine heroin withdrawal to be any more painful than the depth of depression that sometimes would keep me up shaking into the night. This particular evening, after the chant and meditation period, I was feeling as empty and worthless as I had ever felt. After the group filed out from the meditation hall, I stayed around for a while. All was dark, except for the one votive candle that illuminated the photo of the guru. When I felt sure that no one else was watching, I knelt with my forehead on the floor and prayed desperately, "OK, if there is such a thing as shaktipat, let me have it!"

I don't know how to describe what happened

except to say my third eye opened—or something! Something astonishing opened in my mind/soul/being that I had never before experienced, a total expansion of consciousness. I have never tried LSD or hallucinogenic drugs, but from what I have read, my experience seems to have had something in common with those experiences. At the same time, I had a little inkling of what it meant for Moses to be told to take off his shoes because he was standing on holy ground. I was awestruck. I could not sleep the whole night. I knew that something fundamental had shifted within me, something for which I had no resources to comprehend. "Do I have to take on a guru now? Or what?" I was in a full-blown spiritual emergency. I knew I could not continue as I was—receiving the positives from the Siddha Yoga experience, yet on the sidelines of the community, looking in from the outside.

The next morning, as we began our predawn meditation, my soul kept playing the same horrible tape-loop over and over. "What should I do?" I knew that I did not have within me the ability to make sense of my mystical experience the night before. I knew that I desperately needed the help of someone more seasoned than I in the spiritual life. And I continued to feel the weight of my ambivalence and downright resistance about supplicating myself before a guru. Was this willfulness? Ego? I was totally at war within myself. My whole being cried out, "Help me, God. I can't do this!"

Suddenly, totally immersed in the hypnotic chanting and the wonderful smells of incense and the gaudy and bodacious Hindu colors, I burst into laughter. "Jesse, how is this really any different from the Latin Mass? You're surrounded by smells and bells and you are chanting in a foreign language. Is the main reason you are into this because you don't understand it intellectually?" I realized at that moment that, for better or worse, I could not throw away my Western upbringing. That my path is Judeo-Christian. At the very least, I needed to find a way to integrate the real and important new experiences from Siddha Yoga with the real and important experiences from my Christian upbringing. I did not feel free in my soul to take on a guru. My search must lead somewhere else.

ॐ

I first experienced silent meeting for worship with the Religious Society of Friends on the West Coast during the hitchhiking days of my late teens. I had not registered for the draft at the tail end of the Vietnam War and had a natural affinity for Friends because of their peace witness. At this time of transition, I sensed that the non-doctrinal space of an unprogrammed Friends Meeting for Worship might be a place where my Eastern meditation experience and my Judeo-Christian roots could seek integration. I regularly attended small Quaker meetings in the Midwest over the next few years, and there was much that was enriching. There was also a part of me that, wordlessly, continued to yearn for something deeper.

After working with the Nuclear Freeze campaign for a while, I journeyed to Pendle Hill Quaker Center outside of Philadelphia for a ten-week sabbatical. Parker Palmer was there at the time and he was teaching a class on the Trappist monk Thomas Merton that term. When I was nineteen, I had hitchhiked to the Abbey of Gethsemane in Kentucky on a personal pilgrimage to see where Merton had lived out his monastic vocation. Reading Merton's probing dialogue between the mystical traditions of East and West has been an important touchstone for me, and his ever-expanding ecumenical faithfulness provided my one strong continuing connection with the Catholic tradition in which I had been raised. Like so many of my peers at Pendle Hill, I sought out Parker Palmer to be my consultant, the faculty member with whom I would meet weekly to process my experience at Pendle Hill. He's a wonderfully warm and engaging soul and his books had been very meaningful for me. "My consulting load is full, Jesse, but if you're looking for a spiritual director, there's someone I would recommend to you, Bill Taber."

I didn't really know what a spiritual director was, but I was intrigued. Bill and Parker were opposites of each other in a number of ways. Bill had grown up in the tradition of Conservative Friends, although the term "Conservative" is a remnant of centuries-old Quaker realignments and a bit of a misnomer. More than any other branch of the Religious Society of Friends this predominantly rural group of Friends "conserved" the mystical tradition within Quakerism that so easily can become intellectualized in modern urban culture. In that sense Conservative Quakers are really radical.

The serendipity of getting Bill Taber for my consultant turned out to be life changing for me. It is emblematic of my spiritual journey: what I think I want/need is so often not at all what I really need, or what God has in mind for me.

Bill introduced his consultees to an old tradition that goes back to eighteenth-century Quakerism, that of the "Opportunity." When two or three Friends traveled together in the ministry throughout England or the British colonies to bring their vocal and prophetic ministry to Friends' meetings, sometimes under the weight of a particular concern, such as trying to end the practice of slave-holding, the two or three companions would share daily times of silent Meeting for Worship together. When they arrived at their destination, they would often hold special "Opportunities" (Meetings for Worship) in the homes of their hosts, including the whole family and perhaps a few neighbors. Often this type of more intimate waiting upon God can be even more potent than the larger Meeting for Worship on Sunday. For me, that was certainly so.

Bill and I would begin the consultation session with a silent period of waiting upon God. When I was ready

I was encouraged to begin speaking about the current state of my soul. This was totally new to me; I was starving for this kind of spiritual food. It was a qualitatively different experience than a psychotherapy session. In those days it was so much easier for me to focus on what was missing or wrong in my life than to experience being a beloved child of God. The silent "Opportunity" invited me into a space where I experienced God's enveloping presence in a very real and power-filled way.

Whatever came out of my mouth after that time of "sinking down" was invariably much more to the point than my often scattered, surface ramblings. As we began our second session, in the midst of a heart-tendering silence, I suddenly experienced a profound inner "opening," as early Friends would say, that shook me to my core. I did not feel a specific connection to the person Jesus as much as a deep sense of oneness with the Ground of All Being.

The only experience in my life that resembled this at all was that night in the ashram when I received what Siddha Yoga calls shaktipat, the "opening of the third eye." Except this time, instead of feeling terror and being full of frantic questions, I experienced a wonder-filled sense of healing and inner peace. If there had been an inner voice in me to go along with it, it would have said, "This must be the place!" My whole being cried out with joy, "Thank you! Thank you! Thank you!" My whole life I have struggled with feelings of unworthiness. In my youth, the prayer I most related to in the Catholic Mass came right before receiving the Eucharist, "Lord, I am not worthy to receive you, but only say the word and my soul shall be healed." In this encounter with the Holy, for the first time in my life I experienced in my core being that I am truly and unalterably beloved of God, that the Holy One knows and loves me more profoundly than I know myself. The false and toxic sense of separateness and unworthiness that I grew up with was obliterated by this love. As the founder of the Religious Society of Friends, George Fox, said after his great "opening," "All creation has a new smell." For the first time I truly felt my inherent interconnectedness with all of God's creatures.

I knew inwardly that Bill was to be my teacher. Still reeling from what I experienced to be some of the excesses of Catholic hierarchical religion, as well as from hearing one too many stories about different gurus who had abused the trust of their devotees, I had a great fear of religious authority. The type of authority Bill embodied was a gentle, inner authority rather than one based on being in a position of institutionalized authority. I allowed myself to trust him. On Sundays I frequently joined Bill and his wife, Fran, at the small Quaker Meeting they attended a few miles from Pendle Hill, and I took every class that Bill taught.

It just so happened that in that particular winter term at Pendle Hill the whole campus of liberal, non-doctrinal Friends was going ga-ga over Catholic monastic spirituality. In addition to Parker Palmer's class on Merton,

Sandra Cronk was teaching a class on the spirituality of the Desert Fathers and Mothers of the fourth and fifth centuries. I felt like I had landed in a Roman Catholic seminary rather than at a Quaker center. The immediate effect was contact with feelings of anger and betrayal that had come to a head in my death-of-God experience in high school.

Fortunately, I felt enough trust in Bill to bring to our conversations some of those old wounds. Another student, Elizabeth, and I even called a special "Meeting for Anger" one night in the Meeting Room, the space where we held our daily Quaker silent worship. Bill helped to shepherd this special night where the shadow side was welcomed and encouraged to dance. I wonder if, without some opportunity to cleanse the old wound, would I have remained reactive to crucial parts of my own Spirit journey for the rest of my life? And would that have kept me from claiming the path of hospital and hospice chaplain that I currently walk?

The graced time at Pendle Hill and the unusual experience of extended Sabbath and daily worship, study, work, and play within a faithful community provided a hothouse where this new seedling of faith could sprout within me. I gave up plans to go back to the Midwest and resume work there with the Nuclear Freeze Campaign and totally immersed myself in this special opportunity for spiritual growth. After seven months at Pendle Hill and a year in the Quaker community in the Philadelphia area, I continued to feel a profound hunger for more religious study. The Quaker seminary, Earlham School of Religion, provided the next stage of deepening on my Spirit journey, and, eventually, I heard the call to chaplaincy.

I do not claim to understand why I was given these particular extraordinary experiences. I do know that, at that moment in my life, I was truly in desperate straits. Subtlety would not have worked! I needed to be hit over the head with a two-by-four in order to break through the inner constructs of woundedness and unworthiness to which my ego was so deeply attached. As the seventh of seventeen children, I had spent my whole life believing that, to be lovable, I needed somehow to prove my uniqueness. What I received in the experience in Bill's office was something quite different and far more wonder-filled: a sense that, not only am I beloved just as I am, beyond any accomplishments or character traits, warts, and all, but also that—and this is the big one —what was true for me was true for every other human being in all times and places. The Creator loves each and every one of us just as we are. This was not merely about my personal "salvation." I began to have a glimmer of an understanding that my spiritual quest must very much be part of a larger story and engaged within the context of a larger community of seekers on the path.

The transforming experience of God's love and reassurance that particular day at Pendle Hill did not serve as a magic wand to take away all of my angst and struggle. Off and on I still battled depression. Over the years I still sought out psychotherapy and men's groups and other paths of healing. The gift in that mystical experience was an initiation, an invitation onto a new, heretofore unimaginable path that gave my life a real purpose for the first time. In contrast to the experience at the ashram, here I was invited into a community and given a teacher whom I found to be trustworthy. I learned to listen at deeper levels to the Spirit-nudgings within me. As I began walking upon this new path, very slowly, the old anxieties and neuroses faded as my daily life became richer and more joyously full. When I actively followed the authentic path of my true passions/callings rather than being stuck in the familial roles in which I had been imprisoned, as I embraced the path of musician/songwriter and chaplain, I was increasingly surrounded by wonderful people and wonderful opportunities to serve.

My later experience in the Shalem Institute's Spiritual Guidance program provided another crucial place of healing. Over the course of the two-year program I was able to reconnect with deeper streams from my inherited Catholic tradition and to begin to integrate these with the rest of my journey. It was extremely helpful to study the Christian contemplative journey with Christian and Catholic teachers who were open-minded and conversant with Eastern as well as Western traditions.

At one point I invited Bill Taber to be a presenter at the annual Quakers in Pastoral Care and Counseling gathering in Richmond, Indiana. I wanted him to share the rich Quaker tradition of the "Opportunity," which has largely been lost among modern Friends. We were planning to videotape the session and, when I asked Bill for his permission, he responded, "It's fine with me. However, I must warn you that people have previously attempted to videotape me when I have been in the deep spiritual space of a Meeting for Worship, and the video camera usually does not record it." As much as I love Bill, I couldn't help being amused and thinking to myself, "Sure, Bill, whatever you say." When we did the videotaping, Bill and I were in the center of a circle, in a "fishbowl" configuration, with other participants watching our simulated spiritual guidance session from the outer circle. When we entered the period of Quaker silent waiting upon the Lord, the video camera, which worked perfectly before and after this segment, did, indeed, shut down.

I have rarely spoken with anyone about the extraordinary experiences in my twenties. I continued to seek Bill out over the years. I view him as my spiritual father, I, along with many others whose lives were impacted by his quiet wisdom. When Bill was dying of cancer, I spoke to him for the first time about my "initiation experience" twenty-some years previously in our consulting session at Pendle Hill. In my spiritual infancy in my midtwenties, I naively assumed that Bill knew all about it, or perhaps even had some small role in causing it to occur. Actually, he had no idea at all. Then Bill shared with me the spiritual experience that had shaped his life and call as a Quaker minister and teacher. In his early twenties, Bill had a profound mystical experience in, of all places, a Trappist monastery. The fact that this quietly powerful, Quaker mystical teacher had his transforming spiritual experience in a Catholic monastery causes me an even more profound cosmic chuckle than my "Christmas in the ashram" experience did! I continue to revel in this unfolding cosmic sense of humor as I attend my weekly Zen meditation group led by Catholic nun Rose Mary Dougherty and as I go on my first weeklong Zen Sesshin led by a Jesuit priest, Robert Kennedy Roshi.

At his memorial service, and in the reception afterward, story upon story came out about Bill's ability to inhabit liminal space and to invite others into transforming experiences of the soul. In his Pendle Hill pamphlet, The Prophetic Stream, Bill has written about the prophet's role as "making Spirit available" to the community in time of need, of being a lightning rod for God's energy. I do not know that Bill, in his humble servant leadership, would have claimed this role for himself, and I am aware that I am using his words in a different context than he originally offered them. And yet, I wonder if the role of Spirit-Guide, like the role of prophet, is not, at its heart, also defined by this ability to "make Spirit available," to initiate others onto a previously unimaginable path of deep listening and inward guidance. Or, at the very least, defined by the ability to create a sacred, contemplative space where the Spirit can show up as She will!

෴

Jesse Paladowsky is a Quaker, a member of Seekers Church in Washington, D.C., and a board-certified chaplain in his twenty-fourth year of chaplaincy. He worked with pediatric oncology patients and their families for seven years, and for the past seven years, he has served as chaplain for a home hospice in a suburb of Washington, D.C. Jesse is also a professional songwriter and performer and has recorded CDs on Azalea City Recordings. He uses music on a daily basis with his hospice patients and has presented workshops and retreats on "singing in the circle of life and death" for a number of professional organizations. Jesse's website is www.jessepal.net.

A New Image of God, a Veil Parting, and Discovering Oneness

Karen Foley

I think that I need to give you a bit of background before I share my stories: I ignored a call to ministry in my teens because, in the next moment I thought, "I can't be a minister. I'm a girl." I grew up taking religion seriously, said my prayers every night, attended church, Sunday School, youth group, and I sang in the choir when I was old enough. But a painful four-year struggle in high school and college culminated with my leaving Christianity. I could no longer square a loving God with hell or believe that there can be only one "right" religious path. I couldn't just dismiss my religion as "irrelevant" and walk away, as many young people do. I struggled, and found I couldn't be in church. But I had nothing to replace it for years.

After an uneasily agnostic young adulthood, marriage, two young children, and a divorce, in my midthirties I found a home in Unitarian Universalism. Among fellow seekers, my spiritual life grew and, in a year, the call came back with unmistakable force and clarity, this time affirmed by parents, friends, and my minister. I went to Harvard Divinity School and was ordained in 1988.

છે એ

When I had been attending a Unitarian Universalist church about a year (at age thirty-six), I was still not completely over my struggles with faith. However, when I was asked to participate in a "Credo" service, to speak with several other people about our beliefs, I agreed, hoping the exercise would help me give coherent shape to my beliefs. I became deeply engaged in the task. I hadn't used the word God for years and wondered how to express what had been growing in me for the past year. The past few years had been very difficult as my marriage had disintegrated into a struggle with the inevitable difficulties of separation and divorce, single parenting, full-time work, and building a social life.

What had been getting me through all that? It had not been faith in a greater power because I didn't have any; I did not pray; didn't know if there was anything to pray to. And, since my late teens, there'd been no formal religious structure to lean against. As I reflected about where I had turned, what had propped me up and picked me up and helped me stand again, I dis-covered it was people—friends and my church com-munity reached out to me and I could reach out to them. People who essentially said to me lovingly, "Pick up your pallet and walk."

I remember standing in my bedroom when this real-ization struck me. All these people in my life appeared to me as a huge net slung beneath me, that kept me from falling and falling apart, over and over again, and kept on being there for me. When I saw that "net," I exclaimed out loud, "Maybe that's what God is!" It was the first time in more than twenty years that "God" seemed possible.

That moment of clarity, of a strange new way of imaging the Holy that felt very real and true, and absolutely congruent with my experience, has stayed with me all these years. God was becoming a reality to me again, though I didn't quite know it yet. And the image of the net has functioned ever after to hold my sense of what we human beings are and how we are connected. About this time, Unitarian Universalists adopted the term "interconnected web of all existence."

∂৵৹

The sense of a veil parting somewhere high above me, as if in outer space, revealing something I'd never otherwise know about, has happened about three times that I remember. The first two times were when I was in my teens and accompanied glimpses of the possibility of a new way of living or thinking about life. But this last time was more than that.

It was a month before my forty-second birthday and early in my last year of divinity school. The man in my life and I were talking about marrying once I graduated and was ordained. But he died very suddenly of an unclear cause, probably a heart attack. I was with him the night he died. It was an unimaginable loss.

One evening shortly after his death, that sense of a veil parting somewhere high above me occurred again. I was in my house, but don't remember what I was doing or thinking at the time. Suddenly it was as if I saw—though I did not literally see with my physical eyes—a dark sky and a sort of veil that parted against it, very high, as I watched. Behind the veil appeared what we cannot see because it is so far away, or simply in another realm not accessible to our physical senses.

I can't say what I saw behind the veil because it wasn't clear and, as I say, I wasn't seeing in any literal sense. It didn't matter. I simply and suddenly knew, more certainly than any religious doctrine had ever told me or any thinking of mine had concocted, that something vaster than the physical universe lies beyond it, and that I was looking into it, not understanding it, not needing to. I also knew that what lies beyond the veil is beyond life as we live it, and that it holds life as we know it.

Suddenly the expression "death is a part of life" turned upside down. From that moment, I have believed instead that Life is a part of Something much greater than Life, and that Death is an entrance into it.

All this happened in perhaps an instant, but it lives in me and sustains me. I feel this vision was a simple gift. Why is it so hard for us to see the gifts that are in and with us all the time?

ॐ ॐ

My husband, Dan, and I had been dating a few months when he learned from his father's doctor that his dad was hospitalized and probably dying. Dan, his father's only child, flew to his old hometown. He was told his father would die without surgery, but had little chance of surviving even with it. He chose to give his father that slim chance.

On the phone, I felt helpless. I wanted to be with him. I must have asked Dan if there was anything I could do. "You can pray," he said. This was a surprise. Dan had left organized religion behind, with all its beliefs, years ago. As far as I knew, he had no faith in the efficacy of prayer. "Pray for him, and for me."

Well, puzzling as the request was to me, praying was something I could do, so I did. I did not pray for anything specific to happen. I don't ask God for outcomes (except needed changes in myself). I just focused very intently on Dan and on his father and held them up to God's love.

Something happened to me. No words can convey what I experienced, but the best I can do is to say that suddenly my sense of myself merged with my sense of Dan so completely that I felt no boundaries between us. Nothing like this had ever happened to me before and it was confusing. I literally didn't know, for that brief moment, where I began and ended. I was aware both of myself there in my room, praying, and of not being a specific, individual "self." And it was not so much that I was subsumed into Dan as that Dan and I seemed, for that moment, to be one entity.

I told my spiritual director that this scared me. "What is scary about it?" he asked. And when he asked the question, I felt as though my soul rose up out of my body and streamed out the window of his office and scattered itself among all the people of the world. "Because," I said, "if we really are part of each other like that, I'm really part of everyone, and that means I'm responsible to everyone."

Nothing like this had happened before and has not since. I'm not sure I want it to. It is scary. At the same time it is magnificent. And I've known ever since then that we really are part of each other—all waves on the same ocean, made of the same water.

ॐ৵

Karen Lewis Foley is an ordained Unitarian Universalist minister, is married, and is the mother of two young adult children. Although she has served several churches over the eighteen years after her ordination, in recent years she has been led to spiritual direction, small-group work, and retreat leadership. She says that she is finally beginning to say that she has "retired" from parish ministry and calls her present work "freelance ministry." She and her husband, Dan, recently moved to Maine, where she has returned to a passion of her earlier years—writing.

Stars in My Bones

Kathy Morefield

On Holy Saturday 1997, I experienced a marvelous epiphany, a revelation of God through two unlikely sources of grace, the April 1997 issue of National Geographic and The Chemotherapy Survival Guide by Judith McKay and Nancy Hirano.

৵৶

The phone call came during my prayer on Ash Wednesday. I began Lent as I always did, with good intentions and a plan to be disciplined in my prayer life, kind and loving, aware and authentic. But Lent this year would be different. "I have the test results," my doctor said. "You have endometrial cancer." I listened in stunned silence as the doctor explained that endometrial cancer was a cancer of the lining of the uterus. She scheduled surgery for the following week and told me not to worry, that in more than 90 percent of the cases surgery was all that was required. "It's a slow-growing cancer," she said, "and we rarely need to follow up with any other treatment."

Although I hoped with all my heart that she was right, I went into surgery with a looming sense of dread. When I woke in the recovery room, much later than anticipated, I knew something was wrong. I wasn't among the 90 percent. My husband was with me, looking very upset but trying hard not to show it. He told me that the surgery was more complicated than they expected it to be. The cancer had spread throughout my abdomen and the doctors classified it as stage IV, or the final stage of cancer.

Endometrial cancer rarely progresses to stage IV and at the time there wasn't a lot of research available on treatments and outcomes. The hospital oncologist told me that they couldn't guarantee that the standard treatment, chemotherapy followed by pelvic radiation, would be successful and that, once the treatment ended, there would be no way to know if the cancer was gone. My family encouraged me to seek a second opinion. I did so and learned that early results from clinical trials being conducted at the time indicated that whole-abdominal radiation was more effective than chemotherapy in treating endometrial cancer. Suddenly I was faced with two choices, poles apart. It was overwhelming to have to decide between two very different treatments, to make a decision that could mean the difference between life and death. With my family's and my oncologist's help, I finally settled on a combination of both options, a protocol of three sessions of chemotherapy followed by six weeks of whole-abdominal radiation. My first chemotherapy infusion was scheduled for Good Friday.

The day before, Holy Thursday, I met with the radiologist who would oversee my radiation therapy. I left that meeting with a troubled and heavy heart. She was very pessimistic about the outcome of my decision and tried to dissuade me from my choice of treatment. She unleashed a deluge of words about the likely side effects of whole-abdominal radiation, including permanent damage to my kidneys, liver, intestines, and bone marrow, where blood cells are manufactured. She had not conducted whole-abdominal radiation in more than ten years and believed that my plan to undergo chemotherapy prior to radiation would make the side effects of radiation even worse. She said that the doctors at the teaching hospital where I had gone for the second opinion were only looking for a cure (as if I weren't). She went on to say that what doctors failed to inform patients with stage IV cancer is that there wasn't much hope.

There wasn't much hope? I was dumbstruck. I questioned everything. Was I being naïve? Was she right about the hopelessness of stage IV cancer? If my condition was hopeless, why begin chemotherapy the next day? Should I call and cancel the appointment? Would chemotherapy actually set my body up to be devastated by the radiation? Should I go back to the standard protocol, the first opinion, and take my chances? I didn't know what to do.

I prayed my own Agony in the Garden that Holy Thursday. "God, if you are willing, please remove this cup from me." I feared that I was about to embark on the wrong path and I wrestled long and hard with my decision. If I went ahead with the second option (chemotherapy and whole-abdominal radiation) I might live, but at what cost? If I chose the first (chemotherapy and the less extreme pelvic radiation) I might die. I had to decide by eight o'clock the next morning and I didn't know what to do. I tossed and turned in bed for what seemed like hours and finally woke in the middle of the night saturated with perspiration. My hair and night-gown were soaking wet and I remembered the passage I'd read earlier from Luke's gospel: "In his anguish, he prayed more earnestly, and his sweat became like great drops of blood falling on the ground" (Luke 22:24 NRSV). I thought of Jesus and the fear that must have gripped his heart as he anticipated the road that lay ahead. That lonely time in the garden wrestling with the demons of fear and desolation must have been the most difficult part of his journey. But once Jesus made up his mind to go ahead with it all, he had the grace and strength he needed to move through the ordeal no matter where it took him. I prayed for that grace and strength.

I held onto that image of Jesus while wrestling with my own demons of fear and desolation and finally drifted into sleep. I awoke the next morning with a new resolve and a much calmer and stronger heart. I decided to talk with the oncologist before I started treatment. If he agreed with the radiologist's opinion—that chemotherapy would negatively impact the effects of radiation—I would forego the chemotherapy. Fortunately, he did not agree with her prognosis and I started the seven-hour chemotherapy infusion as planned.

The staff and patients at the Infusion Center were wonderful and supportive, and several friends and family members came to cheer me on. I felt fine during the infusion as first the saline solution, then the toxic chemicals flowed into my bloodstream. I continued to feel fine for several hours after I returned home, but awoke during the night feeling nauseated and terribly sick. I went back to the hospital in the morning for an anti-nausea injection and rehydration therapy. When I returned home, I was exhausted and depleted; I felt as if I'd stepped through a door and left my predictable life behind. In that former life I was confident and in control and I had an identity. I was a spiritual director, advocate for the poor, woodworker, volunteer, life-partner to my husband, mother, and soon-to-be-grandmother. Before me now lay a vast emptiness where I didn't know who or what I was. I knew only that I was scared, frail, vulnerable, and certainly not in control.

I collapsed on the couch in our living room feeling too sick and spent to move. On the coffee table next to me was the latest issue of National Geographic. I picked it up and began to browse until I found the article "Time Exposures" by William R. Newcott. It was astonishing! What I read and what I saw was almost unbelievable and unlike anything I'd encountered before. Accompanying the article were extraordinarily beautiful photos of nebulas, giant gas clouds and black holes, storms on Saturn and frost on Jupiter's moons. "Astronomers looked 8,000 light-years into the cosmos with the Hubble Space Telescope," the author began, "and it seemed that the eye of God was staring back." I read that when you look deep into space, you are looking back through time. The Hubble Space Telescope can see 10 billion years into the past, enabling us to witness stars that died billions of years earlier. I wondered how many of the stars we see in the night sky today ceased to exist thousands, millions, or even billions of years ago? The insight gave new meaning to the notion of death for me. If light from stars that died billions of years ago continues to travel through the cosmos, why am I afraid of dying?

I was so inspired by the immensity and awesomeness of the universe, and the Creator of the Universe whom theologian Karl Rahner says can only be described as "incomprehensible Holy Mystery," that I literally forgot that I had cancer. Somehow it didn't matter in the grand scheme of things. The story I had just encountered broke open my sense of the universe and shattered my old image of God. I lost my self in the magnificence of it all and I felt intimately connected to the whole universe, part of something much, much bigger than myself. I lost track of time and space and was filled with that sense of awe that Judy Cannato calls radical amazement. The power of my encounter with radical amazement uplifted and supported me for the next several days and throughout the months of cancer treatments that would follow. In fact, it has never left me. It was a seminal moment that has become the ground of my spirituality and continues to be a source of awe, gratitude, and joy. I've since learned that the DNA that exists in the farthest reaches of the universe has the same composition as the DNA in our bodies. It continues to be recycled through time and space. We literally have stars in our bones.

A few hours later on that same Holy Saturday, I picked up The Chemotherapy Survival Guide by Judith McKay and Nancy Hirano and began to read information that would transport me from the macrocosm of the universe to the equally awesome microcosm of my body. The authors begin with a description of how chemotherapy works: it destroys fast-growing cells in our bodies like hair cells, blood cells, and cancer cells. In order to help the reader understand what is happening—the side effects—in her or his body, they first explain how blood cells work. According to McKay and Hirano, "Blood is the fluid of your life." Red blood cells carry life-giving oxygen from the lungs and nutrients (energy) from the digestive system to every part of the body. (No wonder I felt exhausted and had difficulty breathing.) They pick up waste products and deliver them to the kidneys, lungs, and liver to be filtered and cleansed and eventually recycled or eliminated. Every time we exhale we are releasing the waste products of blood cell activity. The white blood cells discover and fight viruses and infections and cleanse the blood and tissues. Platelets clot the blood and preserve the blood flow by gathering at the site of injury and constricting the blood vessels. These processes take place in millions of microscopic blood cells so infinitesimal that just one teaspoon of blood contains an average of 25 billion red blood cells. There are about 25 trillion red blood cells in the body, 1.75 billion platelets, and between 20 million and 55 million white blood cells. Our hearts pump an average of 600 pints of blood in an hour, 5.2 million pints a year!

These facts exploded into my consciousness. All of this is going on every second of every day in my life without my conscious awareness. Unbelievable! Just a few hours earlier my soul was sailing in the far reaches of the universe, traveling billions of years back in time, and now it moved within my body speeding through minuscule and, to me, invisible blood cells. In a matter of a few short hours I had moved from the macrocosm to the microcosm. From feeling insignificant, I stepped into and experienced my own body as a universe in itself, distinct and marvelous. I was struck by the uniqueness of each and every person, of all beings and of all of life.

I was invited to dance with mystery that day, mystery among the stars in an ever-expanding universe, immense beyond imagination, and mystery within the vast universe of my own body. As I reflect on the experience I wonder, with much gratitude, why both of these incredible experiences happened on the same day through two remarkably different sources—National

Geographic and The Chemotherapy Survival Guide. And why on such an inauspicious day, the day after chemotherapy? I was exhausted, worn out from chemotherapy and my struggle with the demons of fear and desolation the night before. I was forced to let go of many things, including the possibility of a long life and even my own image of myself.

But what was left was an emptiness that created room for God—Incomprehensible Holy Mystery— mystery as distant as the farthest stars and closer than the invisible cells in my own body. I had been, in Gerald May's words, "open, undefended, and immediately present."

The experience of that day continues to evolve in me. As I learn more and more about quantum physics and the new cosmology, my spirituality deepens and my imagination soars. I revel in the interconnectedness of all creation and know that I must participate in its healing and restoration.

From the phone call of Ash Wednesday, followed by forty days of wandering in the desert of cancer, second opinions, loss, and grief to my agony on Holy Thursday and chemotherapy on Good Friday, I journeyed to a profound resurrection of my spirit on Holy Saturday. Easter Sunday was a day of gratitude and joy. I wrote in my journal the week before my first chemotherapy treatment, "I long for hope. Hope like a fire that burns inside me and keeps me going, and along with this hope a passion for life—not a clinging, possessive passion, but a free, celebratory passion. I want to march ahead with hope, not needing to know the outcome." I realize reading this today that that entry is a powerful prayer and that my prayer was answered on Holy Saturday. I didn't know whether I would be cured or not, but I knew that I was healed and that was more than enough.

However we experience it, it is difficult to describe a profound encounter with God and its life-altering effects in mere prose, but poetry can take us right into the heart of the experience. I ran across the following poem by Tracey Marx a few years ago in the 2004 issue of Presence magazine. This beautiful prayer/poem, Space, brings me back to that amazing Holy Saturday in 1997 and is a gift of pure consolation.

Space

If I could write for you a poem of space
I would
outer space where you are tethered
to nothing
but that which sustains you
where you could swim
in the black sea of sparkling stars
hear the whisper of your own resplendence

If I could write for you a poem of space
I would
where you are held
by nothing
but that which anoints you

where you could drift
in the shimmering soul stream
hear the echo of your own emptiness.

If I could write for you a poem of space
I would
sacred space
where you are cradled
by nothing but that which gives you life
where you could float
in the dazzle of a day's dream
hear the heartbeat of your own silence

I can't write for you a poem of space
but I can pray
for wide, wide open
space
and clear cold imagined
space
and gentle grateful
space
Empty us, God
until there is space enough
for the swirling of our own spirit.

Empty us, God
until there is space enough
for You.

In my emptiness, my God, you who are incomprehensible holy Mystery, in my emptiness I met You.

&

Kathy Morefield is sixty-five and has been married to her husband, John, for forty-three years. They have four children and three grandchildren. She has been a spiritual director and retreat facilitator for about twenty years. She has also been a cabinetmaker and has worked on social justice and poverty issues. She and her husband are affiliated with the Catholic mission group Maryknoll, and for the last eight years they have spent a good portion of each year in Cambodia. She lives in Seattle, Washington, in the beautiful Pacific Northwest and says that hiking and walking are a passion for her.

Reassurance in a Hard Time

Cathey Capers

I believe that we live in a world brimming over with the presence of God—if only we could perceive it. The two graced experiences I am going to tell you about were both moments of acute awareness of this Presence. That they occurred in one of the brightest and one of the darkest moments of my life affirm for me the omnipresence of the divine.

The first story attempts to describe a very personal experience of "all my relations." Sitting within this experience offered a keen sense of the Creator's presence and transformed the first syllable of the traditional Lord's Prayer into a prayer of its own.

I understand the second experience best through the poetry I encountered and share of Rilke and Aeschylus. During those dark hours of wakefulness and deep sleep, I felt infused by a Presence I would recognize as the awe-filled grace of God.

These experiences were of God or more simply were God for me.

ं ॐ

Early one morning many years ago I crept from the tent trailer we had parked in the national forest in northern New Mexico. As was my practice at that time, I sought a place apart, to be alone a few minutes at first light. There was nothing extraordinary about this particular morning. My intention was to begin, as was my habit, by praying the Our Father, to be followed by a Hail Mary, and then to simply sit in silence—open to the beginning of a new day.

I settled myself on a decaying log and the beauty around me took my breath away for a few minutes. In the next few moments—I don't know the interval of time—each thing that my eyes came to rest on, seemed to communicate to me personally and deeply. The mountain looming before me, the still water below, the individual blades of grass, the pebbles on the shore, the breeze, the leaves, the log—each was distinctly itself, yet able and willing to be in connection with every other thing. And for that moment and more I, too, was caught in the fold of this intimate yet far-reaching belonging-ness. I would come closest to describing it in words much later, in these few lines:

Valecito
Many years later
I wake
recalling that morning,

the summer I met

the Grand West.

Sitting on a lakeshore

alone, early

Valecito —

still water,

solid mountain;

a single blade of grass

quivering at my feet

amber pebbles

looking up at me.

Sublime unity.

The ancient prayer

Reduced to its first words

"Our . . ."

❧ ❧

To say that my father died suddenly, and unexpectedly, still seems to me, ten years later, the grossest of under- statements. I wince inwardly when asked his age. As if that should diminish the shock. Added to the untimeli- ness of his death was the fact that I had been fearfully dreading the fall of another shoe when his hit the floor.

It was in this state that I lay, the night after his death, on a cot in the room next to what would hereafter be called my "mother's." The house was dark and quiet for a time. Then I heard my mother, trying to muffle her choking sobs. I had never seen nor heard her cry before. It was unbearable.

I crept quietly into the room and sat on the edge of their bed beside her, utterly helpless. When I returned to my cot, I was stifling screams of despair and outrage. At whom, I still can't say.

With my eyes tightly shut against bitter tears, I began, in spite of myself, to feel a growing calm. The strongest sense of reassurance poured throughout and over me like a wave. I fought to dismiss it, vehemently, but could not. There was a little white star-shaped object that appeared under my eyelids along with the expanding realm of peace. I batted my eyes to rid myself of it. It was futile. I surrendered, defeated, and eventually fell into a deep sleep. When I awoke, before dawn, I went downstairs where I would write a eulogy for my father that would close with Rilke's promise:

> And yet there is someone, whose hands
> infinitely calm hold up all this falling.

Some weeks later, in the office of a medical building, leafing through a magazine, I came across these words, spoken by Robert Kennedy at the funeral of Martin

Luther King Jr. While they are originally from Aeschylus's classic Greek tragedy, Agamemnon, they aptly described my experience that dark November night:

He who learns must suffer.

And even in our sleep

pain that cannot forget

falls drop by drop upon the heart

and in our own despair,

against our will,

comes wisdom to us

by the awful grace of God.

In the midst of the worst, God was there. Still. As always.

છ ન્

Cathey Capers says that she "crossed the threshold" into the second half of her life in August 2008, when she celebrated her fiftieth birthday. After traveling and working in the Caribbean, South Pacific, and Africa she resettled in Austin, Texas, where she lives with her husband, sixteen-year-old son and seventeen-year-old nephew. She shares the block with her sister, grown stepdaughter, and son-in-law. She is a "cradle Catholic" who enjoys learning and living with a variety of religious practices and traditions. She is active in the field of dialogue, facilitating conversations that foster inquiry, reflection, and understanding. She is also a founding member of the local chapter of Bread for the Journey, a nonprofit that provides small seed grants to individuals in the community with dreams to improve it. In spare moments she enjoys writing poetry and playing the harmonica and guitar.

Being with My Two Mothers Who Had Died

*Jeanmarie Carleton**

I've had numerous unitive experiences, which seem to me to be seeing the natural world as it really is but on a deeper mystical level that we do not ordinarily see. I am going to relate just one that is still very vivid in my mind. I was stretched out on the couch in our family room, reading. I paused to think about something that I had just read, all the while staring, but not really focusing, on the purple plum tree right outside the tall, wide windows behind the sofa. My husband walked through the room toward the back of the house. A summer thunderstorm had just passed and the sun had begun to shine. As my eyes focused on the tree, my mind was somewhere else until, in full bright sunlight, the tree began to sparkle with a hundred points of light. Diamonds blazing as if the tree were on fire. I have no idea how long the experience lasted as I lost all sense of time and self-definition. As the experience began to wane, I tried to hold onto it. But as all of us know, when it is over, it's over. Except for the joy! The gratitude I feel for being given these experiences cannot adequately be expressed in words.

* Pseudonym

The closest I can come is just to say, "Gloria in Excelsis Deo!

ॐॐ

I will need to give you a little background before I tell this next story: My mother, Jeananne, died when I was born. Her sister, Joanna, raised me, and eventually she and my dad were married. Mama Joanna read New Testament stories to me about Jesus every night before bed. As a very young child, I would often imagine myself gently falling into a warm, safe place in the arms of Jesus.

Mama Joanna and my dad had only one child together, who was named for both of them, JoLee. When she was an adult, JoLee moved to Georgia with her three little girls whom she would raise on her own after a divorce from her husband. On all holidays she would drive the hundred miles to my home in Tennessee to share festivities with my family. Each time she arrived she would "put herself in my pocket," as they say, meaning that she would not have to be on duty 24/7 while she was with her big sister. It was Thanksgiving night and all was quiet in our house.

I woke in the wee hours of the morning and could not go back to sleep. Since this happens frequently, I amble through the soft darkness of a still house, praying as I go. After a while I decided to try to get some more sleep but, so as not to wake my husband, I headed for the back bedroom. Walking down the hall, I thought of my sister's "pocket-putting" and started to wish that I had someone into whose pocket I could put myself.

Ah, yes. Of course! I remembered that I do have Someone into whose pocket I can put myself, just as I used to do when I was a little girl. I accepted the invitation and, smiling, climbed up onto the bed and into Jesus' imaginary lap, pulling up the comforter as I went. My expectation was to pray until I fell asleep. But something else happened. How to express it?

Suddenly both of my mothers were present with me! We had a long, loving exchange of knowing and being known without words. It was our essences that were known and shared in a time beyond time, in a situation of timelessness. I began to weep. My tears were tears of joy. It was the most incredible experience I have ever had. I can never give enough to say "thank you" adequately but try to love and love and love some more. LOVE gave me such a beautiful gift in this experience. Again, Gloria in Excelsis Deo!

❧ ❧

Jeanmarie Carleton is a widow now after many years of marriage to her husband, Richard, a radiologist and Episcopal priest. They had three children together, two girls and a boy, and she now has six grandchildren.

For many years she was a church school catechist who developed her own curriculum and remembers those years as a great joy. She is a 1994 graduate of Shalem's Spiritual Director program and is now involved in many different volunteer activities. Her favorite, she says, is the Victim Reconciliation program (best known as VORP) which gives kids who break the law for the first time another chance. If they finish the program, their offense is expunged. She loves to sing and does so a lot and says that, since she is "Ancient of Days" at seventy-five, there is a lot more but is tired of talking about herself now! However, she does add two more things: "God has been gracious, and I've decided that I would like my middle name to be JOY!"

Through the Shadow of Death

Larry Glover-Weatherington

My wife, Janie, had suffered with type 1 (insulin-dependent) diabetes since she was thirteen years old. For most of those years she led a fairly normal life, although insulin shock was never a stranger. In the last four years, however, the demise of her health was catastrophic: blindness, kidney dialysis, seizures, amputation of her toes and, eventually, her lower leg, surgeries on her eyes, many episodes of peritonitis, and multiple hospitalizations.

Peritoneal dialysis was begun on St. Patrick's Day, March 17, 1987. It was an overwhelming task learning the sterile procedure, which had to be done four times daily. The overall medical regimen was consuming and felt like it was taking over our lives. At one point, when we were talking about it, we made a covenant with God and one another that Christ was going to control our lives, not this disease. This was one of those breakthrough moments of grace that sustained us and gave us renewed focus and hope.

One of my prayers during this time was, "Lord, how do I pray for her?" Over the years we had prayed in many ways. In the last six months of her life, however, God gave me a three-word prayer: "Lord, have mercy." This prayer was liberating for me. I could cry out to God without it feeling like I was telling God what to do. It also gave me a sense of freedom because my emotions and faith were not locked into a particular outcome. I wanted her to be healed and whole again. I wanted our family back to normal with all those daily routines and intimacies of life. Overall, however, I wanted her to be relieved of her suffering. In the mystery of life, if death was the only way for her relief, this prayer also became one of release. "Lord, have mercy." I prayed it over and over again. It was as close as my breath.

Janie died on September 26, 1989. We had been married for twenty years. Our fourteen-year-old son, Andrew, and I arrived at the hospital about three o'clock in the morning after a call that she had "made a turn for the worse." We each took some private time alone with her to say good-bye but it was very incomplete. One does not say good-bye to a relationship of such closeness in a few moments.

One of my first responses was relief. Her suffering had ended. It was, as one author described it, "a severe mercy."[1] Even though we had anticipated her death, we were still caught by surprise. There was no way to comprehend the magnitude of her loss.

---

1. Vanauken, Sheldon. A Severe Mercy. New York: Harper Collins, 1997, 1990. Try to find the hard cover if you can.

On the eve of her funeral I spent the whole night writing a tribute. As a minister most people tell me they want a brief funeral service; I never wanted it to end. It was just what she wanted. The weather was beautiful and people lingered in conversation. It was a surreal but meaningful time.

After the funeral the depth of grief began to grasp me in its clutches. The first routine task of normal life I did was to take my car in for servicing. As I was waiting in the lounge, I began to have a sense of panic. It was my first experience of real panic.

My pastoral care professor in seminary, Dr. Wayne Oates, said the primary dynamic of grief is anxiety. I didn't know what that meant until now. I was beginning to engage life without her presence and I didn't have a road map for that. I have since described grief like the columns in front of the Supreme Court building, with each column representing a major area of life, such as employment, family, faith, home, health. When any one of those columns is knocked out of place, it puts stress on all the others, and the building does not have integrity until the structure has been rebuilt. That is the work of grief, putting the structure of life back into place.

The cycle of regrets began to torment me. Why didn't I spend more time with her? Why wasn't I kinder to her? Why wasn't I more sensitive to her needs? They went on and on without mercy.

The "God questions" also began to emerge. They were frustratingly unanswerable, but very real. It was so unfair. Why did she have to suffer as she did? If she was going to die anyway, why did her leg have to be amputated only six months earlier? Why the seizures? Every aspect of her suffering replayed through my mind and I angrily paraded them before God.

One morning as I was reading the bible, I came to Psalm 77, which echoed my anguished questions to God:

I cried to God for help;
I cried out to God to hear me.
When I was in distress, I sought the Lord;
at night I stretched out untiring hands,
and my soul refused to be comforted.
I remembered you, O God, and I groaned;
I mused, and my spirit grew faint
You kept my eyes from closing;
I was too troubled to speak.
I thought about the former days,
the years of long ago;
I remembered my songs in the night.
My heart mused and my spirit inquired:
"Will the Lord reject forever?
Will he never show his favor again?
Has his unfailing love vanished forever?
Has his promise failed for all time?
Has God forgotten to be merciful?
Has he in anger withheld his compassion?"

(Psalm 77: 1–9)

After taking a semester's break from seminary, I resumed classes in the winter term. My intellectual questions of God were as deep as the emotional ones. One of my courses was titled The Theology of the Providence of God, having to do with God's providential care. This subject also covered theodicy, the issue of suffering. The classical theodicy triangle is this: if God is a God of love, and if God is all powerful, then why does God allow pain and suffering in the world? This question posed a formidable, almost impenetrable problem.

My professor, whose own wife had died six years earlier, intentionally assigned me a paper to compare two of C. S. Lewis's books. In the first book, The Problem of Pain, Lewis carefully crafted a very reasoned and intellectual explanation of the dilemma of pain and suffering. Years later his wife died. He kept a diary of his experience of grief, which was later published as A Grief Observed. In this latter book he referred to his previous, reasoned explanation of pain and suffering as "a house of cards" that came tumbling down, and he was afraid to construct another for fear it would also crumble. So he was content to let the problem of pain and suffering remain a mystery.

As I continued to struggle with this issue, I was led by God's Spirit to the person of Jesus Christ. Through Scripture, spiritual reading, and theological study, I became particularly aware of the humanity of Jesus. The Bible made statements such as, "Jesus wept," he hungered, he was weary, and he slept. I realized I had always focused on the deity of Christ, but his humanity was just as real and meaningful. John the apostle said, "The Word became flesh and dwelled among us."

The redemptive path that Jesus chose involved suffering: temptation, persecution, harassment, and crucifixion. As the prophet Isaiah had said, "he was a man of sorrows, and acquainted with grief" (Isaiah 53:3). God the Father, however, was not a distant observer. As the apostle Paul stated, "God was in Christ, reconciling the world to Himself" (2 Corinthians 5:19).

The union of Jesus Christ with God was brought home to me through a book by Jurgen Moltman, a German theologian, entitled The Crucified God. I began to get a sense of God's identification with my pain—that God was suffering with me in my grief, and that God knew pain and suffering through personal experience. As I thought again about the theodicy triangle, it occurred to me that God does not choose to function through the power of force, but, instead, God exercises power through love. This involves me redemptively in God's effort to alleviate pain and suffering in the world.

Through my journey of grief I had maintained a personal time of worship each morning, which I would conclude by committing the day into God's hands. One morning I had a lengthy to-do list, and, in my haste to get it all done, I jumped out of bed and began my errands—the bank, oil change, and finally the grocery store. When I returned home, I began putting all of the groceries away, when all of a sudden I realized I had skipped my time of worship. I immediately left everything sitting on the counter, went into the living room, and sat on the sofa to pray.

To help me focus, I intentionally created a scene in my imagination. God was sitting on a throne and the floor in front of the throne was a black-and-white checkerboard design. There was a semicircular kneeling rail in front of the throne. I knelt at this rail to pray.

Events then began to unfold that surprised me, which I did not manufacture in my imagination and I am certain of that. I felt a presence behind me and a hand on my shoulder. I immediately knew that it was Janie. I was stunned and did not know what to do. I looked up at God and God said to me, *"Talk to her."* So I began telling her the things that had happened since her death and how Andrew and I were doing. She then whirled around and began to dance in a large semicircle around me. She was showing me that she had two legs now. Then she stopped, looked directly at me, and said, "And I can see, too!" I knelt there and wept. She was OK now. God had made her whole.

Not long afterward, my final resolution of this issue came through one of Jesus' parables. It was an odd passage that I had never before thought of in this context. It was the parable of the wheat and the tares:

Jesus presented another parable to them, saying, The kingdom of heaven may be compared to a man who sowed good seed in his field. But while his men were sleeping, his enemy came and sowed tares among the wheat. But when the wheat sprouted and bore grain, then the tares became evident also. The slaves of the landowner came and said to him, "Sir, did you not sow good seed in your field? How then does it have tares?" And he said to them, "An enemy has done this!" The slaves said to him, "Do you want us, then, to go and gather them up?" But he said, "No, for while you are gathering up the tares, you may uproot the wheat with them. Allow both to grow together until the harvest, and in the time of the harvest I will say to the reapers, "First, gather up the tares and bind them in bundles to burn them up; but gather the wheat into my barn."

(Matthew 13:24–30)

This parable was saying to me that, in creation, God had planted good seed. Evil and suffering were not God's doing. An enemy came along and sowed the evil. God's response did not dispel the mystery for me, but it did unexplainably bring a transforming resolution, that for now the wheat and tares must grow together, but in the end God will sort the evil from the good. Ultimately, God will deal with the evil. In the meantime I continue to pray along with the Redeemer Christ, "Thy Kingdom come, Thy will be done on earth as it is in heaven."

৵৶

Larry Glover-Wetherington is sixty-one years old and a Baptist minister affiliated with the Cooperative Baptist Fellowship. His ministry specialty is that he serves as an intentional interim pastor, or as some call it a transition pastor, who facilitates a congregational process of self-examination during the interim between pastors. "Intentional" means that the congregation takes responsibility for its future direction as it prepares for a new pastor.

He was remarried in 1991 to Miriam Anne Glover and they celebrated their twentieth anniversary in July, 2011. His and Janie's son, Andrew, is now thirty-six years old and single. His passion and hobby is photography and he says that he has a sense of calling to try to produce contemplative photographs. His work can be seen at www.larrygw.smugmug.com.

A Split Second of Seeing and Knowing

Carol Ingells

It was 1980 and I had just finished a lengthy training in Scottsdale, Arizona, when a young friend and I went on a drive up into the nearby Superstition Mountains. By the time we had driven up, stopped to eat, and started down again, it was dark. We drove slowly, as the road was one switchback after another. As we rounded yet another sharp bend in the road, I gasped. The full moon was rising right at the intersection of two mountain peaks and, far below, the moonlight danced brilliantly across a small mountain lake. My friend pulled the car over; we got out and stood silently on the edge of the cliff. I smelled the piñon pines, heard the sounds of night creatures singing, saw the incredible movement of the earth. I literally felt the earth turn! The beauty was so breathtaking that my friend and I spontaneously wrapped our arms around one another in celebration. In those moments I knew that all is one. I KNEW that GOD IS—ALL in ALL. I was complete. It was a time of being one with The One. This given moment created a sense of gratitude in me that has never left me, even some twenty-eight years later. It was given, seen, and gratefully received. And has never been forgotten.

⊰⊱

It was Saturday and the choir was having a final run-through of "The Chichester Psalms" by Leonard Bernstein. My only child, Melissa, about sixteen, was the soloist. I could see her across the chancel from me, standing high in the pulpit—my pride and joy.

I had recently returned from a powerful retreat and was in a spiritually open state. I felt energy coursing through my being. Suddenly, far quicker than I can describe it, I saw the ancestors—Abraham, Sarah, Moses, I don't know who all—seated around a campfire in the middle of the chancel. Right there on the beautiful red paisley carpet! I sang on, ecstatic with the energy of knowing that God is timeless, that God is the same yesterday, today, and tomorrow, that we were singing the same psalms the ancestors had sung (were singing?), worshiping the same God they worshiped, that we were/are truly all one, that linear time actually has little meaning.

I forgot about my daughter, so awed was I at this revelation. Afterward, when people asked me if I wasn't proud of Melissa and her beautiful rendition of this difficult and haunting music, I could scarcely respond. Yes, at some level near the surface, I was proud of her. Still, I felt no exclusive personal connection to her—and yet, I felt totally connected at a very, very deep level, a level deeper than words can express.

Though this was at least twenty-five years ago, I have never forgotten, nor could I forget, that split second of "seeing" and "knowing," and I am ever grateful for that gift.

Though it is sometimes tempting to slough off experiences like these and attribute them to "only imagination," each of them, and others like them, have continually helped me to know that God is directly present if we have "eyes to see and ears to hear." Because of that awareness, countless moments have been graced with a sense of Presence that brings a realization of my place in the whole scheme of things and a sure sense that I am never alone. I can trust in these revelations of God's Presence that come. And, in times when they don't, I have a strong foundation to draw on and a certainty of knowing, because of them, that I and all of God's creation will never be forsaken.

jj

Carol Ingells is sixty-five years old and has been involved in religious education, ecumenical ministry, hospital chaplaincy, spiritual direction, and retreat leadership since the early 1970s. She belongs to the Episcopal Church but is comfortable in many traditions and appreciates the wonders of other religions. She was widowed in late 2005 when her husband of forty years, Norris, died. She has one daughter, Melissa, who is the host of NPR's Morning Edition on WKAR–FM. She now lives in Lansing, Michigan, and continues to lead retreats and do spiritual direction.

The Cantaloupe Moon

Karen Eppert

Late one evening in 2002, I recall feeling very content as I was cruising down the highway returning from a visit with a friend. The radio on, music filled the vehicle, and I was singing along in my less than perfect-pitched voice when I happened to glance to my left. There my eyes fell upon the incredible beauty of an incandescent, glowing, half-orb moon, so magnificent that I was immediately utterly enraptured at the sight of it. A primal gasp of glee bubbled up from somewhere deep inside of me and brushed past my lips. It looked as though God had taken a dipper and scooped out a piece of it, creating the carved cantaloupe appearance of the moon that evening.

Now, although it can truly be said of me that I am a "moon watcher," in all my years of enjoying observing the moon, never had I observed our "sister," as Francis of Assisi called it, in quite the way I did that evening. I was so totally enthralled that, actually, I think I should give myself credit for not running off the side of the road! My instant instinct was to stop everything, pull the car over, and just sit and soak in the sheer loveliness of the moment.

Questions began to surface in my mind: How can one hold so much beauty? How to accord it the importance it deserves? How could one ever praise the Creator of such splendor enough? What can one say but "breathtaking," "awe-inspiring," and, in truth, "beyond the capacity of words to describe"?

I was swept away by the splendor of that moon and found myself moved to a place of utter surrender to Something, or Someone, grander than myself and to a connection with all that ever was, is, or will be. What or who but an omnipresent, love-filled, Divine Being could so shower our senses, inundating them with such precious gifts of nature as surround us. In such moments, our eyes, our ears, our noses and lips see and hear and smell and taste of the richness of all that has been created by such a One. Our hands reach out to touch the beauty, to grasp the essence of pure joy as it drips from the hands of the Creator.

That moon-glow moment of ecstasy, that communion with "all there is" and its Creator so filled my heart that today and ever since, when sorrow threatens to overshadow my life and routine casts its dullness on my soul, all I have to do is to remember that night and, once again, I behold the beauty and experience the grace and goodness of our loving, faithful, and everlasting God.

૰ઌ

Karen Eppert was born into a Lebanese/Syrian family in Utica, New York, and grew up in the Catholic Church. She is fifty-five years old and married and has two adult children and two granddaughters. She describes herself as "always on a journey of self-discovery and spiritual formation" and is trained both for the ministry of spiritual direction and for leading contemplative prayer groups and retreats, all of which are a part of her life. She has identified with the Lutheran Church for some years and is presently an administrative assistant to the ELCA Lutheran Bishop for the Indiana-Kentucky Synod.

God God-ing in My Life

Stephanie Harrison

My first remembered visit with Presence happened before I entered school at the age of five. I was far too young to understand this luminous intersection in ordinary time and space. These things are sometimes hard to talk about and there is not much contemporary modeling for language regarding mystical experiences. Forty-five years later I was able to recall and name this experience as a "vision full of wisdom from God."

I was an only child raised by Irish grandparents in the 1950s' culture of southeast Texas. Given the warm climate there, being out of doors was highly encouraged, as long as I stayed in our yard, front or back. The front yard bustled, neighbors coming and going from their houses, cars traveling up and down the street and children lost in imaginary play on their porches, sidewalks, and driveways. The opposite was true of the yard in back, secluded and tucked away behind the house, especially in late afternoon when my grandmother gathered the last bit of laundry from the line. This setting became my solitary harbor and this is where the vision happened.

In the area farthest from the house and closest to the back of our property a broad-trunked oak tree stood. Its limbs reached out in four directions, three limbs over the fences of neighbors and one limb sprawling across the yard supplying us with shade and shadow. The tree seemed huge; it took me and two other cousins clasping hands to circle the base. I don't remember the tree ever being without its leaves or without the sounds that the wind made blowing through them. The oak anchored our home and my young life. On most days I would catch my feet walking to the same worn spot next to the right hand side of the trunk. There I would lay myself down on my back, becoming attached to the cool earth beneath me. To settle in was to view the familiar, the patchwork sky showing itself between the branches, much like the last piece fitting into a jigsaw puzzle. I felt the intimacy of the giant stalk that rose up out of the ground with great known purpose, part of which was to safeguard me if I should fall asleep. I would begin the silent listening for the beat of my heart. With a deep out-breath, my body would melt into the earth like it does now into my yoga mat.

With eyes closed I sensed the air moving all around me, conjuring up sounds and smells. Sometimes little leaves and twigs that the tree wanted to give me would fall on or around my body, tickling me until I giggled. Other times, I would keep my eyes open watching the cottony clouds and hearing their stories as the shapes transfigured across the heavenly landscape.

On this particular day—this day of vision giving and receiving—something more intentional happened. I was offered a gift whose presence, though for many years not consciously understood, carried me like a current of moving water through the years, changing but always at my core.

I'm not certain of the season; I only know that the grass was thick and green and the breeze was pleasantly warm. As I walked to the tree, I noticed in front of me the field that extended beyond the back chain-linked fence. The wind was moving the high grass, a comb threading through long hair, and the sun tipped each blade with a torch of light that blurred my vision. I saw a field blazing gold, alive like I was alive, breathing, speaking, and reaching out to me.

I squatted down on the ground and looked upward. The leaves and branches were dappled in light, and the blue sky filled with vaporous clouds began to pour through the openings in the tree's canopy. The surroundings seemed amplified as they reached for me, so much bigger than ever before, yet so very personal. My head began to spin and I lay back on the cool, soft grass, my lids closing over stinging eyes. I wasn't afraid; I was in my well-known place under the great protective tree. As my eyes cooled, I began to feel dreamy and I sensed a closeness as though someone were with me. I opened my eyes and looked up.

Everything was exactly how it had always been, except for me; I felt different. For an instant or maybe for a long time, I don't know, I laid there. I remember feeling very quiet like in the mornings after I woke and before I got out of bed, except that I also felt alone. Something or Someone was there, but not a person. When I got older, the same feelings would occasionally heat up in the middle of my body as I sat between my parents in church, listening to the music and gazing upward at the shadowed round stained-glass window, of the kneeling and praying to Jesus.

I never spoke to anyone about these experiences. Even though I had experienced something so different and unusual, I was not afraid and, therefore, didn't run into the house crying. I do remember being subdued and quiet at suppertime. I think, as an only child, that I kept this afternoon like a secret deep inside, and with time and growing older, both this experience and my experiences at church diminished and then were forgotten or, shall we say, held in a hidden place. There was a day in third grade when I was standing on the corner of the gravel playground during recess and realized that my feelings of being different were keeping me away from the other children. I saw a group of girls in the opposite corner. They were laughing and having fun. I decided then that I would do whatever it took to be a part of them. The time would come, in the future, when that choice would be outlived.

Forty-five years after the childhood vision, I was treading up a path into the redwood forests at a monastery in Northern California. I had been awake since

4:30 a.m., gathered in community meditation, morning prayer, and breakfast. I was on the way back to my cabin through the small woods when I caught sight of a deer off to the left. The gracefully elusive creature stood next to a trail as if guarding the entrance. I felt a summons and altered my course to the cabin, following the lure until I verged with the trail leading into the forest. At the time I was not aware of the symbolism of the deer, the animal whose power in nature is to call an individual on a journey: a deer with golden antlers was sacred to the Greek goddess Artemis, and in the legend of King Arthur, a deer leads Sir Gawain into the woods to begin his adventure.

The trail proved narrow, the incline steep; the deer had vanished and my journey became an upward hike into a dark wood. The wide assortment of trees and vegetation on both sides of the trail had enclosed the path into a tunnel, their branches and limbs a thicket above me. Condensed silence having been plentiful for many years cushioned the crackling and crumbling of whatever my feet pounded on as I trudged forward. The flittering of light fell randomly but I was not afraid. Something felt familiar; something other than me was steering my feet to someplace I did not know.

In a moment, there was an unveiling of a small patch of blue; it hung like a funny-shaped moon above and in front of me. Such an exquisite color of blue, lapis lazuli. I was stunned at its beauty yet I continued walking, beckoned on by the surreal image.

The blue patch juxtaposed against the thick brown darkness of the redwood landscape looked like a piece of cloth quilted onto a larger design. As I walked closer the bright color became focused and a view of blue sky appeared at the end of the trail. My imagination wondered if, when I reached the top, I would fall off a cliff or even fall off the edge of the world!

More light fell across my path the closer I got to the patch of sky, now stretching out in all directions. At my back, the spring wind, still cold, was moving me farther up the trail, exhilarating my steps. The wind rose up as I emerged from the tree-darkened tunnel. Something was alive in everything, breathing, heart beating, listening and feeling. I remember thinking that God loved the trees, the wind, the deer, the sky, loved everything, every creature not one atom less than God loved me or anyone else. We were all the same, it is all the same. It is One.

I made it to the top and, in a simultaneous moment, the sky loomed toward me and outward into the heavens, the biggest sky that I have ever seen and a blue that I have never seen since. When I pulled myself away from looking at the sky, I looked down and saw the meadow—a golden field, blazing with sun, moving in gentle waves to the breath of the wind. I stood in awe, in a loud surrounding silence, and then the meadow saw me, and I remembered. We held our gaze and were held in the Gaze, no words, no thoughts, only be-ing, God being, God God-ing, and I was a part of it—again.

I would never be separated again. I experienced an immense space opening up outside of me and inside of me.

Later in the day, I wrote about that morning's experience with the meadow. I wrote about the experience remembered from a child's afternoon in a backyard. I wrote about other times that bubbled up out of my memory. I wrote and wrote and gave thanks for all that had been held for me in secret, waiting to rise out of the dark, rich earth into the consciousness of my ordinary life.

Over the years, I have taken time to record moments of vision, nightly dreams and daily imaginations, even sacred synchronicities that catch my attention. I have begun to recognize God's Spirit asking me for a dance, inviting me to participate and also generously offering me wisdom, self-knowledge and guidance, compassion and love. Sometimes I am offered a not-knowing, an unraveling, a searing pain, a clouded darkness, unresolved questions, and pure chaos. These, too, are dance steps.

Spirit is constantly showing herself, attending, moving, changing, transforming; it's happening to everything and everyone all the time. I experience God as a verb, God-ing, expressing life, bidden or unbidden, happening every minute. These mystical experiences expand my relatedness and response to all creation— earth, animals, myself, others, God. I am comforted as well as confronted, encouraged, and challenged, but always being carried at the center, as a spiritual being, always being carried by and toward Love.

In sitting with others as a spiritual director, I have often asked directees to recall a time and place when they were children and experienced God's presence. If not immediately, at some point they do remember even if the memory is somewhat vague. We begin to investigate the things they loved and that loved them. For me it was trees and skies and fields, but it's different for everyone. We are all mystics having mystical experiences out of and from the Mystery of the great, loving, hidden Universe. God's Wisdom is abundant and available here and now.

❧ ❦

Stephanie Harrison says that she lives her life as a middle-aged, animal-loving, gardening, spirit-watching, and storytelling woman. She married her high school sweetheart, Robin Harrison, whom she remembers kissing after gym class, more than forty years ago. They have two grown sons, Matthew and Adam, and a much-loved Wheaten terrier named "Bunnie." Houston, Texas, has been Stephanie's home all of her life except for the five years after her mother's death when she lived in Oregon. She says that she does not have "big hair," only gray hair.

What Is Happening Here?
What Does This Mean?

Joan Hickey

I'm not sure exactly when this happened—I think prob-ably in the late 1980s or early '90s. I was on the Shalem associate staff at that time and we had all gone out for an overnight retreat/planning meeting at a simple retreat center in the Maryland suburbs. One of our asso-ciate staff colleagues, who was a much-in-demand spiritual director, is also an experienced practitioner of Reiki, and she had offered to do a session of Reiki for any of us who would like that during any of our silent personal times. Since I had never experienced Reiki before, I accepted and scheduled a time.

When my time arrived, I went down to the little room where my colleague had set up the massage table that she uses and climbed up onto the table. She asked if there were any particular parts of my body where I was experiencing pain or discomfort. I told her about the osteoarthritis in my knees—no cartilage left, very pain-ful—and arthritis in my lower back. She told me to just stretch out and that there was nothing that I needed to do; if I felt like taking a nap, that was fine. I closed my eyes and think that I must have, indeed, napped. For a short while I was aware of her hands moving slowly a few inches above my body; I could just barely feel their warmth. Then, the next thing I knew, I heard her saying, "We're through now." I sat up and looked into her beautifully loving face. We gave each other a hug, then I got down and walked toward the door, about seven or eight feet away.

As I reached the door and was about to pass through it, something happened—there was some kind of shift in my consciousness, for I suddenly was looking at my body from behind where I was at the door, and it looked as though my body had been shot through with light in several places. There appeared to be a huge hole from back to front filled with a sparkling light on the right side of my back above the waist and another that went through my left shoulder blade. I wasn't alarmed because nothing hurt, but it was such a strange image— it seemed almost as if I had no connection with that body except to simply observe it. This image went away almost immediately, within seconds.

As I turned into the rather dim hallway to go down to the meeting room where we were to reconvene shortly, I noticed the same amazingly soft, silvery golden light filling the hall. It was not light like sunlight or lamplight—it is still hard to describe. Picture a very, very fine mist in the air, only all of the particles of the mist are light and a light that is so dynamic that it somehow begs to be called "living." I walked into the room. Tilden Edwards, our director at the time, and three of my colleagues were already there, sitting and talking in a normal conversational tone in a front corner of the room on my right. The unusual and beautiful light completely filled the room. I was curious to see whether or not it was also outside of the room, so I walked over to the wall of windows across from the door and looked out onto the small lawn and the woods. The light, with its beautiful color and soft sparkle, was permeating everything. As I stood still and looked, I became aware that there was a deep, deep silence and a deep, deep peace associated with this light. I have struggled for years to find words that might come close to describing what I was seeing and have finally come to settle on "energy field"—I was "seeing" an energy field that, it was clear to me, was Divine. An energy field that was God, or of God.

Soon everyone had gathered and the meeting started. We talked, planned, made decisions all immersed within this Light. I started to think of, "In God we live and move and have our being." Was I having an actual experience of that? I think probably, yes, and it would be impossible to describe what a wonderfully beautiful experience that was.

That was our final meeting, so when we were done, we packed up our cars and headed for home. On the drive home, although I no longer saw the Light of this energy field so clearly, I felt it so powerfully that I knew that it was still there, surrounding and permeating everything. And I began to be aware that that deep, deep silence and deep, deep peace that I had perceived somehow seemed to have moved into the depths of my being. The sense of this quiet but powerful and imminent Divine Presence lasted for five days; after that I noticed that it began to lighten, and by the end of another five days, it was gone. Now, however, I know that it is there everywhere and always, whether I am able to see in the same way that I experienced in those ten days or not. But I believe that deep silence and deep peace that I experienced were laid down in my soul somehow, since that has really never gone away.

One last thought. I have pondered that strange, momentary out-of-body experience that I had just before I walked into the hall for all of these years since that happened. What has come out of that for me is that the sense I had at the time, that "I," the self I know myself to be, was somehow not identifying solely with my body in those few moments, was correct. (Don't most of us have a deep, intuitive sense that we are more than just flesh and bones, more, even, than flesh and bones and brains?) I think the truth is that our "I"s, the selves we know ourselves to be, are more of the Light, that we emanate from that Divine energy field, that we are made more from that Light than we are from any material substance.

Could this be the truest, deepest meaning of the saying that we are all "children of God"?

৵৽

*Joan Hickey is a Catholic laywoman in her eighties, a retired pastoral coun-
selor, retreat leader, and teacher of contemplative prayer practices. She has
been associated with Shalem since 1977 and was a member of the associate
staff for twenty-five years. She was also a member of the adjunct faculty
for continuing education programs at the Virginia Theological Seminary in
Alexandria for sixteen years. She lives in northern Virginia.*

A Transforming Vision

Meredith Moon

When I was a child I often asked adults, "How do you know that God is real?" I never received an answer that convinced me of an infinity I could not see. My question continued in college when one day I asked the chaplain of our Episcopal Club:

"How do you know that God is real?"

"Because of the Bible," he said.

"The Bible is only words written long ago by others; I want to know how you know," I said.

"I believe those words in the Bible."

"I can't," I said.

From then on I called myself an agnostic, a doubting Thomas of seventeen years, one who had to see and experience for herself. I argued long for my point of view, a view that would neither deny nor affirm what religions call "God." Little did I know that the future held a direct experience of infinite reality, a new life of spiritual search and dedication to the Love that had awakened me.

I write now of my remembering, to encourage others to find their own way to the truth through the myriad confabulations of the false self to the real self and oneness with God. It is a journey of transformation that can only begin within and, for me, began consciously when I saw and experienced the infinite reality at the core of being.

Now in my seventh decade, I write from the distance of half a lifetime of an experience that has informed and guided my life and choices since it graced me with the necessity of transformation.

Even though, to outer observation, we seem to be living an ordinary life, there is within us a wakefulness, a light, a wisdom that directs our dreams and knowing and it brings us to the truth of who we are. Just as a caterpillar is destined by liminal disks to become a butterfly, we are destined for evolving consciousness.

My experience is that, once awakened, we are porous to a mystery that interfaces with us, penetrates us, is one with us, teaches us and loves us unconditionally. I call this mystery God. God that is before all religions. God that is the mind of being itself. God that is without beginning and without end. Religions begin and end—they cannot be God, only attempts to frame or hold the mystery in static form. Religions become collective though based on unique, individual experience. Our minds, being limited, attempt to form and define a truth we are too small to hold in its entirety. God is independent of our minds and of our perceptions. God is energy so encompassing that only by degrees can we glimpse and hold a ray of this light.

The Presence

I have seen what I call "God as light" and have experienced as infinite love. This is my story of that Presence, my inner story, of the reality that I know exists.

On December 7, 1970, a Tuesday, after my children left for school, I prepared to begin the four simple tasks I had set for myself that day. I remember wanting to iron curtains. However, I found that I could not focus on them and, instead, would catch myself staring out the window lost in some nothingness. My consciousness was shifting in some unknown way that seemed like a deep dissolving of my accustomed attention. I knew nothing of metaphysics, of alpha states, had never taken drugs nor experienced anything similar to what was occurring within me.

This strange state increased over the next hour as I felt my mind continuing to dissolve, seemingly to change its nature. Lying on the bed on my stomach I experienced an alteration in my perception of my body. I felt my left side becoming very large as if it contained the entire universe. This was not actual, of course, only an interior perception. This frightened me and I placed a call to my doctor, the one who had delivered my three children, telling him of this strange state that I was in.

He suggested that I take a nap and call him back on awakening if there was no change. Given this permission, I fell asleep about 10 a.m.

When I awoke near eleven o'clock, my first thought was that my mind had quite returned to normal, but then immediately I realized that I had two minds, one attuned to everyday life, the mind I was used to, and the other vast and beyond time, the mind I had begun to experience. The linear left brain and the multidimensional right brain were separately active.

I thought, "I must call someone, perhaps my husband," but then realized that he "is not where I am" and would have no way of comprehending my state of being. Next, I thought of my sister-in-law with whom I had recently deeply shared the illness and death of her husband. Realizing that she was at work and not wanting to simply burst into tears (for my normal ego stance was melting completely), I wondered what I might say to her. Then, like a message coming through my head on a ticker tape, not arising from a cognitive mind, came these words, "Christmas is coming. I am going insane; will you still love me?"

Simultaneously I knew both intuitively and instinctively the inner meaning of these words. "It is the time for the Christ to come and I will not be able to bring this about, so will you still love me if I can't bring Christmas anymore?" Since my father's death in World War II when I was ten years old, I had been the one in the family who arranged and brought the joy and magic of Christmas to my three younger brothers: finding the tree, making it beautiful with lights and garlands, wrapping presents, and sharing stockings on Christmas morning. As I had for my brothers, so I continued for my own children, and now, in this strange state of mind, I surrendered, for none of those outer traditions bring the real Christ. Of that, we are incapable.

At the minute those words entered my mind, a being of light appeared at the foot of my bed, filling the space between my ten-foot ceiling and the floor in a great oval of white light. Within this oval the light was compressed into a human shape of light, head and torso, far more brilliant and more dense than the outer oval. I knew without a doubt that this was God, the energy form of the divine. There was no question, no hesitation, no wondering. The reality of the Presence impressed upon me the truth of the One before me.

I began to weep. I felt enveloped by love so unconditional that it was beyond anything I could imagine or hope for. As the tears fell from my eyes, one part of my mind could only say, "You're real, you're really real," over and over again. My more linear mind, the left brain, operating simultaneously but separately, became filled with such thoughts as, "What does one do when God is in the room? Pray? Ask questions? Fall at his feet?" That mind, that limited aspect wondering about protocol (can you imagine God being concerned about such things!) was completely dwarfed by the weeping melting of love occurring in me as I stood before this source of all love.

Then the most amazing thing happened. A visible channel of light came from the center of this being and passed the four feet between us and surrounded me. I was encased in a cocoon of pulsating energy that I could feel even between my feet and the floor. I was completely held in this field ,and then the energy cut through my chest to my heart in a spiral motion as would a corkscrew opening a bottle of vintage wine. I could feel the energy cutting through my tissues and bone but there was no pain or blood. As the spiral reached further inward, I was filled with love, blazing love, radiant love, unconditional love.

I was taught three things by the light. The first and perhaps most important is that we are all loved uncon- ditionally by God beyond all knowing and there is nothing we can do or not do that changes that. The second is that there is nowhere I could go to learn or study this reality, for on earth our knowledge of this source is at a kindergarten level. And third, that there is no death.

With this teaching the "light being" dissolved into many particles and in a stream of light went through my closed window into the outer world. I ran to the window and I could see this light visible in every blade of grass, in every tree leaf. The world pulsates with this light. It was even visible in my own eyes as I looked in a mirror.

I found myself in love with God beyond all human measure. The Presence stayed with me in this incredible form, alive and pulsating, for about a month. It was completely independent of any will or wish of mine. For instance, I wanted to share this grace with a friend of mine who was in a Jungian coterie with me. When he stopped by to visit and I opened the front door to his ring, the divine energy left, exited my body completely. There was no more alive and pulsing vibrancy. I told Jack of my experience of the light's presence but it was only telling about something no longer with me, a memory only. The moment Jack left and I closed the door the light came back, a vibratory field within me. How strange this was! I can only assume that the source is independent of me with a life of its own, a "visitor" from a realm beyond the boundaries of my personal psyche.

Remembering December 7, 1970

Opening my eyes for the first time
I reason but dimly;
Blinded as it were
In the light of my birth.

Every molecule alive!
the very trees speak new forms;
the ground moves while a nimbus ray
encircles earth
making skeletons
of birds.

The light
into my head, white born
light born
energy of presence engulfing,
penetrating my heart
with bursting fire.

I see all
I know nothing . . . yet how impossible
I know . . .

I was changed.

అ❦

Looking back now to the light experience of 1970 I note my innocence. I thought to myself that this experience of presence and love is what everyone knows of God, and I returned to the Episcopal Church with a lighted enthusiasm—only to be shocked by a liturgy that spoke of miserable sinners quite unworthy of friendship with God. I knew I could not be in relationship with a being who loved so unconditionally and say those words. Nor could I say the Creed or anything else that did not seem true to me. This began my separation from the Christian myth built by human attempts to understand Jesus. I see all religions now as forms created about the experience of one exceptional and realized soul that often deny the seeker his or her own inner journey, not on purpose perhaps, but as reflections of a collectively imposed boundary.

As the experience of the white light lessened after about a month, I realized that the power of the energy that had embraced me had pushed my personal dynamics and complexes out of the way and now they were coming back. The light had reached my ego as a strong torch would in the darkness and, as the light dimmed, the darkness returned. Seeing this I knew I must work on myself to become empty enough to again be in the bliss of union, for this was all that I wanted. I had become a seeker and was left to find my way.

Transformation never comes easily, however the pattern unfolds in an individual psyche, and being claimed by God is no assurance of a continuing Presence on the long road to psychological and spiritual maturity. In fact, like Jesus, one is surely to be abandoned in the death throes of a raging upsurge of the unconscious as it melts the very bones of identity only to be met again and loved again and abandoned again until some cleaving makes the two one.

෴

Meredith Moon is a transpersonal psychologist who studied at the Jung Institute in Zurich for a year and a half after having been awarded her Ph.D. As a part of her spiritual journey, she spent a year in India at the Meher Baba Pilgrim Center. She lives in Makawao, Hawaii, where she has a private psychotherapy practice; in addition, she teaches about dreams and symbols and facilitates small groups of people in journeying through their inner worlds. Dr. Moon is also a graduate of the spiritual director's program at Shalem.

How I Learned to Trust God Completely

Judith Halpate

I have always had some sort of a relationship with God. A part of my bedtime prayer was the 23rd Psalm. This gave me a sense that I was cared for and watched over by a loving God and Christ. I came into a deep spiritual relationship with God after participating in a renewal weekend in a small parish in Ohio. It was during our time in that parish that I had my first experience of God's immediate presence.

I had been struggling with the addiction of a family member and was becoming very angry and sinking into despair over the situation. I went to church on a Saturday to receive the Sacrament of Reconciliation, more familiar to most as "going to confession." The priest who was in residence at that time was a deeply spiritual man and had provided good counsel to me before this. I confessed my anger and hate and the struggles that I kept trying to negotiate. When I was through, the priest asked if I might kneel down to receive absolution and reconciliation. He laid his hands on the top on my head and, as he prayed, I felt a great peace and calm fill me. It is not unusual for Catholics to have a sense of relief and peace after confession, but this was no ordinary peace. It seemed to seep into my very soul and cleanse me from head to foot, and it seemed to me that there was a very tangible third presence with us at that time. I knew that we were in the presence of the Holy One and I would not be the same after this. I seemed to know that I could totally trust the God of three persons to be with me and offer me what I needed in all the moments of my life. This experience has been a touchstone for me as I have moved through various life events and struggles. I was thirty-four years old at the time and there were many more testing moments to come.

❧ ❦

As I passed my fortieth birthday I began to notice a change in my prayer life. I found that it was getting more and more difficult to pray with words and I tended to sing my prayer or sing praise often. About two years before this time, I had been given the gift of tongues. That form of prayer was not present in its fullness now. I found that I was more and more simply running out of words. Over a two-year period I found that there were no words left in my prayer. I simply had to sit with God—Father, Son, and Spirit—and be still.

During the next six months I had two profound moments with God. At the time of the first experience, I had sprained my ankle and so I simply decided on that day to lie flat on my back on the floor and be present to

God. As I turned my attention and offered my presence to God, I began to have this vision of the earth, people, animals, countries, sky and trees and stars and planets. Everything was totally connected and I was shown that they were flowing in and through each other and could not be separated. They never were and could not be in the future. There was this deep sense of oneness and connection with all things. As I began to open my eyes and become more attentive to the present moment, I could see this in an indescribable and very real way with everything that surrounded me in and outside of our home. The plants beside the patio door were sepa-rate—and yet connected to me and to each other and everything about me. I picked up my journal and wrote about this but found it difficult, as it still is, to find words that were capable of describing what had hap-pened. After this moment I found that when I heard the struggles of others and listened to accounts of terrible events in the news, I had this deep sense of oneness and compassion for those involved growing in me. My heart was becoming a very tender place. This moment has guided me in providing a hospitable place for oth-ers in the journey to seek God's presence in their lives.

೧ೲ

Not too long after that experience, one day I was sitting in attentive stillness with God and suddenly found myself feeling this very strong sense of evil. It was so powerful that I opened my eyes and noticed that the hairs on my arms were standing on end. My first reaction, of course, was fear. I closed my eyes, after looking around to be sure that there was no other person in the house but myself. As I closed my eyes this powerful spirit began to surround me and I felt as if it were trying to come into me. It seemed to have such a palpable presence that I felt as though I would actually see it in physical form if I looked in the right place. As I felt fear rising within myself, I suddenly took a deep breath and put my hand out in front of me in a "Stop" gesture. I then said, "I have no need to fear you because God is with me and will always stand between you and me. Leave and do not return because you have no power over me." Then I felt a calm and strength surround me and the evil and fear left. I seemed to realize, in the days following, which were filled with difficult decisions and stressful events, that I didn't ever need to fear again. If I made a wrong turn on my journey I would have any help I needed finding my way again as long as I was trying to live life through my faith and trust in God.

&~&

At this point in my life, a great sense of peace has settled into my heart. I totally trust God's faithfulness to me as I try my best to be faithful to the journey. I may not do it well, but I am trying and I believe that is all that is asked of me. If the Churches of this world disappear tomorrow and the world as I know it falls away, I believe that I will still have an inner calm, strength, and hope because my God is with me no matter what life may bring.

৯৯ ৶৩

Judith Halpate is sixty-two years old, a wife, mother, and grandmother. Over the years she has moved many times and says that this has made her life richer in many ways. She has been a member of two faith traditions with most of her years spent in the Roman Catholic Church. She has been a spiritual director for the last fifteen years and has worked with people from many and varied faith traditions as well as with one person who was searching for the God she had been taught didn't exist. She is an experienced retreat leader and has also served as coordinator for several different processes for the uninitiated and the renewal of long-term church members. At the present time she and her husband are kinship foster parents to their oldest grandson. She lives in Pennsylvania.

"*Therefore, since we are surrounded with such a cloud of witnesses on every side we, too, then, should throw off everything that hinders us and keep running steadily in the race we have started.*

Letter to the Hebrews, 12:1
Jerusalem Bible translation

Epilogue Part I

Implications for Individuals and Groups

Probably most of us have heard the old saying that "Familiarity breeds contempt." That may be true but I can't honestly say that I have ever seen it to be so. What I see in myself and in others a good bit of the time, however, is that familiarity tends more to breed a mild form of unconsciousness, a dull awareness in which we neither see nor hear what we would see or hear if we were fully awake and in a bright and clear state of mind. Our eyes might as well be glazed over and our ears stuffed with cotton for all that gets through to us in that state of somnolent awareness.

Is that what has happened to us when it comes to those words that Jesus spoke to his disciples, "I am with you always"? How many times have we heard and read and read and heard those words without their seeming to seriously penetrate our awareness the least bit? (A nice saying, we may think, but what does it have to do with me?) It appears that many, perhaps most, of us do not really believe those words. Is it that we don't believe them because we don't really hear them or that we don't hear them because we've already decided that they can't possibly be true?

The people who have shared their stories for this book, however, the entire "cloud of witnesses," are telling us that their experiences make it clear that those words absolutely are true, literally true, and will always be true, whether or not we are aware of that, believe it, or ever personally have an experience of that Presence similar to their own. They invite us to take those words of Jesus' seriously, not for reasons of dogma but because of the personal experiences over the years of so many people of that Presence.

Or, for some of us, the issue may not be so much that we don't believe that the risen Jesus could be with us as that we think that personal experiences of God's presence are reserved only for very, very holy people, people who are, perhaps, great saints. It would not be surprising if this is so and I think we have the hagiographers, the biographers of the saints, in days gone by to hold accountable for this idea if, indeed, this is a factor in the doubts of some. Today, when we read someone's biography, we expect to learn facts about that person's life, as well as factual accounts of the subject's thoughts and sayings, to the extent possible, and we expect that it will be written from a relatively neutral point of view. That kind of book was not at all the aim of the biographers of the saints over the centuries. Their aim and intention was to edify the populace, to create what we might call a sense of religious shock and awe at the stunning, indescribable holiness of the saint in question, and they had no problem whatsoever in leavening their writing with legends and folk traditions that may have grown up around the saint's life in order to achieve that end.

There are far, far too many cases of this to go into here, though many are so outlandish that, in our day, they can't help but strike us as amusing. For example, here is one of the stories that has been told at least from the Middle Ages, and probably for far longer, about St. Christopher, popular in our day as the patron saint of travelers.

Christopher was said to have been eighteen feet tall and prodigiously strong, and to have had a *"fearsome face."* (Wouldn't most contemporary readers be likely to put the book down right there?) It is also said that, on one occasion, he carried a child who grew increasingly heavy as they crossed a raging river. When they came to the other side and Christopher complained that he had felt that he had been carrying the whole world on his shoulders, the child responded, "You had on your shoulders not only the whole world but him who made it, I am Christ your king . . ." and then he disappeared. And what do we know as fact about St. Christopher? That he was a third-century Christian martyr. That's all. Everything else is legend.

The hagiographers' intentions may have been good, but they did us no favors when they set out to convince us how far below the saints the rest of us are (quite likely true for most of us, so no argument there) and go on to suggest that God's mystical blessings only fall on those of such outstanding sanctity that we "ordinary" folk ought never entertain for a moment the idea that God might ever bless any one of us in a similar way.

Once again, the cloud of witnesses who have shared their experiences for this book would universally deny that they are anything at all like "special holy persons," let alone saints. In fact, one of the main reasons many have given for not sharing their experiences of God before now is that they wanted to avoid being thought of in that light. All see their experiences of God's immediate presence to them on the occasions they have written about in this book as pure gift, undeserved and unearned in any way.

As noted previously, mystical experiences are universal among all of the peoples of the world, and human beings have been having such experiences for who knows how many thousands of years. However, when persons who are adherents of one or another of the world's great religious traditions have such experiences of Transcendence, they will naturally conceptualize and understand the experience in terms of the symbol systems of their own faith tradition. So it should come as no surprise, then, that when Christians have mystical experiences, it seems most often to be the risen Jesus that they experience as being with them in some way. But this is certainly not always the case. Even in this small book, there are accounts of experiences of God spoken of as a "divine energy field" or "Creative Force of the universe," an "indeterminate Light" or "Unbounded Love" and, when we look back over the history of Christian mysticism, we read of many persons whose descriptions of their experiences of God were such that we are led to think of them as experiences of God the Creator (or Father), or of God's Spirit, the "Holy Spirit," as well as of the risen Jesus. Charismatic Christians especially tend to speak primarily of experiences of the Holy Spirit. But in what manner God manifests God's-Self to us is not the issue; the issue is that God does so—and far more often than we are usually aware of—so that, if we wish to be radically in touch with the whole of reality, this is something we should seriously consider taking into account.

One of my teachers once commented that all mystical experiences, albeit given to an individual for God's own reasons, are meant ultimately for the benefit of the community in some way. Perhaps the usual way that becomes real is through the prayers and actions in and for the community of those who have received such graces. But it seems that a wise question to ask might be, "Should this extend to helping the community understand more fully God's real presence among us through the sharing of one's personal experiences of that presence?" This cloud of witnesses has done that, too. Has that been useful for you? Has it enhanced your faith in any way? Might it enhance the faith of your community? Could it lead to the development in the community of greater trust in God? Has it, or could it, foster in any way, a deeper personal devotion to God for individuals? If so, then perhaps we need to find a way for these deeply graced experiences to be shared along with the prayers and actions that grow from them.

This is where we immediately run into problems! The contemplative tradition of Christian spirituality has, through the centuries, always been a bit leery of religious "experiences," with one contemporary spiritual master going so far as to call them "sound and light shows." There is an excellent reason for this caution. For one thing, it is easy, and not rare, for some of us to fall so in love with the idea of mystical experiences that we might begin to covet them and to try to figure out how to have one, even going so far as to make that a spiritual goal. When such a person hears or reads about someone who has had this kind of experience, he or she may begin to ask, "Why did that happen to her and not to me? Why have I never experienced anything like that?" Or, "Why did Jesus come to his brother and take away his craving for alcohol and he didn't do that for my brother?" Do you see the problem? The experience itself, and the importance of having such an experience, can become the center of one's desire while it is God, God's very Self, who ought to be the center of our desire.

The contemplative tradition teaches us that our desire for God, making time for God, our patient "waiting on

God" is what is important. Then we must leave things in God's hands, trusting that God will give us whatever graces we need along the way, remembering all the while that God can always be at work in us in a hidden way, drawing forward our transformation without our having any conscious experience of the divine presence. Although it is perfectly natural for us to want to have some confirming experience of divine reality, any anxious yearning or searching for dramatic experiences of God's presence that may be entertaining and gratify our egos is not in order. This is precisely because those things pull us *away* from the intimacy we already can have with God through our simple, open presence to God in trusting love. Nor are we meant to envy those to whom God has given the particular grace of a mystical experience. Envy hardens our hearts and has the power to carry our egos away in gales of unfitting desires, landing us in a desert farther away from, rather than closer to the God we yearn for. Beyond that, every such experience is, in some way, meant to be a grace for each of us, too, even though we may never understand exactly how that is so. Perhaps just knowing about such experiences, regardless of to whom they are given, is blessing enough for us, for they are always reminders for us of God's real presence in this world at all times and in all places.

There are other issues as well. Perhaps we can see some of them more clearly if we begin with the observation that one of the things that we human beings seem to have a great deal of trouble with is balance, and particularly with balance between our intellects and emotions, or "head" and "heart."[1] We can see this both in our individual lives and, sometimes dramatically, in our various Christian denominations. Some denominations focus almost entirely on an intellectual faith, the "head," and make right doctrine, i.e., getting the words right to express our beliefs, the most important aspect of faith. Sometimes it almost seems as if churches that tend in this direction believe that, if they only get the words right, they have and are holding onto God. Other of our denominations seem to focus almost entirely on "heart," on religious experiences and their feelings toward God. There can be real problems when either focus goes to a radical extreme.

Regarding the predominantly head-oriented churches, a fellow member of the Shalem community, James Banks, commented to me one day about such largely intellectualized churches that "they are losing their members because they have lost their connection to religious experience." His insight seems to be borne out by the fact that many of the people who are leaving these churches are turning toward Pentecostal communities instead. In churches or Christian communities that specialize almost exclusively in a "heart" faith, there is

---

1   *I use the word "heart" here as it is used in today's popular vernacular, as the seat of the emotions, and not as it has been understood in the contemplative tradition from ancient times as our faculty of knowing, different from the mind's way.*

always the danger of over-emotionalism and an uncritical acceptance of any reported religious experience, a situation that has the potential to lead its members dangerously astray.

Clearly, over-intellectualized churches subtly telegraph to their members that religious experiences are not to be talked about if, in fact, they are to be taken seriously at all. On the other hand, "heart" churches, where worship services are structured to elicit emotional religious experiences, make it clear in that and other ways that religious experiences that cause one to feel joyful, even ecstatic, are what they most prize. In such churches there is generally an open invitation to share these experiences and they are, for the most part, uncritically accepted. This can go to such an extreme that members of this kind of congregation who have never had a dramatic encounter with God may feel themselves to be inadequate or even possibly too sinful to have been touched by such a grace. Charismatic groups and congregations especially have often been criticized for seeming to suggest that there is something wrong with those who do not have the "gift of tongues" or have not been "slain in the Spirit."

And so, if it would be valuable for people of faith to hear more fully about the experiences that some of their brothers and sisters have had of God's presence and action in our world today, how might this be facilitated and, at the same time, not so overvalued as to become the primary focus of the community's faith?

I have puzzled over this issue for a long time but thus far have not been able to come up with a perfect answer. At present, my best thought is that one thing that might work well would be to expand the number of small groups in congregations to include some that are specifically intended to be spiritual growth groups. These would be ongoing and permanent groups of perhaps ten to twenty participants, who are meeting for the specific purpose of deepening their relationships with God through various methods of prayer and meditation. In time, such groups foster a deep, spiritual intimacy among the members, which is a perfect setting for the sharing of religious experiences, including mystical experiences. The warmth and support that can usually be found in such groups make them a safe place for sharing. They also provide a setting in which the person who shares is known well and the group can discern together whether, when, and in what manner the experience might be shared with the congregation at large, or if it is best that it remain within the small group. I hope that it goes without saying that no one should ever be pressured in any way to share such experiences. The innate sense of the utter holiness of so many of the direct experiences of God that persons who have had mystical experiences almost always feel often militates against speaking of them at all to anyone. If that is the case, that is exactly where the matter should be left.

In more feeling-oriented churches, conversely, it might be more important for the small group to be a

setting where time is taken to explore a deeper understanding of the meanings of such experiences rather
than to simply rush to report them. Over time, doing so
helps everyone involved learn to discern more clearly
the difference between authentic mystical experiences
and either simple psychological "highs" (good things)
or mental images that may have been mistaken for
something they are not (not such good things). This
could be most useful in terms of putting a ground of
deeper understanding and learning under the emotional delights of experiences of God's love, goodness,
and presence.[2]

Let me say that I do not pretend here, to be offering
a prescription for how to go about this issue of looking
for a balance between "head" and "heart" as it relates
to how we deal with mystical experiences, although I
think this is an extremely important issue. This is because
there is a real possibility of churches or congregations
unwittingly, but actually, doing violence to the spiritual
journeys of their members if they shut them off tightly to
a narrow focus on either intellect or emotions. When an
overly intellectualized faith rules, people are likely to be
hurt by being directed away from an emotional life with
God; this can leave them with a "dry bones" faith of
concepts only, and concepts alone do not usually make

---

2   Many spiritual centers offer training for leadership of such
    groups; Shalem's Leading Contemplative Prayer Groups
    and Retreats program is one of them.

for a very rich relationship with God. On the other hand, when an unbridled, feelings-only "heart" faith rules, ungrounded by any discrimination based on intellectual concepts or on discerning the nature and authenticity of mystical experiences, some people may be hurt simply because emotions are well known for their ability to carry us out well beyond the stratosphere and into a place where illusions can sometimes be confused with reality. No genuine faith can be based on illusion either.

The best conclusion I can come to is to suggest that perhaps all of us, individually and in our religious communities, ought to struggle with this issue and work together to see if we can find a better way to balance our intellects and feelings and ground them in our direct, open presence to God in our spiritual hearts, that is, in the center of our being. After all, they are meant to work together with as much fluidity and grace as our two legs work together when we are dancing, running, or even just out for a pleasant stroll on a nice day. If we are ever able to come close to this goal then we will have moved beyond having to deny or suppress stories of the mystical experiences with which some of us are sometimes graced as well as beyond spending any energy either in coveting or trying to create such experiences for ourselves and, also, beyond making them everything that we live for.

It must be said clearly that mystical experiences are not a usual or ordinary part of our conscious spiritual journeys and certainly not a necessary part. Many of the greatest saints lived out their lives, just as most of us do, without ever having a single, identifiable mystical experience. Such experiences are always gifts, gifts for the individuals to whom they are given and gifts for all of us in that they are ongoing and recurring reminders of God's presence among us always. And let me note here that, although most of the stories shared in this book have come from women, there is no evidence either historically or from the meager contemporary data available that either women or men are more likely to have mystical experiences than the other. The imbalance reflected in the stories in this book seems almost certainly to have come from the possibility that, in our culture and times, women may be somewhat more likely to share such experiences than many men may be.

Someone once asked John of the Cross what we are to do if we are having no experiences of God's love and presence in our lives. His answer was, "Continue in faith and love."

And that is, after all, the truest and deepest essence of the life that all Christians are meant to be living, is it not?

Appendix Part II

Implications for Clergy

Rev. Joseph A. Burkart, M.Div., Psy.D.

Years ago, while serving a small congregation on the Maine coast, I noticed a middle-aged woman who would attend services in July and August and then vanish for the rest of the year. I soon learned she was one of the many "summer folk" who visit our area of the coast in the summer months and then return elsewhere for the winter. One late summer day she invited me over for lunch. She had always seemed a bit aloof to me, so with this invitation offered I was happy to accept. After a congenial interchange she began to relate her story. Some ten years before, her family had been devastated by the unexpected death of her teenage daughter. At one point, in the wake of this, she and her husband had agreed to spend the summer apart, she in Maine and he at their home in Baltimore. She was a practicing psychiatrist in the Jungian tradition and he taught at Johns Hopkins Medical School. Living a solitary life in her summer home she was becoming increasingly depressed. Close friends noticed her isolate behavior, and one came by with an invitation to attend church with her the next Sunday. The woman was initially aghast, thinking, "The last thing I need is to be plunged into some pietistic church service where everyone shows their 'good' side at the expense of honesty about their shadow material!" However, she was so low that simply to be among people seemed like it might be of some help and she agreed to go. So, with grave doubts, she went with her friend to the local mainline Protestant parish her friend attended. About midway through the service she looked up at the altar and there appeared Jesus, beckoning her, rays of light emanating from his heart, and speaking to her the words, *"Come on to me, you who are heavy burdened, and I will give you rest!"* She was flabbergasted and thought that possibly she had flipped over into loony tunes. But she said that she also felt something "let go" inside. "My problems were not resolved," she said, "but some inner templates had seemingly realigned themselves. Interestingly, over the course of the next week or two, I could begin to interact with people and, by the end of the summer, return to my practice."

After the service, she decided that she would share what she had just experienced with the minister. Listening for a few moments, the minister made an offer to take her to the local psychiatric hospital where she might find some help. She said that she didn't have the heart to tell him that she *was* a psychiatrist, so she declined the offer and left it at that. However, a few days later she met the local Pentecostal minister, with whom she also shared this experience, and he understood exactly what she was talking about.

As we talked over lunch, she remarked, "It's interesting that the mainline traditions have little understanding of this phenomenon but have a rich and in-depth academic tradition of research and scholarship, while the more conservative denominations seem to have some sense of this phenomenon which, in fact, interweaves all through the Bible." Continuing, she added, "But the conservative denominations seem to fall short of how 'unitive experience' is never in a capsule but always has to be in connection with a much larger world than we are even aware of as well as having a minimal interest in top-notch scholastic work and dialogue."

Her final remark has left me pensive for years now; when will the two make friends, integrate into something whole? It seems that a good deal about church life is about being good when it seems that it would be more helpful to nurture an environment in which people might be better able to discern the reality of their own spiritual experiences in a context allowing for a more expansive view of the possibilities the experience of being human encompasses.

The reaction this psychiatrist who was a summer visitor to Maine reported as she told her story is far from being unique. Over and over again we hear of similar responses to accounts of profound religious experiences that persons have spoken about. Most clergy with whom I come in contact have a fairly keen sense of what psychopathology looks like. So how is it that so many of us mistake authentic mystical experiences for psychopathology so often? I think that there may be a number of factors at work here.

To begin with, it is one thing to hear someone describe a peach; it is an entirely different experience to taste a lusciously ripe peach oneself. Although we can all be said to be mystics in some sense, and the mystical is not a remote or unattainable event reserved for a select few, the full, luscious "taste" of the mystical/transformational seems less than familiar to most of us. In our objective world of touch and describe, the intangible can always cause suspicion, and the "tasting," when experienced and described by others, is usually left to the realm of poetry and other art forms. This leaves us without a clear way to understand these experiences, even vicariously, through others.

And, secondly, these experiences are mysterious. Pierre de Caussade, in his Abandonment to Divine Providence, says, "The written word of God is full of mystery. His work as expressed in the events of the world is no less so. God is at the center of faith. All that emanates from this center is hidden in the deepest mystery. Obscurity reigns here rather than clear light."

There is the further factor that, although most of us were well trained in seminary in theology and Scripture, in homiletics and in ways of providing good pastoral care for people who are suffering life's assaults, virtually none of us had any serious training in identifying and understanding profound religious experiences and the transformational process that generally grows out of them. Least of all were we helped to learn how to serve as competent midwives to assist at the birth of the deepened faith and spiritual lives of those who come to us with stories of experiences of God that may be unfamiliar to us personally.

Add to this the fact that we may not know the person who brings such a story to us very well, nor the context of her or his life, and we are in a position where we can hardly do anything other than focus on the experience itself when what is really important is what the experience points toward, invites us to: the transcendent significance of the religious experience in one's life circumstances and its connection to the larger world.

We can be helped with this issue by an understanding from the world of spiritual direction that there are two important dimensions, both needed to complement each other, for the authenticity of transcendent experience to be made clear—the "centropedal" and the "centrofugal." The centropedal is the experience itself; the centrofugal refers to the experience itself together with how it connects to the larger world and our response to it.

Clergy are in a difficult spot these days. Simply by the call of this vocation we are confronted with the task of balancing heaven and earth, straddling the crevasse of confusion by providing an equilibrium between the tangible and the intangible. We are, in a sense, asked to live in two worlds, our everyday world and the world of Transcendence, to be comfortable there and to be points of reference where individuals can be helped to see the intersection between the two. This is a tall order and it requires both a profound "in-touchness" with human beings and life, as well as with God, and also well-honed and crisp skills for critical thinking lest we, ourselves, fall out of balance on one side or the other.

Often, when someone reports a mystical experience to a member of the clergy who has had neither experience nor training for dealing with such things, it can be so confounding that a referral will be made rather quickly to a mental health professional where standard diagnostic criteria will be applied and incalculable harm can be done. At times such a referral will be appropriate and at other times not at all; it is of the most critical importance to know the difference.

It seems unlikely that the day will come anytime soon when people who have had mystical or other profound religious experiences will go first, on their own, to anyone other than a member of the clergy for help in understanding such experiences. This suggests to me that we ought to see it as incumbent upon us to familiarize ourselves with the dynamics of such experiences and the transformational process that they engender lest we fail in our responsibility to shepherd the growth and deepening of the spiritual lives of those who turn to us for help in understanding the full meaning of such experiences for their lives. Referring someone to mental health professionals before having discerned whether or not this experience is likely authentic risks de-legitimizing a God-given grace for the person and potentially cutting short the possibility of a much deeper personal relationship with God that we see so often growing out of such experiences.

In a moment I will list a number of resources for you regarding coming to understand mystical experiences more fully, but first I would like to offer a quotation from John Polkinghorne. His words beautifully sum up for me something of the sense of mystery and awe that we can most profitably hold within us as we explore the world of these profound experiences of God:

The poverty of an objectivistic account is made only too clear when we consider the mystery of music.

From a scientific point of view it is nothing but vibrations in the air, impinging on the eardrums stimulating neural currents in the brain. How does it come about that this banal sequence of temporal activity has the power to speak to our hearts of an eternal beauty? The whole range of subjective experience, from perceiving a patch of pink, to being enthralled by the performance of the Mass in B Minor, and on to the mystic's encounter with the ineffable reality of the One, all these

*truly human experiences are at the center of our
encounter with reality, and they are not to be
dismissed as epiphenomenal froth on the surface
of a universe whose true nature is impersonal and
lifeless."[1]*

Resources

1. Spiritual Directors International publishes a directory
called Seek and Find. It is a listing of spiritual guides
around the world who have undergone training and
have practiced for an extended period of time. This
is an easy-to to-use reference, allowing anyone to
find someone in one's own area with whom to work,
consult, ask questions, and become familiar with this
ancient element of the Judeo-Christian tradition. I
might add that this is an interfaith organization, so
one will find guides of various faith paths listed. Their
website (www.sdiworld.org) provides a wealth of
information including events held regularly around
the world.

2. One should not feel shy about locating a contemplative community in one's own area. These are Roman
Catholic, Anglican, or Buddhist monasteries or centers, as well as those of some other faith traditions,
that welcome guests and have accommodations for
extended stays, guided retreats, and educational
events. It is a wonderful way to "taste" the contemplative space that remains the focus of monastic
communities.

3. Ask around to find someone knowledgeable about transformational religious experiences with whom you might talk. My personal experience is that the most visible are often not those of the deepest wisdom and depth. Sometimes a friend's kitchen and a cup of tea is the best resource. Ask questions!

4. The Shalem Institute, a primarily Christian ecumenical organization located in the Washington, D.C. area is a wonderful resource. Shalem offers varied events all year long, from one-day to extended retreats to two-year programs in spiritual guidance (i.e., becoming a spiritual director), leading contemplative prayer groups and retreats, and personal spiritual deepening (www.shalem.org).

5. Contemplative Outreach is an organization started about thirty years ago by Trappist Fathers Thomas Keating and Basil Pennington. They are located at the Trappist Monastery in Snowmass, Colorado, but their "outreach" is extensive (www.centeringprayer. com). As an aside, in the summer of 2008 Thomas Keating came to speak in our small area on the coast of Maine. To our amazement, 450 people turned up and we were left making an attempt to multiply our own loaves and fishes to accommodate everyone. As you can see, his reputation had preceded him.

6. Recently a national effort among contemplative teachers has emerged to encourage seminary curricula to include this material in their course work. The hope is that this might offer an integration of the

cognitive and the affective sides in the study of Christian spirituality. This is the Contemplative Ministries Project spearheaded by David Keller. Interestingly, the project's research has found that medical schools and law schools have taken this integration seriously and Brown University recently added an undergraduate course in Contemplative Studies.

7. Read the great spiritual classics. The span is more extensive than allowed to be listed here, but Teresa of Avila and John of the Cross as well as Brother Lawrence's Practice of the Presence of God are some examples of good places to begin. And, by all means, the work of the contemporary writer Thomas Kelly, A Testament of Devotion, should be included.

8. Not new, as the authors were early pioneers in the revival of interest in spirituality in the 1960s, but still relevant is the early work of Stanislav and Christine Groff, Spiritual Emergencies. Michael Washburn's work, specifically The Ego and the Dynamic Ground and Transpersonal Psychology in a Psychoanalytic Perspective, examines the quantum mechanics of the transformational process mostly, though not exclusively, from a Christian Carmelite perspective. John Nelson's book, Healing the Split: Putting the Spiritual Back into the Healing of the Mentally Ill, examines in detail the discernment between psychopathology and authentic religious experiences and the transformative process. His use of the chakra system as a schematic of the natural progression of

transformative energy, its physical manifestations as well as how it can become stuck, is profound. There is also an intriguing little book, Seeing the Invisible: Modern Religious and Other Transcendent Experiences, that comes out of the Religious Experience Research Center of the Oliver Hardy Foundation founded at Oxford in 1969 and presently located at the University of Wales, Lampeter. It is edited by Meg Maxwell and Verona Tschudin. The particular helpfulness of this book is that it never loses focus on the fact that, whatever we may think of someone's religious experience, it is the transformative influence resulting from it that remains of most significance.

9. An active prayer life, in solitude and in community, as well as the regularity of a spiritual discipline, is an absolute essential. For clergy to be devoid of this would be like a surgeon unfamiliar with a scalpel and unwilling to devote the time and effort necessary to become knowledgeable about it and proficient with it.

You will surely have noted that most of my suggestions here are sources related to the contemplative tradition of western Christianity. This is not at all to suggest that all profound religious experiences, including mystical experiences, grow out of the contemplative tradition. Certainly not! Such experiences are gratuitous gifts of God and are seen to be given broadly to God's people. This is simply because the contemplative tradition has been particularly attentive to such experiences and, over the centuries, has built up much wisdom regarding them and, today, remains the best resource for those of us who wish to come to understand those experiences more fully.

I find myself returning often to some fragments of the quote from John Polkinghorne above: "The poverty of an objectivistic account is only too clear when we consider the mystery of music," and "All these truly human experiences are at the center of our encounter with reality."

My wife has been in scientific research for the past forty years. She introduced me to a colleague who, earlier in life, spent fifteen years as a Trappist monk at St. Joseph's Abbey in Spencer, Massachusetts. He left the monastery to pursue a career in molecular biological research. Once, while out sailing, I asked him how he reconciled the monastic cell with the research cell. His answer: "There is no difference. In both places our search is for reality and, in both places, the closer we come to know something, a growing mystery of what we don't know inevitably emanates from what we uncover. The deepest experiences of the human heart can be approached anywhere as long as we don't limit the world to only the objective and finite."

Appendix Part III

Implications for Mental Health Professionals

Given that studies of the numbers of Americans who have had mystical experiences indicate that approximately 40 to 50 percent of the American population reports having had such an experience at least once in their lives, we can hardly avoid concluding that some number of the clients that mental health professionals see will be among that group, although the percentage may or may not be as high as in the population at large.

So, mental health professionals, whether you are a psychiatrist, psychologist, clinical social worker, pastoral counselor, or professional counselor specializing in a particular field, some of the people you are treating are almost certain to be persons who have had mystical experiences. You may never hear about them, given the protective reticence with which so many people cloak such experiences; but that does not mean that they have not occurred. However, some of those people may want to tell you *all* about them as a way of getting help to process such a different type of experience. As you will have seen from some of the stories in this book, the strangeness of the altered state of consciousness that is involved in many mystical experiences can be unsettling for the subject and sometimes raises questions as to whether something is going wrong with her or his mind. Who better to help answer or settle this question than a mental health professional?

Many members of the mental health community have grown up as members of a religious community, and many who did not were among the vanguard of Americans drawn to the awakening of interest in spirituality that started in the 1970s, and so have pursued that interest and spiritual practices associated with it ever since. You have probably noted that a number of the contributors to this book are, themselves, mental health professionals. Both of these groups are not likely to be intimidated if asked to deal with powerful religious experiences a client may have had but, rather, are apt to be perfectly comfortable in such a discussion. Other clinicians, counselors, and psychotherapists may find themselves in unfamiliar territory, an alien land even, and feel great uncertainty as to what exactly has taken place in the life of a client who reports such an experience.

In such situations, I think most of us, for our own sense of security as well as to provide the best help we can for our client, may be tempted to flee immediately into the security of our diagnostic categories and designate the client as suffering from a specific disease or disorder that we know how to treat. Unless there is unmistakable and inarguable evidence for such a diagnosis apart from the religious experience, I think this is a mistake, even though it may have been made with the best of intentions. The entire issue here hinges on whether or not you, as a mental health professional, can accept the proposition that a dimension of reality exists that transcends matter, and that, on some occasions, it is possible for some human beings to perceive that transcendent reality directly. If you do not or cannot admit of such a possibility, there is virtually no way that you can avoid doing harm to a client who reports such an experience and it would almost certainly be best to recuse oneself from working with that person. If you are open to considering the possibility of such events happening, then continuing with such a client can be a thoroughly rewarding experience for both of you. Your own willingness to face into whatever has happened without prejudgment makes a welcome space and provides encouragement for your client to do the same. Similarly, your unwillingness to accept just anything that you hear without any doubt or question encourages your client to examine his or her experience with some objectivity, a win-win situation. In other words, it is not necessary for a therapist to uncritically accept a client's report of a mystical experience, but it is necessary to be willing to accept the possibility of such a thing having happened and to go from there.

In such cases, I believe the best course is to act on the principle of, "First, do no harm"—to slow down, buy some time, think further about the situation, and do some research. The section "How to Identify Authentic Mystical Experiences" in Part One of this book is an easily accessible place to begin. It may also be fruitful to consult with a colleague or two, preferably ones who are likely to have a different take on the issue than your own, to broaden the possibilities as to how to look at the situation. Hopefully, you will not be under too much pressure from the pertinent health insurance companies, which may want you to provide diagnostic codes quickly, and you will be able to take whatever time is needed with your client to be certain about what is going on. If, in fact, your client has had an authentic mystical experience, something that you as a therapist may never have encountered before, haste can only make it much more likely that mistakes would be made in ascertaining the true nature of your client's experience and what it means to him or her. In arguing for taking whatever amount of time is necessary, let me just say that surely it ought to give us pause to note that the same two questions with which we often begin an assessment for schizophrenia—"Have you ever had any unusual experiences?" and "Have you ever heard voices?"—can just as easily be answered "yes" by a normal person who has had a mystical experience as by a schizophrenic. There being much more necessary than those two questions to come to a clear diagnosis of schizophrenia, however, experienced clinicians will likely have no difficulty in arriving at such a diagnosis if warranted. But it may actually be more of a challenge to figure out exactly what it is that is going on with these other folks. In truth, in attempting to figure out whether a reported mystical experience is authentic or not, we are more in the realm of discernment than of diagnostics, and even many years of experience making diagnoses is not likely to be as helpful as using the basic tools with which we carry out our work of psychotherapy every day together with all of the intuition we may have at our disposal, our best critical-thinking skills, and, possibly, someone more knowledgeable about mystical experiences with whom to discuss the issue—as well as whatever amount of time it takes to arrive at a clear understanding of the experience.

In the United States there are hundreds and hundreds of spiritual and retreat centers sponsored and run by various Christian denominations as well as monasteries of the Eastern and Western Catholic and Anglican traditions, and a number of Buddhist monasteries and centers, also. These are all places where one can consult with persons familiar with the interior landscape of the spiritual life and with issues of religious experiences, including mystical experiences. A number of such centers have been mentioned by those who shared their stories for this book. For those who wish to deepen their understanding of profound religious experiences, such centers can be sources of great help. An invaluable source for the serious study of mystical experiences is the Religious Experience Resource Center (R.E.R.C.) now located at the University of Wales, Lampeter, in Great

Britain. The center was originally founded by Sir Alistair Hardy at Oxford University in 1969 for the purpose of collecting records of mystical experiences from the public. At last count, as this book was approaching publication, there were more than eight thousand accounts in the center's archives. The center publishes a number of books and studies that are extremely useful in expanding one's understanding of mystical experiences and that are readily available for purchase through the university library. Contact information can be found in the appendix at the back of this book.

Every journey of discovery with a client in therapy gives us an opportunity to develop new insights, discover new truths, and come to appreciate more fully the breadth and depth of the capacities of the human heart and mind. Journeying with someone who has, in fact, had an authentic mystical experience may sometimes give us the further gift, through our client's own experience, of being able to catch a glimpse, ourselves, of that Reality that theologian Karl Rahner described as "Incomprehensible Holy Mystery" and that many people have come to call, simply, "Radiant Love."

NOTES

Part One

1. Robeck, Cecil M., Jr. Quoted in "What's Behind Palin's God Talk?" by Tom Roberts in the National Catholic Reporter, September 6, 2008.

2. Wach, Joachim. Quoted in Mystical Tradition: Judaism, Christianity, and Islam, by Luke Timothy Johnson. Lectures on audio and DVD from The Great Courses, produced by The Teaching Company, Chantilly, VA, 2008.

3. Pike, Nelson. Mystic Union: An Essay in the Phenomenology of Mysticism. Ithaca, NY, and London: Cornell University Press, 1992.

4. Johnson, Luke Timothy. Mystical Tradition: Judaism, Christianity, and Islam. Lectures on audio and DVD from The Great Courses, produced by The Teaching Company, Chantilly, VA, 2008.

5. Kelly, Thomas. Reality of the Spiritual World. Pendle Hill Pamphlet Number Twenty One, 1942.

6. May, Gerald. Living in Love: Articles from Shalem News, 1978–2005. Bethesda, MD.

7. Shalem Institute for Spiritual Formation, 2008, p. 18.

8. Ibid., pp. 18–19.

9. Stall, Sam. 100 Cats Who Changed Civilization. Philadelphia: Quirk Books, 2007, p. 32.

10. Robinson, David. Consciousness and Its Implications. Lectures on audio and DVD from The Great Courses, produced by The Teaching Company, Chantilly, VA, 2007.

11. Dalai Lama. The Universe in a Single Atom: The Convergence of Science and Spirituality. New York: Broadway Books, 2005, pp. 11–13.

Epilogue

1. Polkinghorne, John. Belief in God in an Age of Science. New Haven, CT.: Yale University Press, 1998. pp. 18-19

APPENDIX
Contact Information

Readers, as you have gone through the stories in this book, you will have noticed that many of the contributing writers have spoken of spiritual centers that have been important in their lives. Below you will find contact information for all of those centers still in existence in case you might want to be in touch with any of them.

Alton L. Collins Retreat Center

32867 SE Highway 211
Eagle Creek, OR 97022
503-637-6411 or 888-567-6411
Website: collinsretreatcenter.org
Email: alcrc@relianceconnects.com

Bon Secours Spiritual Center

1525 Marriottsville Rd.
Marriottsville, MD 21104-1301
410-442-1320
Website: bonsecoursspiritualcenter.org

The Haden Institute

P.O. Box 1793
Flat Rock, NC 28731
828-693-9292
Website: www.hadeninstitute.com
Email: office@hadeninsitute.com

Manresa Jesuit Retreat Center
1390 Quanton Rd.
Bloomfield Hills, MI 48304-3554
248-644-4933
Website: www.manresa-sj.org
Email: office@manresa-sj.org

Pendle Hill
338 Plush Mill Rd.
Wallingford, PA 19086-6023
610-556-4507 or 800-742-3150
Website: www.pendlehill.org
Email: info@pendlehill.org

Shalem Institute for Spiritual Formation
3025 Fourth St., NE
Washington, DC 20017
301-897-7334
Website: www.shalem.org
Email: info@shalem.org

Shalom Mountain Retreat and Study Center
664 Cattail Rd.
Livingston Manor, NY 12758
845-482-5421
Website: www.shalommountain.com
Email: email@shalommountain.com

The Alister Hardy Religious Experience Research Centre
University of Wales Trinity Saint David
Lampeter Campus
Lampeter, Ceredigion SA48 7ED
United Kingdom
+44(0) 1570 424821
Website: tsd.ac.uk/librariesandcenters/alisterhardyreligiousexperienceresearchcentre/contacts.org

Some Words of Gratitude

First and foremost, I want to express my deepest appreciation for, and to, all of the men and women who shared their stories with me for this book. Without them there would have been no book and so I consider this to be not at all just mine, but their book as well. My thanks go also to all of those writers who sent stories to me that are not included here but are saved aside for another book to come at a later time. Every story has touched and inspired me and all have sharpened my awareness and appreciation for the amazing and seemingly infinite variety of ways through which God's love touches our lives.

I want to thank also, from the depths of my heart, Tilden Edwards, founder and long the director of the Shalem Institute for Spiritual Formation, teacher, mentor, and friend. His incredible gift for evoking the presence of the Holy One with words that can seem so ordinary coming from any other source has been a major gift of grace in my life. I owe a deep debt of gratitude as well to the late Dr. Gerald May, psychiatrist and spiritual master, whose work at the boundaries of psychology and spirituality has richly informed my own thought and work for many years. A most special thank you, too, to Shalem's Monica Maxon for her support, endless patience, and help in chasing down references for me that I had somehow managed to mangle or misplace.

And, indeed, I would like to take this opportunity to express my gratitude to all of my colleagues and associates at Shalem for our time together over these past thirty-five years. Each and every one has enlightened my mind and nourished my spirit along the way.

I think there may be no words to adequately thank my son, Paul, and story contributor Donna Acquaviva for their ongoing enthusiasm and support for this project, as well as for the hours spent bringing their professional editorial skills to bear on the manuscript. They are the ones responsible for bringing it to whatever level of perfection the writing itself might be considered to have attained. I also owe a deep debt of gratitude to my editor at Seraphina Books, Katherine Pickett, who brought my old-fashioned style up to date and put the final polish on this work.

Many, many words of gratitude, too, to the Rev. Joseph "Tony" Burkart, not only for his generosity in writing the part of the epilogue directed to members of the clergy but also for inspiring me all along the way with his insights and deep personal spirituality. I want to thank Tony for companioning me by email, too, well beyond any call of a new friendship all the way through the long, sometimes difficult process of bringing this work through to its completion. I am deeply grateful.

And for my dear friend and award-winning artist, Jacqueline Saunders—a huge bouquet of "thank-yous" for the original watercolors that she did especially for this book; you will have seen one of them on its cover. They are all so beautiful and I am so very honored to have them.

I would be seriously remiss if I failed to acknowledge my debt of gratitude to the generations and generations of holy women and men, some sainted but many not, who have shared their own stories of encounters with the Divine Presence in their lives through their own words or through accounts of their experiences passed along by historians and biographers. To them most certainly must be added the prolific works of scholars, researchers, and writers in the fields of religion and spirituality through the years, and closer to our own time, that of scientists—psychiatrists and physicians with other relevant specialties, psychologists and neuroscientists as well. Just as this book could not have come into being without all of those who contributed their own contemporary stories for it, neither could it have come into being without all of those individuals who came before me in respecting and working to understand these amazing experiences more clearly and deeply.

And finally, I am deeply grateful, also, to:

— Alfred Music Publishing for permission to include the lyrics to On a Clear Day;

— Random House Publications for permission to quote the Dalai Lama from his book, *The Universe in a Single Atom;*

— Pendle Hill for permission to quote from Thomas Kelly's pamphlet, The Reality of the Spiritual World;

— the Shalem Institute for Spiritual Formation for permission to quote from Living in Love, a collection of some of the short writings of Gerald May.

— and to Tracey Marx for permission to include her beautiful poem Space in this book.

Bibliography

Ahern, Geoffrey. Spiritual/Religious Experience in Modern Society. Lampeter, Wales: Religious Experience Research Center, University of Wales, Lampeter, 1990.

Allegri, Renzo. Padre Pio, A Man of Hope. Cincinnati: St. Anthony Messenger Press, 2000.

Alvarado, Carlos. "Exploring the Features of Spontaneous Psychic Experience." European Journal of Parapsychology 12 (1996): 61–74.

Armstrong, Karen. Visions of God: Four Medieval Mystics and Their Writings. New York: Bantam Books, 1994.

Arts, Hedwig. With Your Whole Soul: On the Christian Experience of God. Translated by Sr. Helen Rolfson. New York and Ramsey, NJ: Paulist Press, 1978.

Bacovcin, Helen, trans. The Way of the Pilgrim. Garden City, NY: Image Books, 1985.

Bailey, Raymond. Thomas Merton on Mysticism. Garden City, NY: Image Books, 1974, 1975.

Baillie, John. The Sense of the Presence of God. London: Oxford University Press; New York: Scribner, 1962.

Beauregard, Mario, and Denyse O'Leary. The Spiritual Brain: A Neuroscientist's Case for the Existence of the Soul. New York: Harper One, 2007.

Beauegard, Mario. Brain Wars: The Scientific Battle Over the Existence of the Mind and the Proof That Will Change the Way We Live Our Lives. New York: Harper One, 2012.

Beer, Frances. Women and Mystical Experiences in the Middle Ages. Woodbridge, Suffolk, England: The Boydell Press, 1992.

Besserman, Perle. The Way of the Jewish Mystics. Boston and London: Shambhala Books,1994.

Blakeney, Raymond. trans. Meister Eckhart. New York: Harper Torchbooks, 1941.

———. Meister Eckhart, from Whom God Hid Nothing. Boston: Shambhala, 1996.

Bobco, Jane, and Barbara Newman, eds. Vision: The Life and Music of Hildegard of Bingen. New York: Penguin Books, 1995.

Borg, J., et al. "The Seratonin System and Spiritual Experiences," American Journal of Psychiatry 160 (2003): pp. 1965–69.

Borg, Marcus. Meeting Jesus Again for the First Time: The Historical Jesus and the Heart of Contemporary Faith. San Francisco: Harper San Francisco, 1994.

Borg, Marcus, and N. T. Wright. The Meaning of Jesus: Two Visions. San Francisco, : Harper San Francisco, 1999.

Borysenko, Joan. The Ways of the Mystic. Carlsbad, CA: Hay House, 1997.

Bouteneff, Peter, ed. Daily Readings in Orthodox Spirituality. Springfield, IL: Templegate Publishers, 1996.

Bouyer, Louis. A History of Christian Spirituality. 3 vols. New York: Seabury Press, 1969.

———— Women Mystics. San Francisco: Ignatius Press, 1993.

Bragdon, Allen, and David Gamon. Brains That Work a Little Bit Differently. Bass River, MA: The Brainwaves Center, 2000.

Brico, Rex. Taize. London: Collins, 1978.

Bridges, Howard. American Mysticism: From William James to Zen. New York: Harper and Row, 1970.

Brockelman, P. Cosmology and Creation. New York: Oxford University Press, 1999.

Brown, Warren, N. Murphy, and H. Maloney, eds. Whatever Happened to the Soul?: Scientific and Theological Portraits of Human Nature. Minneapolis: Fortress Press, 1998.

Buber, Martin. I and Thou. New York: Scribners, 1970.

Bucke, Richard. Cosmic Consciousness: A Study of the Evolution of the Human Mind. Hyde Park, NY: University Books, 1961. (Originally published in 1901.)

Burnham, Sophy. The Ecstatic Journey: The Transforming Power of Mystical Experiences. New York: Ballantine Books, 1997.

—— Angel Letters. New York: Ballantine Books, 1991.

Butler, E. Cuthbert. Western Mysticism. New York: Barnes and Noble, 1968.

Castelli, Jim, ed. How I Pray: People of Different Religions Share With Us That Most Sacred and Intimate Act of Faith. New York: Ballantine Books, 2004.

Castillon du Peron, Marguerite. Charles de Foucauld. Paris: Grasset,1983.

Caussade, Jean-Pierre de. The Sacrament of the Present Moment. Translated by Kitty Muggeredge. San Francisco: Harper San Francisco, 1966.

Chalmers, David. The Conscious Mind: In Search of a Fundamental Theory. New York: Oxford University Press, 1996.

———. "Facing Up to the Problem of Consciousness." Journal of Consciousness Studies 3, no. 1 (1995): pp. 200-19.

Chardin, Pierre Theilhard de. The Hymn of the Universe. New York: Harper and Row, 1961.

Cohen, John Michael, trans. The Life of St. Teresa of Avila by Herself. London: Penguin Books, 1957. Reissued 1987.

Colledge, Edmund, and James Walsh, trans. Julian of Norwich: Showings. New York: Paulist Press, 1978.

Colledge, Edmund, and Bernard McGinn, trans. Meister Eckhart. New York: Paulist Press, 1961.

Consolmagno, Brother Guy. God's Mechanics: How Scientists and Engineers Make Sense of Religion. San Francisco: Jossey-Bass, 2008.

Cooper, Rabbi David A. God Is a Verb: Kabbalah and the Practice of Mystical Judaism. New York: Riverhead Books, 1997.

Cousins, Ewert. The Life of St. Francis. New York: Paulist Press, 1978.

———. "Francis of Assisi: Christian Mysticism at the Crossroads," in Mysticism and Religious Traditions, edited by Steven Katz. Oxford: Oxford University Press, 1983.

Crossan, John Dominic. The Historical Jesus. San Francisco: Harper San Francisco, 1993.

Dalai Lama. The Universe in a Single Atom: The Convergence of Science and Spirituality. New York: Broadway Books, 2005.

Dalai Lama and Howard C. Cutler. The Art of Happiness. New York: Riverhead Books, 1998.

Das, Lama Surya. Awakening to the Sacred. New York: Broadway Books, 1999.

Davidson, Hugh M. Blaise Pascal. Boston: Twayne, 1983.

Deikman, Arthur M. "Deautomatization and the Mystic Experience." Psychiatry 29 (1966), pp. 324–38.

De Meester, Conrad. Light, Love, Light: Elizabeth of the Trinity. Translated by Sr. Alethia Kane. Washington, DC: ICS Publications, 1987.

Dillard, Annie. Pilgrim at Tinker Creek. New York: Harper and Row, 1974.

Donovan, Peter. Interpreting Religious Experience. Lampeter, Wales: Alistair Hardy Trust, University of Wales, Lampeter, 1996

Dossey, Lawrence. Recovering the Soul. New York: Bantam Books, 1989.

Dougherty, Sr. Rose Mary. Group Spiritual Direction: Community for Discernment. Mahwah, NJ: Paulist Press, 1995.

Douglas-Klotz, Neil, trans. and commentary. Prayers of the Cosmos: Meditations on the Aramaic Words of Jesus. San Francisco: Harper San Francisco, 1990.

Easwaren, Eknath, ed. God Makes the Rivers to Flow: Selections from the Sacred Literature of the World. Tomales, CA: Nilgiri Press, 1991.

Egan, Harvey. Christian Mysticism: The Future of a Tradition. New York: Pueblo, 1984.

———. "Christian Apophatic and Kataphatic Mysticisms." Theological Studies (Fall 1978): 399.

Epstein, Perle. Kabbalah: The Way of the Jewish Mystic. Garden City, NY: Doubleday, 1978.

Erb, Peter, trans. Johann Arndt: True Christianity. New York: Paulist Press, 1979.

———. Jacob Boehme: The Way to Christ. New York: Paulist Press, 1978.

Evans, C. Stephen. Soren Kierkegard's Christian Psychology. Grand Rapids, MI: Zondervan Publishers, 1990.

Faricy, Robert. The Spirituality of Theilhard de Chardin. London: Collins, 1981.

Forman, Robert K. C., ed. The Problem of Pure Consciousness: Mysticism and Philosophy. New York: Oxford University Press, 1990.

Fortini, Arnaldo. Francis of Assisi. New York: Crossroad, 1981.

Foster, Richard J., and Emilie Griffin, eds. Spiritual Classics: Selected Readings on the Twelve Spiritual Disciplines. New York: Harper One, 2000.

France, Peter. Hermits: The Insights of Solitude. New York: St. Martin's Griffin, 1996.

Goleman, Daniel. Vital Lies, Simple Truths: The Psychology of Self-Deception. New York: Touchstone, 1985.

Goleman, Daniel, and Richard J. Davidson, eds. Consciousness: Brain, States of Awareness and Mysticism. New York: Harper and Row, 1979.

Greeley, Andrew M. Ecstasy: A Way of Knowing. Engle-wood Cliffs, NJ: Prentice-Hall, 1974.

———. "The Sociology of the Paranormal: A Reconnais-sance." Sage Research Papers in the Social Sciences 3, no. 90-023 (Beverly Hills and London: 1975), 61.

———. "The Paranormal Is Normal: A Sociologist Looks at Parapsychology." The Christian Parapsychologist (Journal of the Churches' Fellowship for Psychical and Spiritual Studies), June 1993, pp. 49–55.

———. "Mysticism Goes Mainstream." American Health (January/February 1987): pp. 47–49.

Greeley, Andrew M., and William C. McCready. "Are We a Nation of Mystics?" The New York Times Magazine, January 26, 1975, 6.

Griffiths, Bede. The Golden String. Springfield, IL: Temple-gate, 1989.

———. A New Vision of Reality: Western Science, West-ern Mysticism and Christian Faith. Springfield, IL: Templegate, 1989.

———. The Marriage of East and West. Springfield, IL: Templegate , 1982.

Grof, Stanislav. Beyond the Brain: Birth, Death and Tran-scendence in Psychotherapy. Albany: State Univer-sity of New York Press, 1985.

Hagerty, Barbara Bradley. Fingerprints of God: The Search for the Science of Spirituality. New York: Riv-erhead Books, 2009.

Hamilton, Allan J. The Scalpel and the Sword: Encounters with Surgery and the Supernatural and the Power of Hope. New York: The Tarcher Division of Penguin Books, 2008.

Hammarskjold, Dag. Markings. New York: Alfred A. Knopf, 1964.

Hardy, Alister. The Divine Flame. Oxford: The Religious Experience Research Unit, 1978.

————. The Biology of God. New York: Taplinger, 1976.

————. The Spiritual Nature of Man: A Study of Contemporary Religious Experience. New York: Oxford University Press, 1979.

Harmon, Willis W. A Re-Examination of the Metaphysical Foundations of Modern Science. Sausalito, CA: Institute of Noetic Sciences, 1991.

Harrington, Anne. Medicine, Mind and the Double Brain. Princeton, NJ: Princeton University Press, 1987.

Harvey, Andrew, ed. Teachings of the Christian Mystics. Boston: Shambhala, 1998.

————. The Essential Mystics: Selections from the World's Great Wisdom Traditions. San Francisco: Harper San Francisco, 1996.

Hayward, Jeremy W., and Francisco J. Varela. Gentle Bridges: Conversations with the Dalai Lama on the Sciences of the Mind. Boston and London: Shambhala Press, 2001.

Heffern, Richard. "Consciousness: Life's Biggest Mystery." National Catholic Reporter, February 8, 2008.

———. "Rethinking the Soul." National Catholic Reporter, February 8, 2008.

Heil, John, and Alfred Mele, eds. Mental Causation. Oxford: Clarendon Press, 1993.

Heinecken, Martin J. The Moment Before God. Philadelphia: Muhlenberg, 1956.

Hillman, James. The Soul's Code. New York: Broadway Books, 1996.

Hofstadter, Douglas R., and Daniel C. Dennett, eds. The Mind's I. New York: Basic Books, 1981, 2000.

Hollywood, Amy. The Soul as Virgin Wife: Mechthild of Madgeberg, Marguerite Porete and Meister Eckhardt. Notre Dame, IN: Notre Dame University Press, 1995.

Housden, Roger. Sacred Journeys in a Modern World. New York: Simon and Schuster, 1998.

Hugel, Frederich von. The Mystical Element in Religion. 2 vols. London: Dent, 1908; repr., New York: Dutton, 1923.

Idel, Moshe, and Bernard McGinn. Mystical Union in Judaism, Christianity and Islam: An Ecumenical Dialogue. New York: Crossroads, 1996.

Inge, William R. Studies of the English Mystics. London: John Murray, 1921.

Jahn, Robert G., and Brenda J. Dunne. Margins of Reality: The Role of Consciousness in the Physical World. New York: Harcourt Brace Jovanovich, 1987.

———. "Science of the Subjective." Technical Notes. Princeton, NJ: Princeton University Press, March 1997.

James, William. The Variety of Religious Experience. New York: Random House, Modern Library, 1936.

———. "Does Consciousness Exist?" Journal of Philosophy, Psychology and Scientific Methods 1, 1904.

John of the Cross. The Collected Works of John of the Cross. Edited and translated by K. Kavanagh and O. Rodriguez. Washington, DC: Institute of Carmelite Studies, 1991.

Johnson, Luke Timothy. Mystical Tradition: Judaism, Christianity and Islam. DVD. The Great Courses. Produced by The Teaching Company, Chantilly, VA, 2008.

———. The Real Jesus: The Misguided Quest for the Historical Jesus and the Truth of the Traditional Gospels. San Francisco: Harper San Francisco, 1996.

———. Early Christianity: The Experience of the Divine. DVD. The Great Courses. Produced by The Teaching Company, Chantilly, VA, 2002.

Johnston, William. The Mirror Mind: Spirituality and Transformation. San Francisco: Harper and Row, 1981.

———. The Inner Eye of Love: Mysticism and Religion.

San Francisco: Harper and Row, 1978.

Johnston, William, ed. The Cloud of Unknowing. New York: Doubleday Image, 1973.

Jones, Rufus. Studies in Mystical Religion. New York: Russell and Russell, 1970.

Julian of Norwich. Revelations of Divine Love. Translated by Clifton Wolters. Baltimore: Penguin, 1966.

———. Revelation of Love. Edited and translated by John Skinner. New York: Image Books, 1996.

Keating, Thomas. The Psychology of the Spiritual Journey. Butler, NY: Contemplative Outreach Ltd., 1994.

———. Open Mind, Open Heart. New York: Continuum, 1994.

———. Intimacy with God: An Introduction to Centering Prayer. New York: Crossroad, 1996.

Keating, Thomas, Basil Pennington, and Thomas E. Clark. Finding Grace at the Center. Still River, MA: St. Bede Publications, 1978.

Kelly, Thomas. Reality of the Spiritual World. Pendle Hill, PA: Pendle Hill Publications, 1942.

Khan, Hazrat Inayat. The Inner Life. Boston: Shambhala, 1997.

Kirk, Kenneth E. The Vision of God. London and New York: Longmans, 1931.

Kirvan, John. Where Only Love Can Go: A Journey of

the Soul into the Cloud of Unknowing. Notre Dame, IN: Ave Maria Press, 1996.

Knowles, David. The Nature of Mysticism. New York: Hawthorne Books, 1966.

Kotulak, Ronald. Inside the Brain: Revolutionary Discoveries of How the Mind Works. Kansas City, MO: Andrews McMeel Publishing, 1996–97.

Lanier, Jean. "From Having a Mystical Experience to Becoming a Mystic" (reprint and epilogue). ReVision 12, no. 1 (Summer 1989): p. 41

Lawrence, Brother. The Practice of the Presence of God. Orleans, MA: Paraclete Press, 1985.

Leonard, A. "Studies on the Phenomenon of Mystical Experience," in Mystery and Mysticism: A Symposium. London: Blackfriars Publications, 1956.

Levine, Joseph. Purple Haze: The Puzzle of Consciousness. New York: Oxford University Press, 1989.

Lockwood, Michael. Mind, Brain and the Quantum. Oxford: Blackwell, 1989.

Loder, James E. The Transforming Moment: Understanding Convictional Experience. San Francisco: Harper and Row, 1981.

Louth, Andrew. Origins of the Christian Mystical Tradition: From Plato to Denys. New York: Oxford University Press, 1981.

Magsam, Charles. The Experience of God. Maryknoll,

NY: Orbis Books, 1977.

Marechal, Joseph. Studies in the Psychology of the Mystics. Translated by Algar Thorold. New York: Oxford University Press, 1927.

Maslow, Abraham. The Farther Reaches of Human Nature. New York: Viking, 1971.

———. Religions, Values and Peak Experiences. New York: Penguin, 1964.

Mathew, Roy J. The True Path: Western Science and the Quest for Yoga. Cambridge, MA: Perseus Publishing, 2001.

Maxon, Monica, Lynne Smith, and Rose Mary Dougherty, eds. The Lived Experience of Group Spiritual Direction. Mahwah, NJ: Paulist Press, 2003.

Maxwell, Meg, and Verena Tschudin, eds. Seeing the Invisible: Modern Religious and Other Transcendent Experiences. Lampeter, Wales: Religious Experience Research Center, University of Wales, Lampeter, 1996, 2005.

May, Gerald G. Will and Spirit: A Contemplative Psychology. San Francisco: Harper and Row, 1982.

McGinn, Bernard. The Foundations of Mysticism. New York: Crossroad, 1991.

———. The Growth of Mysticism. New York: Crossroad, 1994.

———. The Flowering of Mysticism. New York: Crossroad,

1998.

McGinn, Colin. The Mysterious Flame: Conscious Minds in a Material World. New York: Basic Books, 1999.

McIlroy, Anne. "Hardwired for God," Globe and Mail (Canada), December 6, 2003.

McIntosh, Mark. Mystical Theology. Oxford: Blackwell, 1989.

McLaren, Brian D. A Generous Orthodoxy. Grand Rapids, MI: Zondervan, 2004.

McMahon, David. Quantum Mechanics DeMystified. New York: McGraw-Hill, 2006.

McNamara, William. Christian Mysticism: The Art of the Inner Way. New York: Continuum, 1981.

———. Mystical Passion: Spirituality for a Bored Society. New York: Paulist Press, 1977.

———. "Psychology and the Christian Mystical Tradition," in Charles Tart's Transpersonal Psychologies. New York: Harper and Row, 1975.

Mechthild of Madgeberg. Meditations from Mechthild of Madgeberg. Edited by Henry L. Carrigan Jr. Orleans, MA: Paraclete, 1999.

Medwick, Cathleen. Teresa of Avila: The Progress of a Soul. New York: Alfred A. Knopf, 1999.

Merton, Thomas. New Seeds of Contemplation. New York: New Directions, 1962.

———. The Wisdom of the Desert. New York: New Dimensions, 1960.

———. Thoughts in Solitude. New York: The Noonday Press, Farrar, Straus and Giroux, 1958.

Miller, William R., and Janet C'de Baca. Quantum Change. New York: The Guilford Press, 2001.

Mitchell, Stephen, ed. The Essence of Wisdom: Words from the Masters to Illuminate the Spiritual Path. New York: Broadway Books, 1998.

Moltmann, Jurgen. Jesus Christ for Today's World. Minneapolis: Fortress Press, 1994.

Montaldo, Jonathan, ed. Entering the Silence: The Journals of Thomas Merton. Vol. 2: 1941–1952. New York: Harper Collins, 1997.

Moore, Thomas. The Re-Enchantment of Everyday Life. New York: Harper Collins, 1992.

Moorman, John R. H., IX Bishop of Ripon. The Anglican Spiritual Tradition. Springfield, IL: Templegate, 1983.

———. Saint Francis of Assisi, 2nd ed. London: Society for Promoting Christian Knowledge, 1976.

Murphy-O'Connor, Jerome. Paul: A Critical Life. Oxford: Clarendon, 1996.

Murk-Jansen, Saskia. Brides in the Desert: The Spirituality of the Beguines. New York: Orbis Books, 1998.

Nadeau, Robert, and M. Kafatos. The Non-local Universe: The New Physics and Matters of the Mind. Oxford and New York: Oxford University Press, 1999.

Needleman, Jacob. A Sense of the Cosmos: The Encounter of Modern Science and Ancient Truth. New York: Doubleday, 1977.

Newberg, Andrew, and Mark R. Waldman. How God Changes Your Brain. New York: Ballantine Books, 2009.

Noe, Alva. Out of Our Heads: Why You Are Not Your Brain and Other Lessons from the Biology of Consciousness. New York: Hill and Wang, 2009.

Obbard, Elizabeth Ruth. Introducing Julian, Woman of Norwich. Hyde Park, NY: New City Press, 1996.

O'Brien, Elmer. Varieties of Mystic Experience. New York: Holt, Rinehart and Winston, 1964.

O'Donohue, John. Eternal Echoes. New York: Cliff Street Books, 1999.

O'Donovan, Leo J., ed. A World of Grace: An Introduction to the Themes and Foundations of Karl Rahner's Theology. New York: Crossroad, 1981.

O'Murchu, Diarmuid. Quantum Theology. New York: Crossroad, 2004.

Ornstein, Robert. The Nature of Human Consciousness. New York: Viking, 1973.

———. The Mind Field. New York: Grossman, 1976.

———. The Roots of the Self: Unraveling the Mystery of Who We Are. San Francisco: Harper San Francisco, 1993.

Otto, Rudolph. The Idea of the Holy. Translated by John Harvey. New York: Oxford University Press, 1981.

Pearsall, Paul. The Heart's Code. New York: Broadway Books, 1998.

Penrose, Roger. Shadows of the Mind: A Search for the Missing Science of Consciousness. Oxford: Oxford University Press, 1996.

Phillips, Dorothy B., Elizabeth B. Howes, and Lucille M. Nixon, eds. The Choice Is Always Ours: The Classic Anthology on the Spiritual Way. San Francisco: Harper and Row, 1975.

Pike, Nelson. Mystic Union: An Essay in the Phenomenology of Mysticism. Ithaca, NY, and London: Cornell University Press, 1992.

Polkinghorne, John. Science and Providence: God's Interaction with the World. Boston: New Science Library, 1989.

Porete, Margaret. A Mirror for Simple Souls. New York: Crossroad, 1981.

Poulain, Augustin. The Graces of Interior Prayer. Translated from the sixth edition by Leonora Yorke-Smith. London: Routledge and Kegan Paul, 1950.

———. Revelations and Visions: Discerning the True and the Certain from the False and the Doubtful. New York: Alba House, 1998.

Pribram, Karl. The Language of the Brain. Englewood Cliffs, NJ: Prentice-Hall, 1971.

Quincey, Christian de. Radical Knowing: Understanding Consciousness Through Relationship. Rochester, NY: Park Street Press, 2005.

Roberts, Bernadette. What Is Self?: A Study of the Spiritual Journey in Terms of Consciousness. Boulder, CO: Sentient Publications, 2005.

Robinson, Daniel N. Consciousness and Its Implications. DVD. The Great Courses. Produced by The Teaching Company, Chantilly, VA, 2007.

Russell, Norman, trans. The Lives of the Desert Fathers. Kalamazoo, MI: Cistercian Publications, 1981.

Russell, Peter. From Science to God: A Physicist's Journey into the Mystery of Consciousness. Novato, CA: New World Library, 2002.

Sachs, Oliver. The Man Who Mistook His Wife for a Hat. New York: Simon and Schuster, 1985.

Sant'Ambrogio, Joan. The Fourteenth Century English Mystics. Unpublished manuscript. Washington, D.C.: 1950.

Schilling, Harold K. The New Consciousness in Science and Religion. Philadelphia: United Church Press, 1973.

Schroeder, Gerald L. GOD According to God: A Physicist Proves We've Been Wrong About God All Along. New York: Harper Collins, 2009.

Schwartz, Stephan. Opening to the Infinite: The Art and Science of Nonlocal Awareness. Buda, TX: Nemoseen Media, 2007.

Smith, Huston. The World's Religions. San Francisco: Harper San Francisco, 1991.

———— "Psychology of Religious Experience." The Roots of Consciousness. Thinking Aloud videotape series, 1988.

Spilka, B., et al., eds. The Psychology of Religion: An Empirical Approach. New York: Guilford Press, 2003.

Spink, Peter, ed. Bede Griffiths. Springfield, IL: Temple-gate, 1990.

Spoto, Donald. The Hidden Jesus: A New Life. New York: St. Martin's Press, 1998.

Steere, Douglas, ed. The Practice of the Presence of God (by Brother Lawrence). Nashville: The Upper Room, 1950.

————. Quaker Spirituality. New York and Ramsey, NJ: Paulist Press, 1984.

Storr, Anthony. Feet of Clay: Saints, Sinners and Madmen; A Study of Gurus. New York: The Free Press, 1996.

Suzuki, D. T. Mysticism, Christian and Buddhist. New York: Harper and Row, Perennial Library ed., 1971.

Swan, Laura. The Forgotten Desert Mothers. Mahwah, NJ: Paulist Press, 2001.

Tarthang Tulku. Time, Space and Knowledge. Emeryville, CA: Dharma Publishing, 1977.

Teasdale, Wayne. The Mystic Heart. Novato, CA: New World Library, 1999.

Tegmark, Max. "Parallel Universes." Scientific American (May 2003): p. 9.

Teresa of Avila. Interior Castle. Translated and edited by E. Allison Peers. New York: Image Books, 1972.

Teresa, Mother. The Blessings of Love. Ann Arbor, MI: Servant Publications, 1996.

————. No Greater Love. Novato, CA: New World Library, 1997.

Underhill, Evelyn. Mysticism: A Study in the Nature and Development of Man's Spiritual Consciousness. New York: Noonday Press, 1955.

————. The Mystic Way: A Psychological Study in Christian Origins. London: Dent, 1913.

————. Practical Mysticism. New York: Dutton, 1915.

————. Mystics of the Church. Harrisburg, PA: Morehouse, 1975. (Originally published London: James Clark and Co. Ltd., 1925.)

Vaillant, George E. Spiritual Evolution: A Scientific Defense of Faith. New York: Broadway Books, 2008.

Van de Weyer, Robert. Hildegard in a Nutshell. London: Hodder and Stoughton, 1997.

van Lommel, Pim. Consciousness After Life: The Science of the Near-Death Experience. Translated by Laura Vroomen. New York: Harper Collins, 2010.

Wakefield, Daniel. How Do We Know When It's God? New York: Little Brown, 1999.

Wallace, B. Alan. Contemplative Science. New York: Columbia University Press, 2007.

Walsh, James, ed. The Cloud of Unknowing. Mahwah, NJ: Paulist Press, 1981.

Wang, Sam. The Neuroscience of Everyday Life. DVD. The Great Courses. Produced by The Teaching Company, Chantilly, VA, 2010.

Wapnick, Kenneth. "Mysticism and Schizophrenia." The Journal of Transpersonal Psychology 1, no. 2 (1969): 49–68.

Weil, Simone. Waiting for God. Translated by Emma Craufurd. New York: Putnam, 1951.

Wesley, John. The Nature of Holiness. Compiled and edited by Clare George Weakley Jr. Minneapolis: Bethany House, 1988.

White Eagle. The Quiet Mind. Liss, Hampshire, England: The White Eagle Publishing Trust, 1972.

White, John. The Meeting of Science and Spirit: Guidelines for a New Age. New York: Paragon House, 1990.

White, Stewart Edward. The Unobstructed Universe. New York: Dell, 1940.

Wilber, Ken. Transformations of Consciousness: Conventional and Contemplative Perspectives of Development. With Jack Engler and Daniel Brown. Boston: Shambhala, 1986.

Wilber, Ken, Jack Engler and Daniel P. Brown. Transformations of Consciousness. Boston: Shambhala, 1986."

———. Quantum Questions: Mystical Writings of the World's Great Physicists. Revised 2nd ed. Boston: Shambhala, 2001.

———. The Spectrum of Consciousness. Wheaton, IL: Quest Books, 1993.

Wills, Garry. Head and Heart: American Christianities. New York: Penguin, 2007.

———. St. Augustine. New York: Penguin, 1999.

Witteveen, H. J., ed. The Heart of Sufism: The Essential Writings of Hazrat Inayat Khan. Boston: Shambhala, 1999.

Wolf, Fred A. The Spiritual Universe: One Physicist's Vision of Spirit, Soul, Matter and Self. Portsmouth, NH: Moment Point, 1996.

Wolters, Clifton, trans. The Cloud of Unknowing. Baltimore: Penguin, 1961.

Woods, Richard. Understanding Mysticism. New York: Image Books, 1980.

———. Mysterion. Chicago: The Thomas More Assn., 1981.

Zaehner, R. C. Mysticism, Sacred and Profane: An Inquiry into Some Varieties of Praeternatural Experiences. New York: Oxford University Press, 1961.

Zimdars-Swartz, Sandra. Encountering Mary: Visions of Mary from La Salette to Medjugorje. New York: Avon Books, 1991.

Zum Brunn, Emilie, and Georgette Epiney-Burgard, eds. Women Mystics in Medieval Europe. New York: Paragon, 1989.

About the Author

Joan Hickey has been reading and researching in the field of mystical experiences for over sixty years. She has a master's degree in pastoral counseling and four years of graduate study in theology and pastoral studies at the Washington Theological Union.

She has been associated with the Shalem Institute for Spiritual Formation for thirty-five years and a member of the Associate Staff for twenty-five of those years and was also a member of the Adjunct Faculty for the Virginia Theological Seminary's Continuing Education program for sixteen years. Now in her eighties, she is retired from her work of many years as a pastoral counselor, spiritual director, retreat leader and teacher of contemplative prayer practices. A lifelong Christian, she comes from a broadly ecumenical family which has members who,

Photograph by Paul Hickey

collectively, belong to six different Christian denomina-
tional traditions. She is a widow, has three adult sons,
one daughter-in-law and four grandchildren and lives
in the Virginia suburbs of Washington, D.C.